Praise for Sonja Klein

"From her ranch, Ambush Hill, in legendary Texas, Sonja produces a stimulating adventure and misadventure book. Readers will be intrigued with her no holds barred essays, worldwide travel adventures and Texas ranch life. The book illuminates the human condition including its joys, heartaches and humor. The book is a literary high quality jewel, not to be missed and a never to be forgotten enjoyable read."
—*The Mindquest Review of Books, Lightwood Publishing*

"According to a Chinese proverb, there are two ways to enrich your life. One is to read 10,000 books. The other is to travel 10,000 miles. Roundtrip from Texas, Sonja Klein's new "travelogue" lets you travel those miles in a single book. Nobody could ask for a cooler traveling companion. Klein, author of Honk If You Married Sonja is a globetrotting hoot. The fifth-generation Texas rancher and cousin of singer-songwriter Lyle Lovett, recounts her journeys to everywhere...with a refreshingly candid voice that adds one or two dimensions to even the most exotic locales we travel to with her."
—*Victor Gulotta, Gulotta Communications, Inc.*

"As we crash through life, we change lives as we change our own...Sonja Klein shares her life's journey through Texas and everywhere else, finding her own adventure and experiencing what life has to offer, sharing what she's learned and what she's failed to."
—*Midwest Book Review*

"Free sprinted Sonja Klein has done it again, serving up a heaping helping of wanderlust for her devoted readers to feast upon. Hop in her back pocket and travel vicariously with this cheeky Texas gal as she explores the world, one adventure at a time. A must read!"
—*Linda Koehl, Singer/Songwriter*

"This book is as interesting as Sonja's life, racy and full of the wit and wisdom of a great Texas 'broad.' Buy several copies and treat your friends."
—*Roxanne Apple*

"Straight from the hip without a quip, Sonja tells it like she sees it, and it is both point blank and insightful. Well worth the time to benefit from her oft too honest observations."
—*Tracy Walsh*

"Sonja describes her adventures across the planet and at home in Texas in a fun and easy manner. She provides interesting detail, personal insight and witty entertainment. The autobiographical sections have the energy and tone of a conversation between friends sharing a six-pack of Shiner Bock on the tailgate of a pickup truck at the ranch of this native Texan. This makes for an enjoyable read."
—*Martin Terry*

"Roundtrip from Texas enabled me to experience more lands and peoples than I can ever hope to experience first hand...still, I feel the fifty shades of Sonja have not all been revealed...yet."
—*Eric Zimmerman*

"I started reading Roundtrip from Texas this morning and ended up being late to my yoga class!"
—*Tami Lynn*

"Sonja is one of the best true life storytellers writing today. She is funny, fascinating, interesting and very informative. Her vignettes about her own life are amazing. And her travel stories are so engrossing that you feel like you are actually on the trip with her...A few hours traveling with Sonja are a true joy."
—*John Gibson*

"CAUTION: Do not pick up this book if you haven't some time on your hands. After just a couple of chapters I found I couldn't stop reading. Sonja's light hearted writing style and fascinating stories are a gagillion times addictive. Cover to cover its a fantastic read. I would recommend this to ALL my friends."
—George Zirfas, Graphic Artist

"If there was a female Gus in Lonesome Dove, Sonja is it."
—*DRK, Executive*

"When I was a boy, Sonja Klein was one of the first grown-ups in my life to show me it was okay to have fun. Sonja is my mom's younger first cousin. My first memories of her are of liking her and wanting to be around her. She always seemed happy and excited about whatever she was doing. She was pretty, wore cool clothes, drove fast cars and raced motorcycles.
"Sonja gave me my first job away from the family farm, working as a 13-year-old floor sweeper and window washer at her newly acquired Honda and Yamaha shop in Conroe, Texas. She taught me that being responsible to my own interests was one of life's greatest gifts. She taught me that's it's possible to be a good, productive person and still embrace with enthusiasm the unknown possibilities every day has to offer."
—*Lyle Lovett, Singer/Songwriter and Actor*

Ambushed by America

More Wit and Wisdom
From Sonja Klein

Sonja Klein

Ambush Publishing
Barksdale, Texas

Ambushed by America
Copyright © 2017 by Sonja Rose Klein

Published by Ambush Publishing
PO Box 192
Barksdale, Texas 78828
1-830-234-3156

Library of Congress Control Number: 2016920598
Klein, Sonja 1942—
    Ambushed by America/by Sonja Klein

ISBN 978-0-9889863-2-9 (trade paper)

2 0 1 6 9 2 0 5 9 8

Cover art designed by Chuck Roach. www.roach-art.com
Editorial production by Angela Smith. asmith1411@aol.com

Printed in the United States of America

Dedicated especially to my family
All of you aunts, uncles, cousins, grandparents, and great grandparents, some of whom I never met. You have given me wonderful memories, and you are my family.

From The Author

At the end, there is usually something left to add. Surrender to the treasures of books instead of engaging in pointless relationships that often end in neglect.

With books one can treat those feelings not recognized as disease and never diagnosed by a doctor. Books are the medicine for afflictions of the soul.

Books keep stupidity at bay and provide love from within. They become lifelong loving companions. Some books are friends who comfort you, others are a slap in the face, and some are like chocolate candy – sweet and satisfying.

I hope this book is one of those.

Acknowledgements

Again the encouragement of family, friends and readers of my first two books has supported me in the publishing of this, my third book. Special thanks to my brothers John, Allan, and David for insisting that I continue publishing. Without Carla Hill and Ed Dondanville, I wouldn't have the free time and peace of mind to write. For my grandsons Theiss and Ryder, I continue to live. And for Angela Smith, my editor and formatter, you are an angel and a kindred spirit and a heck of an editor. To Chuck Roach, the artist behind the book cover, your talent is awesome, and to Eric Zimmerman I thank you for continuing to answer my phone calls and be my friend.

Table of Contents

Ambushed by America

Preface

After writing two substantial books about my world travels, I turned my focus home to America, my plan being to journey the far ends of the earth before limited mobility, but since that has not yet occurred, I was forced to reconsider. After exploring the options and finding no place else beyond U.S. boundaries I desired to visit, America became the playground.

America overwhelms me. The open spaces of middle America, the Great Lakes, the Crazy Horse Memorial, the eastern seaboard, the great northwest, the deep south, Alaska – each of them marked exciting monumental adventures and unforgettable, lasting memories.

How could I have been so stupid. America has it all, whether you prefer jungles, beaches, deserts, mountains, lush streams and rivers, plain hills and rocks. And then there are the people - what an assortment!

All that time traipsing across the planet was well spent. I developed a perspective that otherwise would not have been possible. Learning — wherever it takes place — engages the spirit.

Love for my country and appreciation of its beauty ambushed me, and while this book may be shorter than the previous two, it still took a while and a lot of words for the complete picture to emerge. Sometimes I can be a bit slow.

I think a person will be remembered by shared stories and memories. Perhaps that is all that remains beyond the tombstone and scattered ashes. We can only wonder.

Ambushed by America

Older Woman, Younger Man

I'm an older woman. The oldest man I've ever been to bed with was 65. Viagra made it possible. I didn't know it at the time, and if I had known, I would have been turned off.

After that experience, I gave up on sex, determined to live without it, but fate was kind to me one day as I was dumping the garbage I hauled from the ranch. As a steward of the land I forbid a dump on my property. Many ranchers simply dig a pit, dump their garbage, burn it when it becomes full, and repeat the cycle over and over again. Not me. I pay a monthly fee to deposit my garbage in a trailer in the nearest town of Barksdale.

I also take my cans, magazines, bottles, and plastic to the recycle center 60 miles away in Uvalde. My vegetable scraps are placed in a barrel to provide compost for my garden, and my meat scraps are placed in one of the hog traps I keep baited. My garbage is minimal.

On that day I was retrieving a single white plastic bag from the back of my pickup when a voice called to me from the local cafe across the highway.

"What are you doing Sonja Klein?"

It was Billy, an acquaintance of more than a decade.

"What do you think I'm doing, Billy? I'm dumping my garbage."

I was also on the way to give a talk about writing to the middle school students at the small consolidated school a few blocks away.

Billy looked good. I got in the truck and rolled the window down. He approached the truck.

"You curled your hair."

"Do you like it?"

"Yeah."

"You look good too."

"I had some health problems, almost died. I've quit drinking."

"Have you been dancing lately, Billy?"

"No."

"Call me. Let's go dancing."

Billy is a good dancer. I know that because I have danced with him on a few occasions since our first meeting years ago beside the road. His truck had broken down, and I gave him a ride. When he introduced himself I realized who he was, the son of friends from church. There was

1

a spark between us, but I never fueled the fire though I must admit I thought about it over the years when we ran into each other.

The story is classic. Several weeks later we met at a local benefit. We danced and the rest is history. For once in my life the timing was right. We were both single, had no excess baggage, and the spark became a bonfire – a bonfire that raced through our little community like a raging inferno.

Billy is 14 years younger. After some initial anxiety Billy and I decided the hell with the age difference. If it didn't matter to us, why would it matter to anyone else? We were wrong. The relationship was okay with all the men. Not so with the women. Most of them knew my age. To them I was the older woman seducing one of their young. My reputation was ruined. It bothered me, but not that much.

We talked about it. I told Billy, *"If you were an older man with a much younger woman, it would be okay."*

He agreed. I mentioned several couples in the canyon lands where the woman was much older. The community had accepted them. I asked Billy, *"Why not us?"*

"Because you are the wealthy woman writer and I'm from here. They either think I'm in it for your money or you are a dirty old woman."

"None of that is true."

"We both know that."

"They think I've stolen one of their own, and they're trying to protect you."

"Sonja, I'm 56, been married three times. I think I know what I'm doing."

"I'm over 70 and sure as shit think I know how I feel."

"Just don't die on me."

"I'll try not to."

"I don't want to get married."

"Billy, I'll never marry again, tried four times. Marriage doesn't work for me."

"Doesn't work for me either."

We spend the weekends together, get along great, and the raging fire of gossip is extinguished. Time takes care of most everything, or as Billy quotes his Granny, *"It all comes out in the wash."*

I guess I now fit the definition of a cougar. What a silly term. I'm not that fond of cats.

The Benefit

When a lady we knew developed kidney failure, everyone started praying. A chance acquaintance visiting the ranch on which she and her husband lived and worked as managers offered, "I'll donate a kidney. I have two."

This young man had married the granddaughter of a prominent real estate broker. He was not from the area and worked at a local paint and body shop. In a short period of time he was tested and found to be a match. The odds were in the hundreds of thousands to one. Within a month the surgery was scheduled.

The community sprang into action. While the lady's insurance would pay for the costs of both surgeries, the young man would be unable to work for six weeks. A fund was set up at the local bank. Donations were accepted. Before the surgery took place, the account accumulated several thousand dollars.

A benefit was scheduled. The local paper advertised a silent auction, live auction, music, dancing and barbecue sandwiches

The event was held at the old American Legion Hall. In a town of only 600, everyone attended. Musicians came from neighboring areas to play music in support of these two people now linked by a kidney.

As the doors opened on a Saturday afternoon, people were lined up to buy barbecue sandwiches and lemonade or tea. The donee's husband played the opening music. Men and women viewed the items displayed for the silent auction and wrote their bids. I donated copies of my two books.

As the afternoon progressed the emcee announced a hollering contest. Eight women stood at the foot of the stage for the chance to give the loudest holler. Their ages ranged from young to old. The first challenge was to yell "Prayer and Share."

The second round asked them to scream out "Camp Wood." Some, showing their clever sense of humor, shouted "Vance" and "Barksdale," both very small communities in the area. Everyone laughed.

The winner was chosen and awarded a trophy. The live auction began. The bidding was quite spirited and lasted early into the evening. Pies, cakes, chocolate covered strawberries, brownies, and even banana pudding were auctioned along with jewelry, art work and assorted items. The bidding for the silent auction was over.

More music filled the room and the dancing began. Few danced except for Billy and me. We danced most every dance, often having the entire floor to ourselves. Most of the attendees chatted with each other, sitting on the hard wooden benches. Before the evening ended, several thousand dollars had been raised, and over 200 barbecue sandwiches had been eaten.

That day began a short-lived romance, some good times that will always be cherished, and some not so good, with painful memories that will fade in time.

The kidney donee continues to thrive. The relationship that began at the benefit did not.

Fences

When I purchased my ranch, Ambush Hill, over 20 years ago, there were only a few game-proof fences in the rugged canyon lands west of the Texas Hill Country. The purpose of the high fences was to keep the wild animals out of fields, gardens, and yards, relatively small areas.

Not so anymore. The highways are lined with tall, metal fences intended to lock in the animals and prevent them from ranging across their once familiar habitat.

In the past, the 20-mile drive from Barksdale to Ambush Hill Ranch was once more treacherous than today. One night I counted over 100 deer over a 10 mile stretch. While the game-proof fences have made the roads safer, they are still not hazard-free. The same precautions must be taken for one deer as for many. The driver must still contend with pigs, buzzards, squirrels, armadillos, porcupines, skunks, and turkeys. A collision with a smaller mammal may not be as disastrous as the impact of a deer hitting the front end of a car or pickup, especially without a grill guard, but it is a problem, nevertheless.

Wealthy people from urban areas often purchase acreage in these badlands for the beauty and solitude. Many of them don't last long. The isolation, inconvenience of amenities and distant stores, hospitals, and restaurants soon turns them to desperation, usually after they have spent thousands on fences, landscaping, remodeling or new construction of the classic ranch house, complete with mounted deer heads, leather furniture, lamps made of deer horns, dishes with a western theme and the requisite cowhide rugs.,

City people desire to own, sculpt and control the land. Nature prevents them. The rocks, violent weather and inhospitable terrain prevail. The animals plague their security. The quiet unnerves them to the extent that the buzzing of a bee or fly is to them as loud as a jet plane flying overhead.

The ants, scorpions, spiders, snakes, hornets and biting insects instill fear. Once bitten, a person can become over-cautious. And then there are the ticks and chiggers. Chiggers will change a personality overnight.

Most city people usually last about seven years before they put their ranch up for sale. They return to an environment they can control on a city lot with a yard of green grass around a swimming pool. To them the city is a safe place, a refuge from the creatures and other hazards that come from living in the country.

Often I am asked, "Aren't you afraid living out there alone?"

My stock answer is, "I'm safer out here than you are in the city. Think of all the perverts and criminals within a mile radius of your home. Out here there is no one for miles." Still visitors continue to lock their cars and doors in the guest houses before I remind them that I have no keys for most of the doors.

A thief who wants to steal will break in one way or another. That's what insurance is for and it's not that easy to make repairs in the middle of nowhere. Nothing is simply accomplished with a phone call. There are none or few licensed plumbers, surveyors, or electricians in Real County, but we have plenty of churches and Christians.

Some property not many miles distant from my ranch recently sold to a man from Houston. The first thing he did was hire a fence crew to erect a game-proof fence around his land. Once the fence was in place, the captured deer stood along the fence looking across the road to the pastures they once roamed. The sight of the large herds standing confused and baffled was pitiful. I wanted to stop and cut a hole in the fence, but, of course, I didn't because of the consequences. In Texas we have laws that prevent fence cutting. I wanted to give those deer freedom to wander as before, to give them back their open range.

A recent flood washed away the high fences at the creek crossings. I was delighted to see the deer moving freely once again before the damage was repaired.

City people should stay in the city and leave the wilderness to those of us who are good stewards of the land, who know how to live in harmony with nature, rather than trying to control it. They fail. Nature prevails.

The American Northwest

Every time I travel outside the small, sparsely populated county and leave my isolated ranch I realize what a racial melting pot America remains. Airports illustrate this in the most obvious way.

On this adventure I flew from San Antonio to Los Angeles and then on to Portland, Oregon. The Los Angeles airport offered every kind of food imaginable, from Greek to Thai to Mexican to vegetarian (an old Indian word that means bad hunter). Fellow travelers dressed in shorts and flip flops with more skin showing than not dominated the scene.

A smog reminiscent of China covered the City of Angels, and as we circled to gain altitude, leaving the valley below resembled a toilet bowl that had not been flushed. Flying north, the air cleared and the plane landed smoothly in Portland, Oregon, as daylight faded. The taxi driver or rather the innovative driver of a small coach/van was of Mid-Eastern descent. Fellow passengers were an Oriental lady and a young couple from Jedda, Saudi Arabia. The young Saudi woman was heavily veiled.

The lobby of the downtown hotel teemed with healthy women and men, and early the following morning I understood why. A loudspeaker booming from the Williamette River, a half block away, announced with regularity the heats for the dragon boat races.

I knew about dragon boat races from an earlier trip to Vietnam and Cambodia and pleasantly spent the morning watching the competitive heats to establish the finalists in the various classes.

Some of the boats were rowed by crews of women who had survived breast cancer. Others were paddled by a mixture of gender and age, and some boats were propelled by groups made up exclusively of the young or old. The contestants came from all parts of the United States, as well as Canada.

Portland boasts a population of near half a million and is known as the City of Roses. The city is situated about 70 miles inland from the Pacific Ocean between the Williamette and Columbia Rivers. Williamette is pronounced Will-AM-it, rhyming with dammit, and Oregon is pronounced Or'-a-gen.

The state of Oregon is part of the U.S. region known as the Pacific Northwest. Oregon was inhabited by many indigenous tribes before the arrival of explorers, traders, and settlers. The earliest known use of the name, spelled Ouragon, was in a 1765 petition by Major Robert Rogers to the kingdom of Great Britain. The term referred to the then mythical river of the West, the Columbia River. By 1778 the spelling shifted to Oregon. An autonomous government was formed in Oregon Country in 1843, the Oregon Territory was created in 1848, and Oregon became the 33rd state in 1859.

The diverse landscape from the Pacific coastline to the Cascade Mountains and waterfalls as well as the dense evergreen forests and the high desert of eastern Oregon always attracted my interest, and the historic journey of Meriwether Lewis and William Clark is an epic journey familiar to most Americans.

In 1803 President Thomas Jefferson picked Lewis to lead an expedition through the northwest and gave him the following instructions:

"Your mission is to explore the Missouri river and such principal streams of it as by its course and communication with the waters of the Pacific Ocean whether the Columbia, Oregon, Colorado or any other river may offer the most direct and practicable water communication across this continent for the purposes of commerce."

The expedition journeyed 28 months from 1804 to 1806 and was highly successful due to the ingenuity of its two leaders.

Since the small boat that would take me up the rivers of the northwest would not embark until 5 p.m., I spent the rest of the day at the Saturday market along the river. The market area was crowded with families, children playing in the fountains, and eating a variety of exotic foods including veggie wraps, gyros, and elephant paws, a deep fried pastry covered with sugar that resembled an elephant's footprint.

I purchased a hanging sculpture of stainless steel and a micro-kite only three inches in diameter with a spool of thread to fly it.

A mime painted in silver performed on one of the plazas, and from time to time he would juggle silver balls as children clad only in underwear played in the nearby shallow fountain. Everyone seemed to be having a good time.

The boat docked a few short blocks from the hotel, and as I climbed the gangplank I heard British and Australian accents as well as a few Texas drawls. Only 75 passengers were booked on the ship, and most of them were elderly, but spirited.

After the safety drill and introduction of the crew and staff, champagne and snacks were served before a dinner of salmon or beef tenderloin. I chose the salmon. I skipped the decadent chocolate dessert, enjoyed a last glass of white wine, and slept like a baby as the boat chugged up the river.

The noise of the boat entering the first of eight locks, this one at the Bonneville Dam, awakened me early the following morning. Locks frighten me. As a writer with a vivid imagination I always fear that the walls will collapse, and I will be inundated with tons of water and drown.

After clearing the lock, the boat docked and we disembarked to tour the Bonneville Dam. A park ranger delivered a lecture with technical detail explaining how hydroelectric power is generated. The fun part of the dam tour was the fish ladders. I couldn't take my eyes off the huge salmon negotiating the swiftly flowing water ladders to swim upstream and die.

The tour guide spoke of protecting the salmon from sea lions and raptors under a federal protection plan, the Marine Mammal Act. I learned that a salmon has a four-year life cycle.

The Bonneville Dam was built during the depression to generate jobs and fulfill the president's promise to provide electricity to all Americans. The dam creates the first in a series of navigable lakes that are part of the Columbia-Snake Inland Waterway, a water highway running 465 miles from the Pacific Ocean to Lewiston, Idaho.

After leaving the dam we boarded a coach for a 35-mile scenic drive where we saw 70 waterfalls, including the beautiful Multnomah Falls, the tallest falls in Oregon at 640 feet. Since it was a Sunday, the site was crowded with tourists of many nationalities.

Returning to the ship I enjoyed snacks and a glass of wine before dining on lamb and tender scallops. The remainder of the evening was spent cruising through the spectacular Columbia River Gorge, which, at 80 miles long and up to 4,000 feet deep, cuts the only sea level route through the Cascade Mountains. I learned that much of the land along the river was owned by the Bureau of Land Management.

I skipped dessert and the lecture, which was to focus on the effects of world wars, the Manhattan Project, and public works efforts during the depression.

We passed Table Mountain, which in 1699 slid into the Columbia

River, blocking the river flow to the extent that a person could walk across it. Mother Nature prevailed and the river unclogged itself.

As an early riser I enjoyed a light buffet breakfast of quiche, fruit, and a bagel as the ship entered the state of Washington. The land became much dryer, having an annual rainfall between 12 and 18 inches. More locks and dams were encountered as the boat slowly eased up the river. The skies were clear, the weather was warm, and on the banks of the river I observed the world's largest apple orchard, over 20 square miles, owned by an individual.

As we transited McNary Dam the boat arrived at the confluence of the Columbia and Snake Rivers. More than 200 wineries covered the hillsides, and I saw the wheat fields of the Palouse, one of the nation's top wheat growing regions. The waters of the river changed to a blue green as we cruised by massive wind farm turbines.

After a salad lunch and some writing, a short nap was my reward before a dinner of haddock and grilled vegetables. During cocktail hour I discovered just how out of touch I am with the cocktail scene as I heard drinks being ordered with "exotic" names such as Dark and Stormy, Bee's Knees, Berry Drop, and Flying Cucumber. I stuck with red or white wine.

The lecture that evening centered on the history of the area. About 10,000 years ago, the area was inhabited by ancient man. The natives of the interior traded with the coastal tribes and later with fur traders from Great Britain, Canada, and the eastern United States. Initially relations were friendly until the white man's greed and disease enraged the natives.

The Lewis and Clark Expedition was mandated by the federal government and took place from 1804 to 1806. The report was a great one, lauding the bounty of the northwest.

Missionaries arrived in the 1830's. The Whitmans established a mission but were later slaughtered by the Indians.

Indian wars resulted in the 1850's as more land was taken from them and their numbers were decimated. During the 1870's the remaining Indians were sent to reservations. The Indians were finally given citizenship in 1924, too late and not enough to compensate for the loss of their lands and people. Today the natives can fish for salmon with fewer restrictions than the rest of the population.

The following day was clear and cool as we cruised the Walla Walla Gap and the lower Snake River before docking and boarding a jet boat. On one side of the river was Lewiston, Idaho, and on the other was Clarkston, Washington. I learned that most .22 caliber rim-fire bullets are made in Lewiston and that jet boats are also manufactured in the area.

As we left the port the jet boat cruised past interesting lava formations, an Arabian horse farm, a cattle ranch, and stopped at Hellsgate State Park on the Snake River. The fruit trees were laden with apples, pears, and figs. We picked fruit from the trees, and I ate some ripe figs. As we continued up the Snake for the 49-mile trip we met rafters and kayakers going downstream and spotted big horn sheep and mule deer along the river.

Sturgeon, bass and salmon attract fishermen to the area, and we observed camps, accessible only by water. As we reached the confluence of the Snake and Salmon Rivers, we turned around, not going all the way up the Snake to the dam.

On the return trip we stopped at a farm and enjoyed a lunch of barbecued pork tenderloin, potato salad, and baked beans. Carrot cake was served for dessert.

Returning to our home on the ship, cocktail hour began. Crab claws and fresh octopus salad were served. I could have made a meal with the snacks. That evening my culinary feast continued with prime New York steak served with red potatoes and squash ragout. My steak was nice and rare. I took only one bite of the dessert, which was poached pears in gingerbread cake.

We began the return journey, stopping in Walla Walla after passing through the eastern Columbia River Gorge. Walla Walla is an Indian name, meaning land of many waters.

Most of the morning was spent at the Fort Walla Walla Museum, a large complex including a pioneer settlement and exhibit halls showcasing early farm machinery, sheep wagons, buggies and sleighs, farm wagons, hand tools, early vehicles, a Nez Perce tepee, and a territorial prison.

A light lunch was served at the Dunham Cellars Winery, plus a tour and wine tasting. The Northstar Winery, a larger more commercial winery, was next on the agenda, and the remainder of a long day was spent at the ruins of the Whitman Mission, a National Historic Site.

The story of the Whitmans has been portrayed as a tragic event. As I walked through the visitor center and left the rear of the building to stand on the Oregon Trail, I was offended by the presentation, which depicted the Whitmans as victims of the savage Indians. While their motives might have been Christian, our nation's treatment of the Indians was not. The Whitmans had no business interfering with a centuries-old culture that lived in harmony with nature. The natives lived peacefully until the white man exploited them.

Continuing down the Columbia River, we stopped in a town called The Dalles to visit the Mary Hill Museum and the Columbia Gorge Discovery Center. I spent the rest of the afternoon walking the streets of The Dalles after being told it was the only town in the United States that began with the word "The." I knew that was false because a town north of Houston, Texas, is called The Woodlands. The town was small, and many of the storefronts on the main street were vacant. I visited a fly fishing shop and an antique store and noticed a Chinese restaurant and a Mexican restaurant.

Leaving The Dalles we cruised down the river passing irrigated fruit orchards and fields of corn, alfalfa, and wheat. Barges moved slowly, carrying wheat to the port of Astoria.

The following morning we docked in Astoria, Oregon, known as the Graveyard of the Pacific. Astoria lies 12 miles inland from the Pacific Ocean and is known as the world's most dangerous harbor because of the ever changing bar at the entrance. Over 2,000 ships have been sunk and over 700 people killed.

The port conducts much trade with China, shipping out wheat and lumber. In addition, Idaho's famous potatoes are exported as frozen French fries. Fertilizer is barged up the river to the Columbia Basin and the Palouse. The first United States Post Office west of the Rockies was established in Astoria in 1847, and the city is known as the salmon canning capitol of the world.

As I visited the Maritime Museum in Astoria, I entered the large gift shop. Admiring many of the items for sale, I discovered most of them were made in China, Mexico, and Honduras. I have never understood why the tourist gift shops in America sell goods not made in America.

We sailed from Astoria that evening and enjoyed an evening of boiled shrimp with our cocktails. The Captain's dinner began with a lamb chop lollipop, cucumber salad, prime rib with a vegetable blend, and finished with baked Alaska Ali Baba. I enjoyed the entire dessert. The ship docked in Portland. The journey was over.

There are always defining moments on my adventures. The scenic moment of this trip was the 640-foot waterfall. An instant when I saw a glimpse of God occurred on the ship as I was leaving the lounge and turned a corner. An old man traveling with his wife suffering from advanced Alzheimer Disease went with her into the women's restroom.

I have always insisted that adventures and journeys are mostly about people, not places and things.

5 Ashrams, India, and Self-Realization

An ashram is a spiritual hermitage, a usually secluded residence of a religious community and its guru, usually a Hindu, devoted to toil, austerity, penance, and inner reflection. Life in the ashram is a journey on the ancient path of timeless spiritual wisdom that emphasizes personal freedom and practical ways to lead a meaningful life. The guru instructs the seeker or student in the basics of sadhana, the cultivation of a daily personal practice, and seva, being of selfless service in the world.

By weaving the practice of sadhana and seva into the fabric of daily life, the student achieves a sense of peace and fulfillment and becomes better equipped to meet any challenges with calmness, grace and skill. The vibrations emanating from the student spontaneously touch others, contributing to greater harmony in families, communities, workplaces, cities, nations and, ultimately, the world.

Mother Teresa and Gandhi were teachers of this spiritual movement. Others seek to achieve enlightenment by traveling to India and immersing themselves, living in an ashram. For this privilege they pay dearly.

I have traveled to India and experienced a culture that practices religion as a routine part of daily existence. In contrast, religion in America is pursued primarily on Sundays, with the rest of the week usually given to self-indulgence.

Citizens of communist countries are the exact opposite of those in countries like India, Bhutan, and even Morocco. While Bhutan is Buddhist and Morocco is Muslim, they still spend a good part of each day immersed in their religion.

I do not understand why Americans and Europeans endure the expense and journey to India to experience poverty, sacrifice, and hard labor to discover the silence of their souls. I can walk out my door on the ranch and experience the wonders of nature and the heavens, observe sunrises and sunsets, feel the wind, hear the birds and insects, and smell the grape-like scent of the mountain laurel blooming in the spring. I can quiet my inner chatter easily by digging in my garden rather than cleaning toilets in the dormitory of an ashram. I can breathe the fresh air that blows from the south instead of inhaling the exhaust fumes from an overpopulated India. I can enjoy the fresh fruit and vegetables from my own efforts rather than experience diarrhea caused by food to which I am unaccustomed. If I want to find that quiet inner self, I can take that journey by lying down on the sofa and closing my eyes.

Perhaps the reason for traveling to India might be lack of self-discipline, something most Americans are lacking. But the expense of an ashram in India doesn't make sense to me. Sacrifice and deprivation are not necessary for obtaining spiritual enlightenment. The journey to heaven or nirvana should be one of joy and happiness, not pain and sacrifice. I maintain that the answers lie within each of us and that attainment is achieved through personal reflection and meditation, something that everyone is capable of doing on their own, in the comfort of their own culture.

Begin your personal journey by searching within. You don't have to go to India. The answers are right here at home.

6 Money

Money is only important in that it provides freedom, freedom to be who you really are and freedom to do what you please. Money is not for material gain. There are those who love making money, who live for the game of increasing wealth.

You can sleep in only one bed, drive one car, propel one boat, and watch one TV. There is no need for second homes, two boats, or three cars.

Possessions can own you. You become so trapped in taking care of and protecting your assets that they become a burden, constricting freedom. I have owned a second home and it was a trap. I found myself worrying about the yard, the security and spending time going back and forth to take care of the property.

Renting a house or condo in a resort area is now my preference. A second home will cost in excess of $100,000, and for that amount a person can rent a pretty nice house and not worry over the maintenance, insurance, and safety. You have freedom to exert choices and locations rather than being confined to spending time at the second home. The world beckons.

The tax advantage could be considered, but then money becomes the influential and confining factor.

Freedom is the biggest issue with me. I have to be free whether it be in financial matters or in a relationship. I don't want to monitor stock investments every day. I prefer having a competent broker who is smarter than me, a bond broker who is more informed, a banker I can trust, an attorney who does what I tell him/her, a doctor who likes me, a lover I can depend on, and business partners who are honest.

While I expect my money to work for me, I don't want more than I need. Instead I want just enough money to have fun and be free. I once read, "Find what you love and let it kill you." I adore fun and happiness and love, and I'll gladly let those things kill me. What a way to go!

Hats

My daddy always wore a hat, a white Stetson. So did his brothers — all five of them. My mother wore hats, too, many of them red. My father bought them for her. After my father died, she wore cowboy hats, probably because she owned a racehorse and was into the cowboy scene. Her closet was then full of cowboy shirts, Levis, and boots, in every color imaginable to match the hats.

I also wear hats. Two shelves of my closet are devoted to them — hats for the beach, hats for dressing up, cowboy hats for winter and summer, and caps for keeping the hair out of my eyes when I do ranch work or have no desire to comb my hair.

Hats draw attention to the wearer. A woman in a hat is always noticed. In the past, men always removed their hats when they entered a room. Not so today. Hats are worn in restaurants, caps too, some of them backwards. Most men still take off their hats and caps in church, probably the last bastion of hat etiquette.

Many homes in Texas display a hat rack or stand near the front door. Mine is made of tarnished brass and was given to me long ago. My favorite hats and coats are carefully balanced on the curved prongs.

My boyfriend keeps three hats and two caps on the rack, an old beat up felt cowboy hat for feeding livestock and chasing goats and sheep, a nice straw hat for dancing, and a couple of caps, a nice one and an old one for climbing trees. My favorite is the old beat up felt hat because he looks so cute wearing it. He likes my old faded blue straw Stetson that was my mother's. So do I.

8 **Alcohol**

I recently attended a Crawfish Boil at my brother's ranch in the east Texas Piney Woods in the Trinity River bottom. Since I live over 300 miles to the west of his ranch, I arrived the day before, looking forward to enjoying a visit with my three brothers, along with other family members and friends.

When I reached the ranch, I called my boyfriend, who I had reluctantly left behind, from the phone in the guest lodge. I assured him that I arrived safely and innocently gave him the number of the landline at my brother's house next to the lodge. It was a mistake.

Over the course of the evening he called, interrupting the visit. I could tell he was drinking, fighting his chronic alcohol problems. Avoiding rude behavior I kept the conversation as short as possible and as the evening drew to a close I retired with a book and slept peacefully, having only indulged in a few glasses of wine before supper.

The following morning I awoke refreshed and descended the long staircase in my brother's ranch house to the kitchen for some coffee. My sister-in-law entered the room and handed me her portable phone.

"Do you recognize this number?"

"Yes, it's Billy."

"Look at the time he called."

The numbers read 12:06 a.m.

"Sonja, he sounded inebriated."

"I'm sorry. I apologize. He shouldn't have called that late."

I was embarrassed, but relieved that my brother John was not present. He can be brutal.

I walked over to the guest lodge where preparations were underway for boiling 400 pounds of crawfish along with corn, sausage, potatoes, and garlic. Kegs of beer were being iced in plastic barrels, and I helped as instructed until I felt useless.

When I returned to the main house, I was alone so I found a book to read and settled myself into an armchair and ottoman, attempting to escape from my embarrassment at the late night call. The phone rang. The caller ID identified Billy's number. He was sober and apologized profusely. It helped a little. My nephew entered the room, and I tried to tone down the conversation since it was obvious he was listening. I then went out to the porch to continue talking and end the call.

Feeling a bit better I returned to the lodge and as I approached, my brother John said, "I hear you gave your boyfriend an ass chewing." Everyone laughed and the party began. As usual, I had made a mountain out of a mole-hill.

Later that evening after the party ended, those of us spending the night retired to the deck to watch the sunset over the Trinity River bottom. My niece and three couples continued to drink but switched to champagne to celebrate her 50th birthday. My afternoon buzz had ended and I preferred to remain sober for an early morning departure back to my ranch.

As I tried to engage some of the younger crowd on politics or world events or the economy, one of them interrupted. *"I don't read the newspapers or watch much TV. I drink instead."*

I retired early, the subject of drinking on my mind. My three brothers and their wives drank, my children and their spouses drank, most everyone drank alcohol. On occasion some of them drank too much, including myself. I think that alcohol keeps this country going. In fact it keeps the world pretty well sedated, along with prescription pills and illegal drugs, not to mention the toxic substances that are likely added to our food.

Alcohol is an escape for the poor as well as the rich. Beverage preferences vary only according to the size of their bank account or money in their pockets.

Bars, convenience stores, and dance halls flourish from the sale of drinks. The court system is clogged from DUI offenses. People are in prison for drinking and driving. Rehab centers, counseling, and probation offices extort money from drunks.

I'm beginning to think that alcohol keeps the economy grinding and the citizens complacent. Perhaps it has always been so.

In many ways drunks built this country. The oilfield and construction workers, the Americans who labored on the railroads, pipelines, and power lines all drank the minute they got off work, but the next morning at daylight they were back on the job. The alcohol eased their aching backs and muscles and relaxed the tension from the danger and stress of their jobs. Even some of our so-called best presidents were drunks.

What is the definition of a drunk? I don't know but what I'm sure of is that if you get up and go to work every morning — whether it be on Wall Street or Oak Street or a construction site or offshore on an oil derrick — you are not a drunk. What you do in your spare time is your private business, only as long as what you do does not harm others or put them at risk.

Las Vegas

Remember when Las Vegas was classy and elegant, when gamblers wore three- piece suits and their ladies wore long, glamorous dresses? Not so today. Back in the 1970's, the blackjack and crap tables were surrounded by beautiful people. For a short while I was there with my second husband wearing designer gowns and diamond jewelry. We stayed at the Tropicana in a two story elegant hotel room with a grand piano and free food and drinks.

Recently a girlfriend called and asked, *"Would you like to go to Vegas with me for two days and a night of gambling? I have a free room in the old part of Vegas at the Golden Nugget."*

The answer came easy.

"I'd love to go, but I don't gamble."

"Don't worry, we'll just play the nickel slots."

"I've never heard of nickel slots."

"They have them."

After checking in the hotel early in the afternoon, we played the slot machines with modest gains, which translates to breaking even. We dolled up for dinner (translate overdressed), dined very expensively in the hotel dining room and spent the night playing the nickel slots, drinking champagne.

My friend remarked, *"It's getting daylight. Maybe we should get some sleep,"* I was shocked. *"I can't believe I'm drinking champagne this early in the morning."* We returned to the room, took a shower and dined on the breakfast buffet, desperately trying to act sober. The slots treated us well. We won enough money to cover our meals and the taxi ride back to the airport. The elegant casinos must be out on the strip, but the common folks are downtown, playing the slots, dressed in Bermuda shorts and wearing flip flops. I'm glad gambling doesn't excite me. I'd rather throw my money out the window or give it to someone rather than lose it to a casino. If I'm going to gamble I prefer to do it elegantly and not with nickels. It's my good fortune I haven't had the opportunity.

10 On Writing

I don't write for money or fame. I write because that is who I am. I am a writer. It took years for me to discover that writing is my game. If I don't write, I don't exist. I write because I have to.

When I worked for a contractor at NASA back in the 1960's, I was an editor and proofreader. As a young person I wrote stories and was published in the school literary magazine. In college several of my professors remarked that I wrote well and offered encouragement.

My bachelor's degree is in English, and I have been an avid reader and lover of books my entire life, thus rendering me a social isolate. Books are my psychotherapy. Reading a book is my escape from normalcy. Some consider me an eccentric. I don't care. I am a wordsmith, a communicator and an entertainer, but yet a solitary soul capable of shutting out the world and living in my own fantasy world. As a writer I live in a world of make believe.

My imagination runs rampant. I conjure scenarios that are fascinating and bizarre but mostly fun. I write not only to stir emotions – laughter, tears, anger, hurt, resentment – but also to stimulate thought and inspire learning.

Mostly I write in the early morning. I sit at my desk. The view is magnificent. I watch the birds, see the cliff across the canyon, the wide Texas skies, and I am at peace. The words flow easily. I never suffer from writer's block.

I write poetry, essays, short stories, screenplays, movie scripts, full length non-fiction, and full-length fiction. No matter the genre, I try to do it all. Much of my inspiration comes from people. Life is about people not things.

Thoughts come to me when I drive. I never listen to the radio; rather, I write stories, allowing my imagination to run wild. What fun to embark on a long road trip and savor the freedom of letting my mind roam free.

Often I'll start writing a book, not knowing where it will lead, never outlining, just taking off with an idea. My writing comes not from within but from without. When I begin a book, not knowing where I am going, a moment occurs that is as exhilarating as experiencing an orgasm. Simply said, it feels that good. And that is when I know I am me.

I go through periods of not writing when I am preoccupied, but still I either blog, email, or write something of value. If I don't write, I read. It is not unusual for me to read five books in a week. If I have some good books downloaded on my Kindle I have been known to binge until I have read them all.

I read on every subject because learning is my thing – my passion. Whether it's philosophy, history, travelogues, humor, or mystery I demand that the book I'm reading be well written and the content enlightening.

I believe that artists have a tendency to seek out hard times just as flowers turn their faces to the sun. From those hard times comes the inspiration for creating.

I do not enjoy verbose literary missives. I prefer clear, succinct text. I don't enjoy horror, vampires, rapture, or weird subjects, but I am drawn to topics such as remote viewing, visiting the other side, space aliens, seeing the future, traveling into the past, and reincarnation.

Books set in distant lands, written by international authors, appeal to my sense of adventure. I love reading about and studying other cultures, venturing into their countryside, villages, and markets.

Books on the writing experience help me better understand myself. I find it comforting to read other authors explaining the process of writing and realize that I share many of the same emotions. In a way they affirm who I am.

I'll never forget a quote I once read, *"I shall live bad if I do not write and I shall write bad if I do not live."* That says it all.

11 Rebellion

Rules are made to be broken. If I don't run a stop sign by coasting or park in a wrong place or break some cardinal rule, I consider the day a lost cause. Rebellion is part of my life; being a Texan may have something to do with it.

The Texans rebelled against the Mexicans, fought and killed for the land and formed a country. The classic story of the Alamo is known throughout the world. John Wayne made Texas famous when he starred in the movie depicting the valiant fight for independence. Once the Mexicans were defeated, the Indians were next.

Today most citizens follow the rules without questioning. I don't. In fact, I like breaking the rules. It makes me smile.

Recently I was on my way to Uvalde for a supply run with many stops scheduled for the day. As I approached the town, road work was being done on the highway, likely to repair damage caused by big trucks traveling the main route from the oil fields in the Permian Basin to the new oil boom area in southwest Texas, the Eagle Ford Shale.

One lane was blocked. A portable red light and barrier stood guard. No one was in sight. I looked ahead. The road appeared clear. I drove my pickup on the one lane only to encounter a pilot car coming toward me leading a caravan of vehicles. He stopped, rolled down his window, and yelled. *"Didn't you see the red light? You should of stopped."*

I played the helpless, dumb old lady. *"Oh no. I'm so sorry. I didn't see it. Should I turn around?"*

"No, just stay here until I get back."

He motioned me to the grassy shoulder. The short delay had given some cars behind me the courage to follow my lead. There were four of us. I drove on, smiling.

In my rear-view mirror I watched him stop each of the following cars. In time they followed me. It occurred to me then that there were others like me who embrace rebellion. I knew it would be a good day.

Sometimes I carry rebellion a bit too far and suffer the consequences.

Several years ago I stood in a long line for an airport security check. I reviewed the list of "You can't take that with you." Among the prohibited items were cigarette lighters. The man behind me withdrew one from his pocket and prepared to drop it in the receptacle provided for such disposals. In a reckless moment, I asked for the lighter and boldly put it in my purse, passing through security with impunity, in the process losing sight of the lighter's owner.

On the return trip, having forgotten the lighter in my purse, I failed to pass security, instead being taken to a cubicle to endure an embarrassing lecture that almost caused me to miss the flight, in retrospect pretty stupid.

During a recent visit with my daughter in Marfa, Texas, we were sitting on the porch enjoying the Big Bend landscape and the colorful sunset. The evening became one of confession. My daughter admitted that most of her life she had been a bitch, rebelling against every rule, imagined or real.

In truth she was kicked out of three high schools in one year, and my mother once said, *"That child will never finish high school."* That was one of the few times my mother was wrong.

She now holds a master's degree in botany, works as a consultant, and is the mother of two young boys. On that fine summer evening she apologized for the worries she had caused. "I fought the rules because I didn't want to follow them, especially when I saw you being nice when you didn't have to. I thought you were a hypocrite. Now that I'm a mother I realize I have to play the game for the benefit of my children and husband, but that doesn't mean I like it."

I almost cried with relief that she finally understood me.

My son and his wife also played the game. He abandoned college, worked in bicycle shops, and later achieved an associate degree in fire fighting. I personally believe he would have been happier working with bicycles. He spent eight years as a firefighter in the Houston area. His wife worked at a hospital as a physical therapist assistant for more than eight years. After more than a decade, their house and cars were paid for, they had money in the bank, and they quit their jobs, bought a house in Colorado, and have changed careers. I am proud of them.

In America we are free to cut our own trail. How great is that?

12 Boston

For a change in my normal travel patterns, I decided to fly from San Antonio rather than drive to Houston, reason being that I would only be gone three days, making the parking and logistics easier.

The day began on an exciting note. Before dawn, my ranch manager arrived for work and called from the guest lodge down in the creek bottom (cell phones don't work, thankfully, in this remote part of Texas) announcing that a new lamb had been born during the night. We had penned the ewe several weeks earlier as she was showing all the sure signs of impending birth. She was big enough to pop, and at last she produced a healthy lamb.

I loaded my small overnight bag into the pickup and stopped down by the barn for a last minute conversation with the manager who was all smiles. We had also trapped two feral hogs in the hog trap, and for a change they were a good eating size. Previously we had trapped five small hogs, too small to butcher. We gave them to friends with the patience and facility to fatten them. I instructed the manager to process the hogs for the freezer and left for San Antonio.

I stopped at Garven's Store to purchase some buffalo and venison jerky as a gift for the man I was meeting in Boston, a publicist for my soon to be released book. The day of our meeting was coincidentally his birthday.

I had planned on long-term parking adjacent to the airport, but the lot was full. My other choice was to park in short-term parking for $24 dollars a day or drive to off-site parking for $8 per day. Being early, I chose thrifty.

The short flight to Houston was followed by a smooth connection, and I at last settled down to a relaxed flight in first class to Boston.

My seat-mate for the Boston flight was a very tall, very young man. Mark was a talker from Houston. He was well informed on world affairs and was soon telling me of his school debate on China. I didn't completely agree with his opinion concerning the current relationship between the U.S. and China but declined to argue with him, delighted to speak with someone his age who at least had an interest in the world beyond Texas.

When he noted that the movie *"Argo,"* was playing on the screens before us, I admitted my ignorance and let him set my screen to watch the movie, welcoming some relief from his chatter about the new Pope of whom I was unaware.

While the engine noise prevented my hearing every word of the movie, I was entertained and impressed by the film, which had won the Oscar.

The conversation with Mark continued. I was shocked to learn he was only 14 and an eighth grader. This, I realized, was the new generation. I was disappointed to hear that he wanted to live in Germany and believed in the social welfare system and big government spending to provide for the masses. Not wanting to engage in a heated conversation, I inserted a few contrary comments, which he seemed not to hear. He praised his middle school of 1,800 students but then added that 65 of the 148 students in his class were failing physics and chemistry. When he left his seat to use the bathroom, I feigned sleep and was relieved that the plane landed ahead of the scheduled time.

The night was cold and clear as I engaged a taxi to relay me to Newton, a suburb of Boston. The driver was Jamaican and had been in the states 11 years. I found his English difficult to understand.

When he delivered me to the hotel, the price on the meter read $48. He turned to me and asked, *"Cash?"* I nodded.

"It's $60."

I suppose my look was incredulous.

"The extra is for the toll roads."

Rather than argue, I paid the fare and checked into the hotel, going to my room, which supposedly overlooked the Charles River. The only thing I cared about was the soft bed.

Reflecting on the taxi ride, I felt I had been swindled for only the second time in my world travels. Both incidents had occurred in my own country, the other one being in San Antonio when a taxi driver late at night charged me $20 for a short mile trip, citing a $20 minimum.

I read too late, slept fitfully, and made coffee as I watched the Charles River emerge in the gray-colored dawning.

I met my publicist in the lobby, shared a long breakfast and conversation, and signed a contract for a national publicity campaign. Victor was professional, had excellent references, and exuded confidence. I felt we were a good match. Meeting him face-to-face established a good rapport between us that predicted a good relationship for the future of the book and others to come.

Wired on coffee after our goodbyes, I arranged a taxi for the following morning, asked the desk clerk to print out my boarding passes for the return flight, and returned to my warm room to read the Wall Street Journal from cover to cover, discovering that Greenland hosted only 57,000 inhabitants and was closely tied in governance with Denmark.

The weather remained cold, but some of the clouds dispersed. I spent most of the afternoon becoming reacquainted with my iPad's keyboard and word processing program. Three months had passed since I last used it on a trip to Southeast Asia.

I wrote an essay and ordered a burger from room service. The ranch and a new lamb awaited my return.

13 Love

I don't believe in lasting love between a man and a woman or two of the same sex. I do believe strongly in love of children, family, a higher power, and love of land. Those loves last forever.

Having been married four times and involved in some temporary relationships, I have come to the conclusion that this magical thing called love between two adults, no matter their gender, is temporal. I cannot imagine living with the same person for 50 or 60 years and having sex with the same person for that long. Boring is the word that comes to my mind.

In fact, I know of few marriages — including my own — where either spouse has been faithful. What most people call love is lust, chemistry, and conquest.

I don't know why a stupid piece of paper can do so much to alter a relationship. The marriage certificate is a powerful game changer for the parties involved. I tried it four times. It never worked for me. Yet, there are those who profess to be happily married; what happens behind closed doors is most likely another story.

We all wear masks. Whether it's a woman who wears makeup or a man who acts macho, we conjure for ourselves an appearance that we feel is what others expect of us, and in so doing become something we are not. Only when we discover that we have lost our spirit and self can we begin to fix the problem. In the case of marriage, that usually means divorce. Then we do it all over again with someone else, put on another mask, and continue the game.

In marriage we stifle the things that construct our happiness in order to please our partner. Marriage is a trap designed to stifle the freedom we need to become our better selves.

We all crave love and adoration and will do most anything to attain that high, that special feeling that makes the skin glow like a ripe peach. When that wears off, usually not much is left.

Respect is the key to maintaining a relationship. I have been with couples who abuse each other verbally or talk about each other when one is absent, embarrassing for me but not for them. The respect is gone. The game is being played.

My philosophy about game playing is if I don't play, there is no game. It takes two unless you play solitaire.

Solitaire has worked for me for almost 20 years. I think I failed at marriage because I rated sex way too high on the list. When the glow of sex wore off and the revelation of deceit appeared, I fled. During the second marriage I remained because of my children. There was no time for much else. When they reached high school, I bailed out of the marriage. I'm still not sure why I remained married for 15 years, perhaps because I felt safe or because he spent over three years in prison. Raleigh was a hell of a man.

The third time was not a charm, but a big mistake. It was an attempt to be respectable and ended up being the shortest marriage. Number four was the predictable reunion with an old love. He died before the relationship had a chance to go south.

This current relationship is fortunately marriage-free. We tried living together to no avail. Now he visits and I don't have to comb my hair or wear matching clothes or hold in my stomach. We enjoy each other's company as well as our solitude. Today, solitude rules. I wave when I pass him on the road.

I still don't understand the love between adults. Perhaps I am a slow learner.

The Family Reserve

At a recent Lyle Lovett concert in San Antonio, Lyle, a cousin on the Klein side of my family, sang a song called "The Family Reserve." The lyrics mentioned some of the characters in the Klein family who have passed, and their names brought memories long forgotten or neglected. Tears came to my eyes at the guilt I felt for neglecting the impact they had on the Klein generations that followed. Whether "Family Reserve" meant those of us still living or the reserve strength they imparted, it really didn't matter. For several days I had the blues, often crying as nostalgic scenes and pictures floated through my consciousness.

Lyle first mentioned Skinner, his uncle and my first cousin. Skinner farmed and had a dairy. He drove a Mercury and drank beer all day. Then there was Eugene, Skinner's brother. Eugene farmed, worked in the family dairy and promoted oil and gas leases. Next came Aunt Ella, my father's sister. She was one of a kind, a unique individual with whom I spent many summers. Aunt Hannah was another of my father's sisters, forced into an arranged marriage with a man she didn't love and who drank much and worked little. She had a nervous breakdown, was given electric shock therapy back in the early 1950's, and never fully recovered. She divorced when divorce was not acceptable, at least not in my family. My father Alvin was mentioned last.

Oh, how those memories came flooding back for days after the concert. Lyle did not mention his grandfather, Adam Klein, who wore overalls, farmed, and chewed tobacco; or Uncle Alec who died in his 50's leaving nine children; or Uncle George who was a serious alcoholic most of his life; or Uncle Johnny who was the director of the Lutheran Deaf Institute in Detroit, Michigan, before he retired and lived well into his 90's; or the third sister to the Klein brothers, Aunt Mary, who died in childbirth. I recall each and every one of them from the eyes of a child to the years of my early adulthood. And then there were many of the first cousins, most of them older than me because my father married at age 46 and started a family much later than his siblings. I know the superficial story of them all. Among those first cousins are/were doctors, grocers, lawyers, teachers, business owners, bankers, accountants, oil company executives, house wives, a preacher, a high school coach, farmers, a restaurant owner, a nurse, and a retired colonel. One thing they shared in common — they all worked. Not one of them ever went to prison or accepted welfare. Most of them were Lutheran, and they honored family. Today the descendants of my first cousins have broadened the family base. They are religious, educated, and contribute to society. My cousins and I have hopefully instilled the family values given to us by the preceding generation.

I find it shocking that I am now among those of us in the top remaining generation. None of the aunts and uncles on the Klein side of the family are alive, and quite a few of my first cousins have also passed beyond life on earth.

I believe the remaining family members know our roots are deep and our branches will continue to be strong. That is their legacy. We are the family reserve.

The Yard

I don't know why my yard is so popular with the wildlife that inhabits the ranch. Thousands of acres surround the few acres enclosed by a game proof fence that comprise my small piece of the rough terrain in southwest Texas. I only want a bit of land on which to grow a few herbs and flowers, and the fence supposedly grants that privilege. It doesn't.

The deer remain outside but are the only ones. Every sort of varmint imaginable has invaded the yard. There is a white hooded skunk that scampers away in the predawn darkness when I descend from the bedroom to enter the main house.

The coon trap I keep baited between the house and the utility room, a short walk away, yields at least a couple of coons a week and an occasional possum. Three porcupines, big ones, have been killed in the last two weeks a few steps from the back door. I have nothing against porcupines except that they kill trees. My boyfriend is a tree man. He hates them more than I do. He's a good shot and killed them all with a pistol. Three more porcupines have been killed down at the guest lodge in the creek bottom. Over the years the porcupines have killed three apple trees, a peach tree, and severely damaged my pear tree and an apricot tree. Wire cages now prevent them most of the time from continuing their destruction, but the wire cages provide a leg up for the raccoons to feast on the fruit. I have since removed the wire cages and closely monitor the fruit trees for missing bark.

Armadillos dig up my yard. Billy killed one of those last week. Cliff swallows nest under the eaves of my roof, and this year an orange oriole nested near the swallows. Rock squirrels and brown squirrels eat the bird seed.

Twice I have spotted bobcats in the yard and once even a small wild hog that I shot. Cottontail rabbits ate the petunias until I changed to periwinkles. They don't eat those.

A pair of roadrunners nest beside the propane tank. I like them. They eat snakes.

The coon trap down at the barn also nets a few coons a week, and one week a gray fox was in the trap. Billy shot him too. Foxes eat baby lambs.

The surveillance camera at the hog trap captured a jaguar, a lethal spotted cat, which was quite surprising. Two mountain lions or cougars have been spotted, not to mention the 30 wild hogs trapped in the last few months.

Two ringtails were killed in the yard this spring. I don't like killing anything. I just want a few acres of space. Why do these critters love my yard? I know they were here first but the wild country provides room for all of us. I know I can't win against Mother Nature. She's a formidable force, and God gave those animals claws. A fence doesn't keep anything out that wants in. I guess I'll have to live with them but not as close as the back door. There is a limit.

The Bridge Players

There's not much to do living in the middle of nowhere. There is a saying, "We are all here because we're not all there."

I love to play bridge. Being from a large German family that played games when the family came together — bridge, dominoes, or cards — there was always a game going.

I can't remember when I learned to play those games. If one of us kids walked through the room and an additional player was needed, we were drafted and taught how to play. One thing we learned — you play to win, but keep in mind, it's just a game.

There are several bridge clubs that play once a month. I have been invited to join them but prefer to be on the list as a substitute. I don't like living on any sort of schedule, and I know my boundaries. As a result I have the opportunity to play at least once a month.

All of us are senior citizens, and camaraderie and tolerance dominate our bridge days.

Margaret walked with difficulty so we let her stay in the same chair when it came time to change partners. She died recently. Carol doesn't hear well. That's okay, too. Some of us blank out at times. We refresh each other's memory. Shirley deals with an aging husband. Some of us are widows. We have dealt with loss. Rosemary lost her hair from chemo. It has grown back.

Many of us drive crooked, winding, gravel roads to reach our destination. Sometimes we meet at the post office or bank and ride together. Tillie drives from Leakey, over 25 miles. For me the drive to town is 20 miles. Often we meet at Fat Boys Barbecue and play in the second dining room, eating barbecue before the games begin.

When we play at Carol's, the drive is up and around some mountainous terrain, the road in some places being one way around the precipitous turns. Nuts and candy are on the tables, and music is often in the background. Sometimes it is a symphony or opera, which I find disconcerting. I prefer the table chatter.

The conversation doesn't focus on hair styles or fingernails or small children or school but rather on world events, history, books, and the vagaries of aging, not always pleasant but pertinent.

At a recent bridge game at Fat Boys Barbecue, we were settling at two tables. We often each put up a dollar, and the high and

35

second highest scorers divide the $8 pot. Hesta made the remark, *"I better hide this money. I'm not comfortable with it being out on the table."*

I asked, *"Why not? I don't think anyone will be robbing us."*

She replied, *"No, it's not about that. This is the game room, and Chug the owner might get in trouble if someone thinks we're gambling in here."*

Hesta was serious.

Shirley sat at the table with Hesta, Carol, and me. As she relaxed, she sighed and said, *"I'm so tired. I had 18 people sleeping in my house over the Fourth of July weekend."*

Before she could finish, Carol interrupted. *"What did you do with 18 people all weekend?"*

Shirley continued, *"That's not all, they also brought five chickens, three pygmy goats, a puppy, and a dog."*

I added, *"That's crazy. Who would bring five chickens and three goats plus dogs? There has to be a story behind this."*

Shirley told her tale. *"Well, the grandson and his wife were given the chickens on the way here. They were in a cage, but we had to put them on the back porch to keep varmints from killing them. We let them out during the day but had to watch out for them because of the dogs. Herding chickens at night into a cage was not easy."*

Hesta asked, *"What about the pygmy goats?"*

Shirley answered, *"They came with the grandson and his wife who are expecting their first baby. The wife's mother doesn't think her daughter will be good at parenting so she gave her the three goats to raise and awaken her motherly instincts. She keeps them in the house."*

I spoke, *"Yuk, goats in the house. You can't housebreak a goat. That has to be nasty."*

Shirley answered. *"It was, along with the puppy who was also not housebroken."*

Hesta advised, *"Shirley, every time you come to play bridge you say you are tired. I think you need to get more rest and quit all this entertaining or get some help."*

Shirley agreed. *"I've spent the last two days in bed. I feel almost normal today."*

The bridge game began. In the course of the afternoon, Clarice was my partner. I bid one heart. Clarice bid five hearts. The miscommunicated bidding resulted in going down a few tricks. When the hand was over, Hesta spoke up. *"Clarice, what did you mean by that bid? I've never heard of a bid like that?"*

Clarice stiffened, *"I knew she had two aces and didn't know if she played the club convention asking for aces."*

Hesta continued. *"You could have bid four no trump, asking for aces."*

Clarice repeated that she knew I had two aces and that it was a legitimate bid.

Hesta did not give her any slack. *"Well, I've been playing bridge for 50 years, and I've never heard of such a bid."*

Everyone smiled and we continued with our afternoon of bridge. There were no hard feelings because we are kind and forgiving, although we do tell the truth. Gossip is not on the table. Political views are accepted without question. Respect prevails.

Rosemary moved to Austin. Carolyn's husband died. She moved to Kerrville. Carol no longer drives. Two of the husbands have recently suffered heart attacks. The ranks are thinning but the game goes on.

17 Adventure

An adventure can be defined as a mundane task or trip that turns out to be more or different than expected. In reflection, most adventures are fun, sometimes not so much.

Living on a remote ranch provides opportunity for all sorts of adventures. Just the other day Billy and I drove down to the barn, loaded up the fermenting dog food, fish food, and corn that we call hog bait slop, a cooler of beer, and some sacks of corn. The purpose was to fill the wild game feeders, bait the hog traps, and sit in the shade of some big oaks on the back of the ranch, and drink a few beers. Sounds simple enough. Not so.

The fuel gauge on the Jeep registered one fourth full, sufficient to drive the few miles up the hills to the higher elevations on the ranch. I changed the memory cards on the surveillance cameras while Billy baited the hog traps and added corn to the feeders.

We tolerated the summer heat in the shade of a Spanish oak and drank a beer. The Jeep started easily but before we journeyed too far, the engine sputtered and died. *"We're out of gas."*

Since we were headed downhill, we gave the Jeep a push and coasted over the rough rocks and caliche until the Jeep came to a stop. Ahead were a few humps too difficult to push over. On one side of the narrow road was a high, steep hill. On the other side the terrain dropped sharply to a canyon far below. Billy sat down in the shade of a cedar and opened a beer. I asked, *"Who's going to walk back and get the diesel truck?"*

Billy answered, *"If I have to walk down this fucking mountain, I will die of a heart attack."*

I stood. *"I'll go."* The temperature that afternoon approached three digits. Shorts and sandals were not very appropriate for an afternoon hike. My cap had blown off on the coast down the mountain.

The walk was longer and warmer than expected. I drove the diesel over to the shed and loaded up a gas can and a tow rope just in case. It was a good decision. On the drive up the mountain I soon realized that if the Jeep didn't start we would have to tow it with the diesel in reverse down the mountain.

Back at the stalled Jeep, I found Billy sleeping under a cedar tree.

Thanks to the Environmental Protection Agency or some other

government regulatory body, the nozzle of the gas can would not fit in the gas tank of the Jeep. BIlly attempted to make a funnel out of a water bottle. It didn't work. He connected the two vehicles with a rope, and I backed up the diesel with Billy driving the Jeep. The road was narrow with little room for error, backing slowly until arriving at a point where I could turn the diesel around and Billy could coast down to the creek bottom. We left the Jeep in the pecan trees and returned to the house. The long afternoon had worn us down. I remarked, *"What an adventure. We could have really had a wreck."*

Billy answered, *"It wasn't as hard as jacking off with a hand full of stickers."*

My reply, *"Actually that was kind of fun."*

"If it was that much fun, why don't we go up there and do it again?"

I asked Billy, *"What would you have done if I said I couldn't make the hike to get the diesel?"*

"I would have gone to sleep and walked down in the morning when I was fresh."

The next afternoon we decided to go fishing. I had some worms and planned to fish for perch. Billy had bigger ideas. He was after bass and catfish. After setting up our chairs, cooler, and tackle box, BIlly patiently rigged my new rod and reel with cork, hook, and sinker, even put the worm on the hook. No one had ever done that.

He handed me the rod and reel and I tried to cast it. It would not cast. I have always used the old fashioned open reel, not those new closed spinner things. Billy is a serious fisherman, very serious. On top of that he is crazy. He shook his head while I tried adjusting the tension. The cheap China piece of shit would not allow me to cast.

As he shook his head in disbelief, he rigged one of his rods and reels, baited a new worm, and handed it to me. I shook my head. *"I can't cast one of these. I've tried before. I can't do it."*

"What do you mean you can't do it? You just press this button and throw it out."

"I can't do it."

BIlly patiently demonstrated the correct technique and cast the bait, handed me the rod, and watched the cork disappear as I reeled in a big sun perch. Before I could take the fish off my hook and put it in the bucket, Billy did it for me, re-baited the hook and handed me the rod. I cast into a large willow tree. He shook his head, untangled the line, and handed it to me again. An elm tree was my next catch.

"I knew better than to go fishing with a woman. I knew this would happen. We've been here an hour, and I haven't gotten a line in the water."

"Billy, I really know how to fish, bait my hook, take the fish off the hook, and clean fish. You just walk on down the creek. I'll be fine. I'll figure this out. You make me nervous."

He couldn't leave fast enough. I struggled with the reel and managed to catch a few more trees and even some nice big perch. He caught a mess of bass. We threw them back.

As we returned up to the house, Billy drove the pickup almost to the living room window. I commented, *"Don't drive into the house."*

"Why not, I've done it before."

The following day I mentioned to Billy, *"I'm going down to the guest lodge to do some weed eating. Is there gas in the weed eater?"*

"You don't need a weed eater. Just take your rod and reel."

Of course the light weight weed eater wouldn't start, and neither would the heavy duty one. I remarked, *"What else can go wrong?"*

"The day isn't over. We still have time. It's not dark and we're not asleep yet."

18 **Who Am I**

Today I don't know who I am. Most of the time I do. I think it was an email from my brother Allan about my book and our family heritage. For some reason it made me sad. I couldn't quit crying. To combat the watery avalanche I drove down to the barn, baited a coon trap, threw a dead rock squirrel out of another trap, fixed a surveillance camera aimed at one of the deer feeders, and drove on to the guest lodge to do some weed eating around three blueberry bushes and a cherry bush.

Then I sat down on the rock patio in the shade and cried. I cried, missing my mother and father, my grandson, and my daughter who sometimes hates me because I adopted her. She blames me for all the bad choices she has made and has spoken cruel words that can never be erased.

I cried for my cottage cheese upper arms, the sagging wrinkles on my lower face. I cried for the bruises and broken veins on my legs. I cried because I am 73 and my boyfriend is 59.

I don't think I know who I am. I try to define myself by my family. My three brothers all live in fabulous homes. One owns three homes, the other owns a ranch and a mansion, and the other owns even a bigger ranch with a mansion and guest lodge. Two of them have swimming pools. I live in a 60-year-old house with louvered windows from the 1950's.

Yes, I have traveled all over the world but I haven't found a place I fit except this remote rocky rough ranch in the middle of nowhere. My brothers and their families wear nice clothes, expensive jewelry, and hobnob with other wealthy folks. My second hand Rolex runs 15 minutes fast every day. My diamonds and jewelry are locked away in a safe deposit box. I wear turquoise and silver, not gold.

My boyfriend is a tree climber who smokes, cusses, and drinks beer, not expensive wine or martinis. He has never held a passport. He doesn't own a suit. We laugh, we dance, we cook, and we fill deer feeders and shoot hogs. He would be uncomfortable around my family. I go to their fancy parties and cultural events. I play the game and try to blend. It doesn't work. I am different.

I have never fit in, never had many close friends, and escape through reading. I am a writer. I live in a world of make believe. I see God in nature, not in a fancy edifice.

I go several days without combing my hair. My nails are clean but not manicured or painted. I don't visit beauty parlors or pampering spas. On the ranch I wear clothes that don't match. In fact, I revel in my bizarre outfits, plaid shorts, flowered shirt, socks that don't match, and even the multi-colored elastic band that holds my hair from my face.

My bank account is excessive. I can never spend all the money I have saved and invested. I could have a mansion, a swimming pool, or anything I wish. But none of that means anything to me.

I save rubber bands and paper clips and recycle as well as compost all food scraps. I have a garden that requires hard work.

I turn off my air-conditioning at night and only during the heat of the day do I turn it back on. I unplug the coffee pot when I am finished. I enjoy the breeze blowing through the screen doors, even when it's hot.

I keep my hummingbird feeders and bird feeders full. My flower beds have weeds, as well as flowers. The brush grows wild around my home. I like it that way.

My cell phone is older than dirt, and I only used it to send and receive calls. My son gave me a newer model when he upgraded his. There is no cell service at the ranch, and it is never turned on. I have never texted anyone, nor do I know how.

Physical work makes me feel good. Fun and relaxation are difficult. Dancing is the best. Passion energizes me and permeates everything I do.

I have never been afraid and meet problems head on. I don't know how to take it easy. I am adventurous, but mostly in my mind.

I am a rebel. Don't tell me it can't be done because I will do anything and everything in my power to make it happen. I will attempt almost anything but physical danger. Giving up is not in my DNA.

I love to grow things whether it be flowers, trees, herbs, food, or animals. I am not afraid of killing or cleaning an animal or fish or bird to eat. I know how to use a gun.

I am a failure at marriage and relationships. I've been married four times. Never again. My father was the most honorable man I have ever known. I don't believe in lasting love between a man and a woman.

I have always taken charge, no matter the task. I don't know any other way to live.

There have been times in my life — some rough ones — when I have hit the wall, when I've known deep in my heart there is nothing more I can do to solve the problem. I have learned that when I hit that formidable wall to turn it over to God, the God to whom we all pray whether it be Jehovah, Allah, Buddha or Jesus. That is the moment of surrender, of absolute helplessness, the instant of relief, the turnaround that never fails. That is what I call faith, the faith that passes beyond all understanding.

At times I long to be like everyone else. My wealth allows me the freedom to be eccentric, crazy, or unique. The most unhappy I've ever been is when I've tried to conform. I only fooled myself, no one else. By the time I was 50, I learned to quit trying and instead be true to myself. I am who I am.

Who am I? I don't know. Perhaps I'll find out when I go back to where I came from, wherever that may be.

19 The Ultimate Rich Man's Hobby

Men indulge in expensive hobbies – yachts, airplanes, hunting, fishing, golf, motorcycles, race horses, and girlfriends.

Women, on the other hand, sew, cook, play bridge and bingo, groom their bodies, go to book clubs and luncheons and showers and committee meetings, and volunteer. As a reward for our less expensive pastimes, we are given cars, jewelry, and nice clothes, not much of an equal trade in my estimation.

Skiing, rafting, camping, swimming, and horseback riding are classified as family outings and usually include the wife and children.

I know men who think nothing of flying to South America for a week of bird hunting at an estancia where their ammunition bill for the week is $6,000. Alaska is another favorite destination for hunting or fishing.

But I think the ultimate rich man's hobby is running an exotic game ranch. The opportunity to spend megabucks is endless. It all begins with the purchase of the ranch. Then there are game proof fences to erect, animal stock to purchase, and the famous lodge to build. The toys are various - bulldozer, tractor, four-wheelers, Jeep, stock trailer, flat bed trailer, blinds, feeders, pens, a large barn, watering troughs, hay racks, maybe even a horse or a mule. The maintenance and labor required to keep such an operation running is no small matter.

Many of the ranch owners build a landing strip for their plane and guest houses for their friends. Some build lakes and furnish them with canoes or kayaks and stock them with fish so that everything is available. I know of some who even construct a shortened golf course and, of course, tennis courts, something for everyone.

The creation of their own world is intoxicating and extremely expensive. They are masters of their universe, the ultimate power trip.

What is gained? A large tax write-off, their private resort, an all-consuming money drain, and perhaps a bit of fun.

I believe life is about people, not things. Having friends to enjoy the game ranch is a bonus, but the work and time consumed may destroy the pleasure factor. On a ranch the work is endless, never finished. Danger is always present, especially when dealing with wild animals.

Animals die, floods wash away fences, equipment breaks, employees steal, and accidents happen. As in life, pain comes with pleasure.

Knives

The first time Billy arrived at the ranch for dinner, he brought a gift. It was a knife, and I could tell he was proud of the purchase. The knife was made from a file and had a lovely inlaid wooden handle. It was the size of a small paring knife, and most likely cost over $30.

My mother taught me the custom associated with giving someone a knife. The recipient must always pay a token amount for the gift; otherwise the relationship would soon be severed. When my mother bought a set of expensive knives for me early in my first marriage, she asked me for a dollar. I gladly gave it to her.

I paid Billy a dime for the knife. He was not familiar with the custom but gladly accepted the 10 cents. Most of all, he liked the knife because it was sharp, very sharp.

He asked, *"Do you have a whetstone?"*

I opened my knife drawer and showed him my sharpening stone. He deemed it was not the right kind and promised to bring me the correct stone and oil to keep the knife sharp. That's when I knew he would be back.

The next time he came he brought an old stone and a small can of oil. They and he serve my knife well.

From my mother I learned to maintain my knives and sharpen them on a whetstone. She cautioned me never to put the knives in the dishwasher as the heat would dull them.

Many times I have visited friends and family and volunteered to help in the kitchen. Often their knives are so dull, they wouldn't cut a noodle. I am particular about my knives.

Texas men value their knives and guns. Rarely do I find a man without a knife in his pocket or a gun in his car or truck. Billy carries a small yellow lightweight knife.

Weekly he sharpens the knife he gave me as well as the one in his pocket. He tests them by shaving the hair on his arm.

Some of the local men carry their knives in a scabbard on their belts if they wear one. If they do, the buckle is usually a large decorative one. Close dancing is known as shining the buckle.

Every store, from the local Get N Go to the feed store, the hardware store, auto parts house, and the tourist shop, sells knives, and none of them are cheap. The knife maker often is associated with the quality of a knife, and some are as famous as the crafters of hand-made boots.

The knife Billy gave me that first evening he came to the ranch lives on the tile countertop in my kitchen. He keeps it sharp and uses it often. While our relationship has been a roller coaster ride, I know the dime I paid for that knife was well spent.

21 The Family Farm

The family farm goes back five generations. My great grandfather immigrated from Germany and settled north of Houston, Texas, in the middle 1800's. Successive generations lived on the land, plowing the soil and raising livestock. The Kleins are people of the land, going back to the 1500's, farming in Germany and then Texas where the opportunity for free land and the lack of available land in their native country encouraged them to journey across the world and settle in a new place. They were brave people.

Now the family farm is being sold to developers planning to build modest mansions.

My three brothers and I made the decision to sell. Common sense required it.

We are all aging as disgracefully as possible, and with many heirs, wish to keep estate matters as uncomplicated as we can.

Farming is in our genes. Today we all own ranches and continue to grow things and have animals, only in areas of our choice. Houston has grown around the farm, and it is no longer feasible to hold land where value is determined by the square foot.

The only consolation is that my brother David still lives on the land. He retains a small portion of what was once a prosperous farm where cotton, sugar cane, potatoes, and vegetables were grown in the sandy soil.

Tears flow when I think of selling the farm. The farm never had a name, unlike the current trend of naming one's ranch and then erecting an elaborate and expensive gate to signal its unique name. My father always called it the farm.

Memories of the farm overcome me. I've even returned to grinding my teeth at night, averse to the idea of selling the farm.

As a child I spent most every weekend and summer at the farm. Daddy grew peanuts, corn, and vegetables, mainly for our personal use. We cut hay for the few cattle he raised.

I drove the old gray Ford tractor while my father and brothers harvested the corn from the stalks and threw them into the trailer behind the tractor. We gathered pecans from the orchard and picked blackberries that grew wild along the banks of the pond. We fished, shot bullfrogs, hunted rabbits and squirrels, and fought the crows that came to steal the pecans in the fall.

We butchered calves and hosted family gatherings. We stayed in the camp house, a series of garages connected by a screened porch.

Many afternoons were spent on that porch, cooling off during the hot summer months. There was no air-conditioning or TV, and the telephone was a seven-party line.

I recall Daddy showing Mother that the gun was not loaded, pulling the trigger, and shooting a hole in the porch ceiling. I remember my youngest brother coming in from working in the field and saying to Mother, *"I'm a tired turd."* He was only eight.

We were all shocked. Mother asked him, *"David, where did you hear that?"*

He answered. *"My brother John said I was a tired turd so I guess that's what I am."*

When the pond dried in the late summer we seined the trash fish, leaving the gar, Grinnell, and big catfish to die on the banks.

Those were the days when wild horses roamed the coastal prairies and not all the land was fenced. We had horses, some good and some bad. The quarter horse named Nellie was prone to run away with its rider. Baby and Dolly were apt to roll over while you were in the saddle or run for the barn. We rode them bareback or saddled, and it's a wonder we weren't crippled for life. We didn't know any better.

My brother Allan rode a horse called Sandy. I think he was the best horseman of the four of us children. I can't remember how many times I fell off a horse. Nellie once ran away with Mother, and she was thrown and broke her heel. Daddy was charged by a crazed heifer when we were penning cattle. He was in his 70's and riding Nellie. He suffered a broken shoulder and collar bone and some cracked ribs. Mother took him to the emergency room at the small community hospital in Tomball. They taped him up, and she brought him back to the farm.

The state of Texas awarded a plaque to the family commemorating over 100 years of the farm being in the same family and in continuous agricultural use. The plaque will remain on the few acres retained by my brother David. I'm thankful for that.

As time drew near for the closing, I realized I was being a crybaby. I came to the conclusion that I was trading my undivided interest in the farm for a ranch; in other words I was expanding my backyard or sandbox, the land on which I played. I thought of my ancestors. They did not hesitate to leave the land on which they had farmed for over 400 years and journey to Texas.

I was only 370 miles from my roots, and like John Adam Klein I established roots in new land, Real County.

My portion of proceeds from the sale of the farm will be spent on the purchase of the ranch adjoining the property where I now live. Rather than pay capital gains on the profit, I am doing a 1031 tax exchange, buying additional real estate with the proceeds.

When asked what name I would give my new ranch, I replied. *"I'll call it the farm."*

22 Estate Planning

Over three years after my mother's death, my brothers and I settled with the Internal Revenue Service, paid additional estate taxes, and dispersed most of the assets. The high-priced attorneys naturally received their share.

The ordeal seemed endless. After filing the federal estate tax return, the Pennsylvania-based IRS agent requested more documentation and information going back a number of years. The result was an accounting nightmare. Fortunately, two of my brothers are Certified Public Accountants, not in practice, but very knowledgeable.

When the Pennsylvania agent retired, we requested an agent based in Texas and were told the Texas agents were overloaded. The case lingered for months even though we requested the fast track, whatever that means in government terms. The case did not move. Another agent on the verge of retiring worked on our estate return before passing us on to another agent.

Finally faced with the choice of litigation and more attorney fees, we settled for a sum larger than any of our individual shares in the estate. We could not win and simply paid our tax.

In many ways it was a wakeup call. We faced a similar situation with my father's estate back in the 1970's. The IRS challenged that estate return, also, and after paying exorbitant attorney fees, we settled rather than go to court.

Duly, we all began planning our own estate tax programs, forcing us to confront the uncomfortable reality of our own deaths. And while hearses don't pull U-Hauls, I did want to leave something to my children rather than have the government take more than its fair share.

My brother David recommended an estate attorney in Houston. Since I had a book signing and other business in Houston, I reluctantly scheduled an appointment in the Galleria area, dreading the drive into the heart of the city.

My son accompanied me because I believe four ears are better than two. The office was in a complex of high-rise buildings. We parked and found the right office tower, riding the elevator to the 22nd floor.

The large and elaborate waiting room was well stocked with candy and fancy coffee. We were on time for the appointment, which had been scheduled months before.

Five minutes after the hour, I was ready to flee. Scott and an associate approached the two of us eight minutes after the hour. We followed the two of them to a conference room.

In the hour we were there, he recommended setting up an LLC, limited liability corporation, an FLP, a family limited partnership, and two guarantor trusts, the purpose of which was to put my real estate holdings in these entities and reduce the estate tax liability for my two children. In addition I was advised to execute a durable power of attorney, a medical power of attorney, a directive to physicians, and some other form.

Being a single woman of substance, I find relinquishing control abhorrent. My freedom has been hard fought.

Scott gave me the figures of how much I could give tax free and then the 40 percent rate for the remainder, explaining how placing most of my assets in the entities he suggested would save my heirs estate tax assessments.

Of course, these entities would be required to file K1 tax returns on a yearly basis, and those returns would be a part of my children's annual tax returns. I would also have to obtain certified appraisals on the real estate and oil royalties owned before placing them in the proper entity.

I am experienced in accounting procedures, and all I could think of was the nightmare of preparing those returns, obtaining appraisals, and the record keeping as well as the cost. After all, I am German.

My son and I took notes, asked questions, and paid attention. Scott drew a chart, explaining the process. I asked him how much to prepare a will. The fee was $3,750. I asked about the formation of the interlocking entities, and he said the fee would be about $30,000, depending on the cost of the appraisals and such.

I thanked Scott and his associate and said I would be back in touch. It was early in December and he assured me that there was no hurry to act before the end of the year, that the laws would not be changing before year's end.

On the drive back to Tomball, we were silent, overwhelmed by the information overload. My current will was a simple one. At least I had that.

The following day I sold books at a Signature Event in The Woodlands and then drove to my brother's ranch in Crockett for a party and business meeting with my three brothers.

Finally, on the long drive home from east Texas to my ranch in southwest Texas, I took advantage of the silence to think. Just the logistics involved in this estate planning scheme overwhelmed me. My freedom is important. My joy is writing, reading, gardening managing the wildlife and livestock on my ranch, and traveling for research for my books. This whole estate planning thing seemed a bit time consuming, to say the least.

In fact, I was so occupied with this matter that I spent the rest of the month and most of the holidays worrying about my decision. I put pencil to figures more than once. The numbers did not lie. I knew the facts. And then I decided to give more to charity to remove funds from my estate and lower the tax liability. Once I played with the figures, I came to the conclusion that this country has been good to my family who immigrated here in the mid 1840's. Why not give them their share and maintain my freedom? If my children couldn't be happy with the money left to them, then it was their problem.

I had wasted over a month on indecision. I could not write and seemed to be busy doing absolutely nothing. In the meantime, I had purchased the adjoining ranch since my brothers and I had sold the family farm, and in order to avoid capital gains tax on the substantial profit, I executed a complicated tax free exchange on the real estate deal.

The adjoining ranch enhanced my ranch, but I now had three more houses and two barns to maintain. Thus my period of being busy but accomplishing little for fun and freedom, as well as writing, lasted another month.

And then the day came. I decided to write a new will, execute the power of attorney, the medical power of attorney and directive to physicians, but not the other stuff. I called an attorney friend of mine, explained what I wanted in the new will and the accompanying documents, and breathed a sigh of relief.

I awoke the next morning at 5 a.m., put on the coffee , and sat down to write. I was back on track. Wise or stupid, I did it my way.

Months later with no results from my attorney friend, I called. He prepared the durable power of attorney and the directive to physicians but had done nothing on the will, giving an excuse that amounted to, "I don't want to prepare your will."

He did forward those standard documents, which I executed, accordingly. I again put the pencil to my existing will and rested.

The next time I spoke with a girlfriend in Kerrville and asked about her estate planning, she recommended an attorney in Kerrville. I made an appointment, visited with him concerning my estate, and was assured that the assets were sufficient to satisfy the government tax and leave my children a nice amount.

Then I really rested, but didn't tell my brothers. I didn't wish to suffer any more anxiety.

23 **The Border**

When someone asks me where I live and I try to explain, I always mention that I am less than 100 miles from the Mexican border. That always raises the question, "Do you ever have problems with illegals?"

"No, I never have, but there's always a first time."

In the 20 years that I have lived on the ranch I have seen them walking down the county road. On several occasions they have banged on my gate with rocks, and I have walked unarmed to the gate and offered them water and food. They politely accept and continue on their journey. An interesting observance is that however many you see, there are always more hidden in the brush.

The homes on the ranch, as well as the barns, are unlocked. The keys are in the vehicles – the tractor, Jeep and two pickup trucks. I am not afraid, living alone. The worst they can do is kill me, and I am prepared to die.

What alarms me is the information that I obtain from friends who have family or friends in the Border Patrol. I often ask them, *"What's going on with the border these days?"*

I don't like what I hear. *"They're focusing on guns and letting the illegals come through."*

"They're apprehending more OTM's, double from last year." OTM is an acronym for Other than Mexican.

"They are catching Chinese and Mid-Easterners."

The bi-weekly Uvalde newspaper reports drug seizures worth millions of dollars and often cites the numbers of illegals intercepted.

The startling news is that many of the illegals are sent to camps and imprisoned where they then do contract labor for county officials and local landowners. Minors are detained and sent to live in large homes where the owners are compensated for their keep. The owners of these facilities own more than one, and the properties are held by limited liability corporations. In other words, it is a money-making industry. The border patrol agents are paid to deliver them as far as Conroe, over eight hours east of Del Rio. Supposedly, the minors are held until family members are contacted, and they are sent elsewhere.

The latest shocking news is that illegals who are apprehended in deep south Texas, the Brownsville and Lower Rio Grande Valley area, are bussed to Del Rio and then released across the border at Del Rio into Mexico with no money or contacts, only to find themselves at the mercy of the drug cartels.

The war on drugs can be compared to the war on poverty, an abysmal failure. The good news is that with the legalization and taxing of marijuana in some states, perhaps the drug industry will be affected.

As long as border patrol agents are corrupt, however, dope will be imported. I have heard stories of bales of marijuana being seized and warehoused in Del Rio. The bales are marked with case numbers. Later those same bales are discovered on the market or in the desert being seized once again.

None of this information is reported by the media. I recently viewed a TV broadcast that said that over a million illegals have returned to Mexico due to lack of jobs in America. That may be true, but I believe it is hype to further advance the idea of amnesty.

Many of the politicians have promised to secure the borders prior to passing legislation granting amnesty. The truth is that the border can never be secure. Look at a map of the United States. We have thousands of miles of border — land and sea. It is impossible to police. Any hole closed will open somewhere else. Recent politicians in favor of a wall tout the success of Israel's wall. I cite the Great Wall in China. That wall did not prevent the invasion of China by the Mongolian hordes.

If amnesty is legalized, then a giant administrative government agency will be created and administered by typically inept bureaucrats to process the applicants.

There is no quick fix. I say give them credit card identification when they enter the country and let American Express, Visa, or Master Card administer the information. They are efficient. Our government is not.

Time has passed. Politicians are again defending a wall, advocating sending millions of them back. The border patrol is letting them come into the country in blatant defiance of the injunction against the president who is appealing the ruling that the executive order is against his authority.

Stories from border agents abound. Existing laws are not being followed. The media remains silent. America has a problem. I don't have a solution.

Europe is being invaded by refugees. They are experiencing the same situation. Some of the smaller European countries are erecting fences. Terror and violence dominate the news, and some blame it on global warming, saying that climate change is driving people from their land due to drought and flooding. They are idiots. Climate change has cyclically occurred for millions of years.

Open borders, amnesty, fences, walls, compassion or civil unrest, violence, and terror don't offer many good choices. I'm glad I'm not a politician.

24 The Tractor

When I purchased the adjoining ranch, I didn't plan on having a $70,000 bright blue tractor with front end loader, brush hog and hay forks, as well as an air-conditioned cab with Panasonic Stereo. At least that's what the owner said he paid brand new for the piece of equipment. I'm happy with my orange Kubota diesel four-wheel drive tractor.

The blue tractor should be plowing fields in south Texas or cotton fields near Abilene. The longer it sits in the barn, the more it depreciates. When I let everyone know I had a tractor for sale, a rancher nearby showed interest. He definitely wanted it but would have to sell his old tractor first.

In order to determine the value of the New Holland tractor, I called the New Holland dealer in Uvalde. The dealership would sell the tractor for 10 percent commission. With the information I fed the salesman from the owner's manual, he estimated the value at $33,500. The tractor is a 2006 with less than 100 hours of use. I suppose the years depreciate the dollars.

Friends came by for a visit. I gave them a tour of the new property and mentioned the tractor. They advised me to put it on Craig's List. The cost would be zero. Following their advice, I took pictures, downloaded them on Craig's List, and set the price reasonably at $31,000 and received five phone calls the same day.

I emailed the interested parties more pictures and specifics on the tractor. One of them planned to come see it on the weekend, but tempered his upcoming visit, commenting, *"The book value of the tractor is between $22,000 and $24,000 and a tractor that has been sitting in the barn may have problems."* I listened politely.

Then a lady called, declaring vehemently, *"I want the tractor. Is it sold?"* I replied honestly.

"No, but a man is supposedly coming this weekend to look at it."

"I have the money and want the tractor."

"The tractor is yours. Us girls have to stick together. Do you have a farm or ranch?"

"I have a hay operation south of San Antonio and will bring you the money Monday. Where are you?"

"I'm north of Uvalde. I can meet you at the bank in Camp Wood."

"How many banks are there in Camp Wood?"

"Just one. It's a small town of about 500. The bank is on the left."

When the other interested party called to say he was coming to look at the tractor, I told him, *"It's sold. I'm sorry."*

He was kind. *"Keep my number and if the deal doesn't go through, call me."*

I spent a cold Monday morning waiting for the call. She called about noon. *"I've been in court all morning. I'm a federal agent. I'm picking up the check in Kenedy from Farm Credit tomorrow morning at 8:30 and will call you when I get to Uvalde."*

After I hung up the phone I moved to the computer and looked up Farm Credit in Kenedy. There was an office with a phone number.

I drew up a bill of sale with the pertinent data, elated that the deal came together so rapidly.

She called about noon. After completing the conversation I called the Farm Credit office in Kenedy and verified that a cashiers check issued to me had been drawn. I drove to Camp Wood where she arrived at the bank a few minutes after I entered the warm lobby. We introduced ourselves and sat down at an empty desk. She handed me the check for the full amount of the asking price, and I proposed that we notarize the bill of sale. She replied. *"I don't need it notarized. I looked you up on the Internet. You're a writer."* We signed and dated the bill of sale, shook hands one more time, and rose to leave.

"I have a 1,200 acre hay operation out of Floresville and own the antique mall there, too. Stop by some time. I have some interesting stuff."

I asked, *"What kind of federal agent are you?"*

"DEA."

Paranoia set in. I thought of the illegal drugs I consumed in my earlier years.

As we parted she said, *"I'll have a guy that hauls for me come and pick it up. I'll let you know when."*

The following week she called, informing me when the man would be arriving, and gave me his cell phone number. He called from Barksdale. I met him at the gate with my ranch foreman, but when I saw his truck and huge trailer, I had my doubts that they would pass through the narrow gate to my barn where the tractor sat waiting.

The foreman and I had thoughtfully started the tractor prior to the transport.

We drove the young man to the barn. He agreed it would be best to drive the tractor to the gate and load it there. The trailer was very tall. I had my doubts that the tractor would leave the ranch but left the loading up to the savvy men. It took a while, but before they loaded it I noticed the crossbar above the gate, wondering if the tractor on the trailer would pass below the bar. I was correct. My foreman drove the tractor through the gate and they loaded it outside, along the road. Crisis averted. I smiled as I saw the tractor leave the ranch.

A month passed and the rains came. When the rains come, Bullhead Creek, which runs through the ranch, comes down with a vengeance, flooding and washing away everything in its path. Unfortunately, the crossing on the property of the new part of the ranch is in the path of Bullhead Creek.

The tractor's purpose was to repair the crossing when the creek flooded. There was no tractor, so I called a local man who had a bulldozer and a bobcat. He worked two days to repair the crossing. The bill was $800. I still came out ahead and figured I couldn't live long enough to spend $31,000 repairing the crossing. I made the correct decision.

25 Do You Take American Dollars?

After traveling to all the countries in the world that I wished to visit, I decided to write about America, my plan being to spend my later years in the only country in which I choose to live. Of course the state of choice is Texas, home to five generations of my family.

I decided that I had visited enough temples, mosques, cathedrals, museums, waterfalls, mountains, lakes, oceans, islands, seas, ancient ruins, and monuments. When I told my son Joe of my plans, he advised, *"Well, I hope you write an essay about taking American dollars."*

I laughed, remembering the trips taken with him and his wife Carla. Together we visited Australia, New Zealand, Austria, Slovenia, Serbia, Bulgaria, Romania, Hungary, and Croatia.

Currency exchange can be a problem. I carry cash, no travelers' checks, and I do not own an ATM card. Much of it is either carried inside my shoe or in my bra. Bras make good pockets.

Many times on my adventures I observe tourists searching for an ATM machine or a bank to cash travelers' checks or exchange dollars for the local currency. I don't like to waste time on such transactions and instead always ask, *"Do you take American dollars?"* Most countries do and return the change in their monetary units.

There are exceptions. Communist countries insist on payment in their money. In Bhutan I spent ngultrums.

My son was always embarrassed when I asked if vendors would take dollars. He swears he will engrave on my tombstone, *"Do you take American dollars?"*

I would rather the inscription read, *"She had fun."*

Not Perfect

When I was 48, I thought I was perfect. My health was good. My teeth were white and even, and I wore a perfect size 8 petite. My hair, though fine and thin, was adequate, my skin was clear, and my eyes blue, but reading became a challenge. At first I held the text farther and then reluctantly resorted to buying reading glasses. Soon the reading glasses rested on a cord around my neck. The glasses trapped a lot of crumbs and food. I read a lot, three or four books a week.

I quit my job, reunited with a love from the past, purchased a ranch in southwest Texas, and planned to live happily thereafter. Not so. Within three years he was dead of cancer. I was devastated and spent the next months in solitary, grieving. When I decided to live again, my mother advised, *"Go have your eyes checked, and get some decent glasses."*

Being a dutiful daughter, I heeded mother's advice and made an appointment. I think the glasses saved my life. When I put them on for the first time, I felt safe, as though no one could see my grief because it was concealed behind my glasses. They became my shield, a barrier from the pain within. I only removed them to sleep and bathe. Without them I felt exposed, and with them I hid.

Life continued. I traveled, wrote, and tended the sheep, garden and ranch. Then as I drove at night, the highway signs were surrounded by sparklers, a gradual thing until the vision in the left eye became quite blurred.

Again my mother came to the rescue. *"Make an appointment with my eye doctor. You have a cataract. He's good and removed my cataracts."*

I followed her advice and scheduled surgery, supposedly a simple thing. It wasn't. The surgery lasted two hours. I knew something was wrong. The doctor admitted that he couldn't insert the lens but did something else. I was too overwhelmed to question him further and when my vision returned, it was perfect, or so I thought.

Months later in a frustrated and angry mood I tilled the garden. When I returned to the house for a cold beer after a day's work, I couldn't see out of that left eye. I first thought I had ruptured a blood vessel but checked that suspicion on the computer. My symptoms described a detached retina, and time to treat it was of the essence. The following morning I called an eye doctor in Uvalde, explained the emergency, and drove to his office. After an examination, he agreed, *"You have a detached retina. Go straight to San Antonio. We're making the appointment."* The second doctor made the same diagnosis, emphasizing that time was crucial. Surgery was scheduled for the next morning.

Following surgery I learned that my retina had detached completely. A silicon band had been placed around the retina to hold it together. The retina is similar to layers of wallpaper and attached to the back of the eye. That was the explanation. In addition to the silicon band, a gas bubble had been inserted into my eye, the purpose being to push the retina to the back wall of the eye to facilitate re-attachment. The kicker was that I had to lie flat on my face for two weeks until the bubble dissolved. The other option was to completely lose vision in that eye.

The doctor was emphatic. *"I don't mean walking around with your head down. I mean your head must be parallel to the floor 22 hours a day."* I understood. Being a good German I follow instructions well. The task was not easy. I had no knockout pills or company. I divided the days into segments where I could be up at 15-minute intervals. The first few days I slept a lot. I couldn't read or watch TV. I refused to listen to TV or music. Instead I embraced the solitude until I went a bit crazy. The last week was utter hell, and the last few days I can't even remember, but my sight returned. I saw the last of the bubble dissolved, and though everything was blurred I had limited vision.

Follow-up visits to the doctor revealed no change, and I canceled the last appointment and began to travel, that is until I felt a film growing over the bad eye. A doctor's visit confirmed my suspicions. Surgery to remove the film succeeded, and I was soon on the road again. The vision remained the same until I discovered my sight was deteriorating.

This time the pressure was low, inflammation was present, and I was given drops to reduce the swelling inside the eye. All went all until I walked into the sliding glass doors at the ranch lodge. My knee hit first and the intense pain disguised the bump to my forehead. The eye filled with blood. A Sunday emergency trip to the eye doctor in San Antonio revealed bleeding within the eye, but the retina was still attached. The doctor was more interested in who hit me than in saving the eye. When I assured him I had not been assaulted, he gave me a shot in the eye. It hurt. The blood slowly dissolved after sleeping for a week with my head elevated on three pillows.

I quit tilling the garden and heavy lifting until I discovered my vision was once again distorted. The inflammation had returned. Another shot in the eye and close monitoring followed in the months ahead.

I booked a riverboat trip in the American northwest, cruising the Columbia and Snake Rivers from Portland, Oregon. Midway through the cruise, I left the riverboat and retired to a jet boat to speed up the Snake River. When I returned to the boat that evening I saw a floating rectangle and hundreds of black dots floating before my good eye, similar to a flock of gnats. I imagined a broken blood vessel, but for three days, the floaters persisted.

Upon my return, an immediate trip to the eye doctor revealed that the good eye experienced a tear in the retina. This was catastrophic. My good eye was weak. The retina specialist used a laser to repair the tear. This procedure was done in his office. They clamped my head in a vise, deadened the eye (not enough), and zapped me more than once. Nothing had prepared me for the smell and the intense pain. A shot in the eye was nothing compared to this experience.

Follow-up visits determined the tear was repaired. To not think of my eyes as a potential disaster with blindness was difficult. I was afraid to shovel or hoe or do anything strenuous. Today the right eye remains good, and the left eye is stable with prednisolone drops two times a day.

My one luxury consists of a pedicure every month. Since my right toenail is discolored from a childhood incident when I dropped a can of peaches on my big toe, I attempted to hide it by painting it red. I wear sandals a lot. The red toenails were so distracting that I removed the polish and instead went for a pedicure and had them painted either white or silver. The polish covered the flaw. But then I realized that the left big toenail turned white without polish. I continued the pedicure routine until one day I looked up the reason for a white toenail on the Internet. The answer was shocking. I had a fungus, common. I didn't think it was common on my foot so I continued my Internet research to find a cure. Prescription creams were not highly recommended. Urine and Clorox appeared to be the most effective. For a week I peed in a cup and poured the urine on my toe. In addition I soaked my entire foot in a strong Clorox solution every day for a week.

With that malady supposedly conquered, I rested. Not for long when I realized my hair was thinning and my hairline part was widening. I changed shampoos and began eating foods rich in Vitamin D. There aren't that many so I began to take cod liver oil. I hoped it would work. It didn't.

And then my bad eye became irritated. It felt like there was sand or gravel in the eye. I rubbed it a lot, dealt with tears running down my face, and finally went to the doctor. The diagnosis was too much Vitamin D, calcium deposits on the eye.

The cornea specialist to whom I was referred ground the deposits off the eye in his office. It wasn't too painful, especially after other eye experiences.

On a follow-up visit, the cornea doctor observed that the good eye was developing a cataract. I worried for weeks before agreeing to cataract surgery. This went well, and the vision is perfect. I wear protective polycarbonate glasses for the good eye, just in case.

My teeth were the next to fail. I cracked a molar eating a baked wasabi green pea. The tooth, as well as another cracked molar, were extracted, and I wear a partial plate.

Everything else remains perfect as possible at 74 - no joint pain or gastric problems, and lots of energy. My love life sucks, the eyes are weak, and I have an excuse to be lazy. It could be better, but it could be a lot worse.

27   **Home Remedies**

My first memory of a home remedy was painting creosote on the wound of an animal, a young stallion on the farm who tangled with a barbed wire fence, presumably looking for romance. His name was Stormy. He died.

The second memory includes the four of us children. Whenever we had a cold or the flu we were given a warm cocktail of whiskey, hot water, honey, and lemon. We liked it. I'm not sure it cured us, but we definitely felt better.

I'll never forget the summers I spent with my Aunt Ella camping and fishing on Spring Creek, north of Houston. I somehow managed a splinter in the palm of my hand. The hand became infected, and red streaks crawled up my arm. Aunt Ella cut off a piece of bacon fat, placed it on the embedded splinter, and wrapped it tight with a dish-towel. Within a few days, the splinter came out, and the red streaks retreated.

When my children were small and we were living in Louisiana, my daughter Molly had frequent earaches. My Cajun husband's mother recommended blowing cigarette smoke in the child's ear. It soothed the pain. My husband Raleigh was a smoker. At that time I was too. The second remedy was to put a warm towel around the child's neck. That, too, eased the pain and allowed some much needed sleep.

When hornets and wasps stung us, I made a paste with water and baking soda to relieve the pain and draw out the poison. Baking soda provided relief.

From Louisiana I moved to a ranch in southwest Texas via the north Houston suburbs for a few years. All sorts of thorny plants, cactus, and biting critters inhabit the wild terrain. For cactus splinters, a corn pad or duct tape usually helps. For scorpions, centipedes, ticks, and red bugs there are all sorts of remedies. For red bugs or chiggers, I use Absorbine Junior. I have often wondered whether Absorbine Senior exists.

For tick bites I use toothpaste. I was in the habit of using toothpaste and baking soda on scorpion and wasp stings, but my boyfriend turned me on to Clorox. Clorox worked wonders when a scorpion bit my big toe.

Picking okra or figs can cause skin irritation, an itchy, uncomfortable prickly sensation. A vinegar wash usually takes care of that.

Since I live 60 miles from a community hospital, home remedies prevail in most cases. The only exceptions might be a snake bite or a bite by the dreaded brown recluse spider. In either of those instances a drive to the hospital emergency room is mandatory.

I recently discovered via the Internet an amazing remedy for the itch, the itch that accompanies the bites of chiggers, ants, scorpions, and the dreaded spider. While the baking soda compress, ice, Absorbine Junior, and an antihistamine alleviate the swelling and pain, the itch that will change a personality and render a person cranky has previously been incurable, something to be patiently endured.

When my boyfriend was bitten several times on the arm by an unidentified spider, the first line of remedies worked except for the itch, the desire to tear the skin apart. As a last resort I went to the Internet and discovered that heat delivered with a hair dryer to the affected area will remarkably alleviate the itch. The blog was written by a fellow Texan, and I immediately knew he was on to something.

According to the blog and the comments, the heat releases the histamines that cause the itch. It worked. My boyfriend could sleep and did not scratch his arm raw. Thank heaven for the Internet. It likely saved my relationship.

Recently I have been plagued by toenail fungus. All of a sudden the left big toenail became white, just partly. Then the entire toenail turned white. Stupidly I ignored it and resorted to having my toenails painted to cover the fungus, enjoying a pedicure every couple of months.

When I mentioned the white toenail to my card-playing lady friends, they admitted the same problem. The Internet provided home remedies - vinegar, Clorox, hydrogen peroxide, tea tree oil, and even urine. For a while I peed in a cup and then poured the urine on the toe. All of the remedies created new growth at the base of the toenail, but when I abandoned the regimen thinking the fungus cured, the fungus spread once again.

Back to the Internet for advice. Throw away your polish because it reinfects the toenail. That is a problem. I'm now using tea tree oil twice a day on the toe, and the next time I go for a pedicure I'll take my own polish, but I suspect the fungus won't disappear until I quit having pedicures.

I do remember my mother getting a staph infection from a pedi-cure. At least that's what she told me.

I wonder if fingernails harbor fungus. I don't do manicures, so I don't know. What I do know is that I planned on spending the winter with no pedicures, a daily regimen of tea tree oil, and wearing socks and boots to cover the infected toe. Surprisingly by spring, the toenail was normal. Australian tea tree oil cured the fungus.

Somewhere on the Internet, I read an article about healing with aromatic oils, namely frankincense and myrrh, and how rubbing the oil over a diseased part of the body, as well as on the bottom of the foot, produced cures. The gifts of the Three Wise Men from the east to the baby Jesus - gold, frankincense, and myrrh - made sense, the most valuable gifts to bestow on the Savior.

Of course, I ordered a bottle of frankincense oil and now rub it on my chest and the bottom of my feet to overcome the effects of smoking. Needless to say, I am well-oiled.

28 **Regulations**

In the 20 years since I have moved to my ranch in southwest Texas, changes in the American way of life occurred, not necessarily to my liking. At first they seemed ordinarily small, but added and accumulated, the changes are substantial.

I thought I remained hidden from the mainstream until I was given an address, supposedly for access to emergency service, a way to find me if I dialed 911, which is preposterous given that it takes at least an hour for an ambulance, sheriff, or the border patrol to reach my ranch. A sign hangs crookedly on my gate, "We don't call 911." Out here in the remote canyons, a person is primarily on their own, no matter what happens.

The terrain is rough, rocky, and not profitable. Native game and exotic animals, those which imported have escaped, run freely. At least they ran freely until city people purchased property and game fenced their perimeters, I suppose this was an attempt to own the animals in the same way they pretend they own the land. Nature owns the land. We are only its stewards.

To supplement income many of us lease the hunting rights to men who appear in camouflage and shoot up the countryside while riding around on four wheelers and drinking beer or whiskey. As soon as Texas Parks and Wildlife realized they might be missing revenue, they required that the owner who leases to hunters must sign up and pay a fee of $70 per year for the privilege of leasing their own land. I don't know the penalty if you get caught or how you can be apprehended for leasing your land without a permit.

I run a few sheep and goats to keep the agricultural exemption and thus lower my property taxes. When I received a letter from the United States Department of Agriculture that I must obtain a registration number and tag all animals I trailer to the livestock auction, I dutifully filled out the form and received a package with numbered tags and a device for inserting the yellow plastic tabs in the ears of all animals sold. All of this was free, though I believe the government surely spent millions on the production of the kit, along with creating a bureaucracy to implement the rule. Subsequently, the program was never enforced, and the last time I attended the auction with animals to sell, they didn't even ask if I had a number, much less if my animals were tagged.

When the Internet first arrived, the local telephone company provided access through a dial up modem, which often didn't work. Now we have the option of three speeds, in escalated prices. Cell phones still don't work, but with WiFi, high priced instruments can access the Internet.

In the past, sales tax for ranch purchases and supplies was exempted, that is, until the government stepped in and required an exemption number that must be filed with the vendor. Again I filled out the form and was assigned a registration number and a piece of paper signifying the same.

When the license plate renewal for one of my trailers was due, I sent in the $7 for the tag, along with a copy of my insurance card. I received a return letter saying the fee was $70 unless I submit a copy of my agricultural number. I complied, asking myself, *"When was this law passed?"*

And then there is the medical profession. Every year I visit my doctor for a checkup, consisting of complete blood workup and summary examination. Being over 65, I have Medicare and a medical supplement. The blood work has always cost less then $200. This year, because of the new government insurance, the bill was over $700 for the same test, same lab, and same place.

Today you can receive a citation for your license plate light not working, for seat belts unfastened, for wobbling on the highway, or driving without insurance. Yet motorcyclists are allowed to ride without helmets, and smoking is not allowed in bars, but drinking is encouraged. I say leave us alone. We are adults and should be able to name our poison. Marijuana is legal in some states but will land you in prison in other states.

The Border Patrol is not deporting illegal immigrants, therefore not enforcing the federal laws. Some laws are enforced, others are ignored. I believe the law is the law. Not so anymore.

Our justice system is in shambles. Social Security benefits are reduced if you earn more than a specified amount. That is my money earned from years of working. Yet welfare, Medicaid, and disability benefits are increased. Free cell phones are issued to citizens living below the poverty level.

If you live below the poverty level, you can file an income tax return and receive money, termed unearned income tax credit, even though you did not pay one penny in income tax. I do not understand that. Over 50 percent of Americans pay no income tax.

Did you know that I have to buy a fishing and hunting license to hunt and fish on my own property? Before long I'll have to buy a gardening license to grow fruit and vegetables to consume.

Over the counter medication is readily available. Billions of dollars are spent on supplements that are not regulated by the government. Yet we are warned that most of them are flushed down the toilet after passing through the body, contaminating the water supply, not to mention the prescription medicines that join them. Perhaps we have a population sedated by the water. I have even read that fluoride added to the water supply acts somewhat like a sedative. And speaking of water, think of how many people spend a dollar or more for a bottle of water, not from springs but from municipal water supplies. Add it up; we are paying more for water than for gasoline. How stupid is that?

29 **America Hunts**

Americans love to hunt. I have traveled the world and very few cultures, if any, are avid hunters, except for extant primitive cultures in Africa or South America.

Perhaps the older civilizations have eradicated most of their native animals or become too populated to live in harmony with nature or cannot possess weapons. Americans are armed and pursue native species or imported ones. We know how to hunt.

I live in the Texas Hill Country where the scenery is similar to Africa. Animals thrive in the rugged canyons and along the spring-fed creeks and streams. Fences do not appear to contain them, and those enthusiastic land-owners who import and attempt to fence in exotic species are often disappointed.

Exotic game ranches dot the area and have been in the business for decades. They sell the animals at auction or sell a hunt to sportsmen. Often the kill is not very sporty. The animals come to the feeder, the hunter sits comfortably in a weatherproof blind and selects the animal with the most spectacular horns.

Similar to golf, fishing, skiing, or most hobbies, hunting is not cheap. A three-day hunt usually begins at $2,500 with no guaranteed kill. Camouflage clothing, guns, ammunition, and booze are all extra.

When I purchased my ranch, my husband and I originally intended to raise a few goats or sheep to qualify for the agricultural exemption, thus lowering the property taxes. We soon discovered that fences will not contain goats and that the land was too rough, the rainfall too unpredictable, and the native game too populous. The domestic animals compete with the native and exotic species that escape, despite game-proof fences.

My husband died and as the years passed I leased the ranch to hunters on a yearly basis. At first I had a group from the Golden Triangle – Orange, Beaumont, and Port Arthur, Texas. They were a friendly group, soon taking possession of my ranch with four-wheelers, blinds, feeders, and family and friends. I felt invaded and as I raised the price every year, finally priced them off the ranch.

My second group of hunters were from Louisiana. They, too, were a friendly group, bearing gifts of shrimp, crawfish, and boudin, but eventually they too became invasive, bringing wives, girlfriends, children, and even a dog or two. Quarrels among themselves saved me the effort of raising the price.

When hunters vacate a lease, they always leave behind stuff - blinds, feeders, dishes, microwaves, toaster ovens, coffee pots, buckets, rope, bedding, and a dirty, deteriorated hunter's cabin.

Being German I painted and cleaned the hunter's cabin and pursued a dream to sell weekend hunts or recreational visits to the scenic ranch I named Ambush Hill. My desire was to utilize the beauty of the isolated ranch and make a few dollars, as well as control the native and exotic species, to be a good steward of the land.

The first experience was a disaster. A Texas Sports Writer's Convention was scheduled for Uvalde. The newspaper called for volunteers on nearby ranches to host the writers for a free weekend before and after the convention. I offered my modest accommodations.

A well-known sports writer from Fort Worth visited and before the month was over, he had published in the Sunday edition of the Fort Worth Star-Telegram a front-page feature on my ranch with spectacular pictures and contact information. I was inundated with calls from persons eager to visit the ranch. They wanted to bring dogs and children merely to sit around a campfire. I declined the children and dogs and agreed to an older couple's visit. It rained, they were disappointed, and I spent the day after their departure scrubbing the mud off the floors and cleaning the cabin. Obviously, it was not worth it.

Then my daughter and her boyfriend moved to the ranch. I remodeled and added on to a guest house on the ranch, and the dream of selling hunts was re-awakened. We rehabilitated the feeders and blinds, purchased game cameras, fixed the Jeep that the Louisana hunters had abandoned, and produced flyers and business cards, as well as ran ads in the local newspaper. It was a disaster. The relationship between my daughter and her boyfriend fell apart, she returned to school to complete her master's degree, and the two-year project netted one hunter who killed an aoudad for $750.

I returned to my solitary life, writing, gardening, traveling, and tending the few sheep I kept to maintain my agricultural exemption. The hunter's cabin and beautiful lodge I built for my daughter stood vacant. I hired a local man and friend who drove out to the ranch several days a week to help with chores I disliked or was unable to complete alone. In addition, he stayed at the ranch when I traveled.

And then I acquired a boyfriend, also a local, who was hunting savvy. Again the dream of guided hunts surfaced. Either he knew someone or was related to them. He networked. I created a brochure. We kept the eight feeders full, retrieved memory cards from the surveillance cameras, and eventually became familiar with the animals on the ranch, both native and exotic.

Reviewing the memory cards provided interesting information. We saw sika, aoudad, mouflon, sika grande, elk, axis, and fallow, all imported exotic animals. The native white tail deer, wild hogs, Russian boar, javelina, and turkeys were equally in evidence. I won't fail to mention the skunks, raccoons, squirrels, foxes, bobcats, mountain lions, porcupines, as well as the abundant birds. The ranch was a paradise and a zoo.

The boyfriend handed out brochures and called friends and relatives. I updated my website to include the photos. He returned one day with a card from the bulletin board at the local feed store. The card named an outfitter with professional credentials. I called the man and discovered, coincidentally, the man owned a ranch near mine and conducted guided hunts all over the world. In addition, he fed, lodged, and babysat the clients. The match was made in heaven.

The outfitter visited the ranch, was impressed, and the deal was struck. I would receive a per day fee for each paid hunter's lodging and we would split the harvest fee. He would furnish the food and clean my facilities.

The boyfriend moved away, and I awaited the hunters. Disaster ensued. The outfitter called. Four hunters were booked. They would be staying at his ranch for two days and then they would migrate to my ranch, along with a chef, three guides, and two animal experts from Texas A & M. Only the four hunters would be paying the lodging fee. The remainder of the entourage would be boarding free.

The date was set. Three days prior, I called the outfitter, not once but several times. He did not return my call. Finally, the day before the hunters were scheduled to arrive at his ranch, he called to say, *"I'm on the way to your ranch to show a client your property."*

I replied. *"No you are not. You don't have permission to show my property to anyone without prior notice. You have not returned my calls."*

His excuse, *"I've been in Houston remodeling a rent house."*
"Cell phones work in Houston."
"Our plans are to arrive at your place on Saturday."
"No, I don't think so. The way I work is that you call, I meet you at the gate, you pay me the harvest and lodging fee. I conduct business in a professional manner. Our agreement is canceled."

He replied, *"What I am I going to do?"*

My answer, *"Not my problem."*

For me it was another hunting deal gone sour. Great hopes, expectations dissolved. Considering my previous experiences, what else could I expect?

Smoking

Yes, I have smoked. Neither of my parents smoked. My father was an executive with Humble Oil and Refining, later to become Exxon. When he attended out-of-town business meetings, he usually returned with a big cigar in his pocket.

I recall him sitting in his chair, taking the paper ring off the cigar and giving it to me. I was thrilled to put it on my finger and watch him blow smoke rings. I loved the smell of the cigar. To this day that smell brings back the fond memory.

I smoked in college because it was cool and I could do it. I dated a guy who smoked Lucky Strikes. I remember the Marlboro Man.

Today it is not cool to smoke. People frown on smokers. The price of cigarettes is ridiculously expensive. In southwest Texas, many of the cowboys and ranch hands dip snuff or chew tobacco or smoke. Small town bars still allow smoking.

Smoking is not allowed in many city hotels, restaurants, or bars. The cities have ordinances prohibiting smoking. I cannot fathom how the smokers let that happen when motorcycle riders averted a requirement to wear helmets. We all have to wear seat belts, but motorcycle riders don't have to wear helmets. Hard to understand.

Recently a major pharmacy chain stopped selling cigarettes, in conflict with selling prescription drugs. Prescription drugs present an equal danger, similar to cigarettes.

Vaping, smoking vaporized nicotine, now offers an alternative to smoking. But preliminary research proves that the vapor is just as dangerous as the smoke. The liquid that comprises the vapor contains harmful chemicals, and many of the delivery devices and the fluid originate in China. How dangerous can that be?

Most of my friends smoke; my housekeeper smokes, my ex-housekeeper smokes, the mail carrier smokes, my boyfriend smokes, my boyfriend's landlord dips snuff, my ex-ranch worker smokes, and my new ranch worker smokes.

Options to aid quitting the habit include hypnosis, pills, patches, and gum, all costing money. I have read that quitting cigarettes is harder than resisting heroin.

What can I say? We all die. Pick your poison.

31   Ask To Be Given

A friend asked, *"Would you see if your boyfriend could use his truck and your flatbed trailer to clean out two sheds and the barn on my other property and bring the stuff to my house in town so that I can have a garage sale to raise some money to pay my credit card debt? I'll pay him."*

I hesitated, thinking quickly before I made my reply. *"He is a tree climber, he trims trees for a living. I don't think he would do that. What about your four children? Can't they help you?"*

"I asked them. The two boys are busy constructing homes. The girls are busy, too, one with a new baby and the other with a new business she purchased."

"Well that sucks. They're your kids. They can spare you a day. Mother's Day is coming up. If they can't help, then ask them to give you some money to pay someone to do the job. You've sacrificed a lot in your life for your children. It's time for them to step up."

I gave her the name and number of a man who often helps me on the ranch.

I reflected. Asking isn't painful, at least physically speaking. A "no" is not the worst thing in the world. Most of us ask a lot in prayer.

I learned in a marketing course that it takes hundreds of no's to receive one yes. Of course, that applies to sales but there is truth in it.

When I purchased my treasured Navajo coat and learned the price was over a thousand dollars, I asked if the manager would take $600. The answer was yes.

Years ago in the 1970's, my brothers prompted me to ask our mother what she wanted for her birthday. Her response, *"I would like a four carat diamond ring, one carat for each of my children."*

I was stunned, but when I relayed the news to my brothers, they said, *"Do it. You take care of it and we will pay our share."*

I called a friend in Baton Rouge, Louisiana, who owned a jewelry store. He mailed me three boxes, each containing several diamonds close in size to the four carats. I selected an oval diamond of 4.02 carats, put a note in the box with $6,000 cash, and mailed them back. He designed a gold ring with my mother's initials scrolled on one side and my father's on the other.

When the ring was complete I made a turnaround drive to Baton Rouge and surprised my Mother with the ring on her birthday. She treasured that ring. It now resides in my safety deposit box.

My brothers and I recently sold the family farm. I was faced with paying a huge capital gain tax or doing a tax free real estate exchange, known as a 1031. I searched the area for property to buy and then on a whim phoned my neighbor, asking if he would be interested in selling his ranch. In a month the property was mine.

The answer was yes.

32 Louisiana

Often it is said, "Louisiana is another world." Having lived in south Louisiana, I heartily agree.

Spanish settlers arrived first in Louisiana, then the French and Acadians. The Napoleonic Code governs the state, a set of laws different from any other state.

I loved living in Louisiana, probably because I was married to one of them. In the Cajun state, family and who you know determine success, and if you are an insider, they will take care of you. The chez babe philosophy abounds. If you lose your job or get divorced, you just move your trailer in Mawmaw's back yard and eat well.

Whether it's shrimp, crab, crawfish, or a big garfish roast, the food is excellent. Boudin, cracklings, alligator balls (not the balls you think), smothered chicken, and French bread are part of the menu, and the sauces that enhance the food are to die for.

Back when I was young and fresh I lived in Baton Rouge and taught school in the swamps around St. Amant, south of Baton Rouge. I never dreamed that I would marry two men from Louisiana.

I lived in the French Quarter in New Orleans — heaven for an unapologetic foodie. But I loved the Cajun lands of New Iberia the best, perhaps because I raised my children there. I went to cock fights, dog fights, horse races, and shady bars, where the card games were conducted in back rooms and girls were available upstairs. The Cajuns are the happiest people I have ever met. They love to play and have fun, living fully their motto, "Let the good times roll."

The festivals are family affairs - the Crawfish Festival in Breaux Bridge, the Shrimp Festival in Lafayette, the Sugar Cane Festival in New Iberia. There are no pretenses, just drinking, eating, dancing, and music. And the music is like nothing else.

An interesting fact about Louisiana is that most of the people who live there are born there. They don't leave and if they do, they return before they die. I once read that in the town of Jeanerette, over 95 percent of its residents were born there.

In Louisiana, fishing, food, and oil are king. Gambling is a way of life. Most bars have back rooms where you can bet on most anything. Dominoes and cards are played with passion. Cheating is expected. Drive-through bars are in most towns.

I recall a day when a girlfriend called and asked if I wanted to ride with her to the country outside of New Iberia to pick up a load of horse feed. Since my children were safely in school, I agreed. First we stopped at a drive-through bar for a giant daiquiri, then purchased the feed, and stopped for another daiquiri on the way home. Those were the days when everyone drove and drank. I was looped when I picked up my children from school, nothing to be proud about.

When the oil boom collapsed, hard times erupted. Home sales dropped, unemployment was high. My church initiated a brown bag program and provided a thrift shop. The churches banded together and established St. Joseph's Diner where I helped to feed hundreds of people a hot lunch on week-days.

Cajuns take care of their own, but I must admit that they might not be so caring if you are a Yankee or an outsider. One of my boyfriends related an example of this in New Iberia. After one of the hurricanes, not Katrina, he and some friends from Michigan drove to New Iberia for the purpose of obtaining work during the cleanup. Their vehicles had Michigan license plates. Before they settled in the motel, the sheriff's deputies arrived and in effect said, *"**Leave town if you want to stay out of jail and keep your equipment. We don't need any Yankees to help.**"* They wisely left.

In later years when I returned to New Iberia for a visit, I found the town unchanged. It was good to know that some things remain the same.

33 The Pity Party

I found myself a bit tearful the past week, the reason being that the romance I enjoyed was over. Of course I blamed myself, a total failure at relationships, marriage, and romance. For a few days I despaired of growing old, being alone, doing nothing but writing, working in the garden, and doing ranch chores. My world travel days appear to be over. There are no more waterfalls, monuments, mountains, cathedrals, mosques, ancient ruins, or shining seas and beaches that appeal to my sense of adventure.

I believe adventure is key to discovering where we truly belong. I belong right where I am, at Ambush Hill in Real Country, Texas. Travel plans in my declining years will focus on America, not so much for the scenery as to feel the pulse of the American people. I believe our world is changing, and America is in crisis, one reason being too much government control.

I am aging, in good health, and still full of passion for learning. My pity party started with feeling sorry for myself and progressed to missing my mother and father, friends who are dead, and romantic failure.

The pity party ended accidentally. I had driven my truck up to the house to retrieve some batteries for the game surveillance cameras. A friend came up the hill, and we met on the steep incline. I was driving down, and he was driving up. There is no room to turn around, and the loose caliche road can be slick.

I backed my pickup all the way up the hill into the yard of my house. He followed, got out of the truck and remarked, *"I would have bet $100 you couldn't have done that. I know many men not able to carry that off."*

That's all it took. The pity party was over. I merely replied, *"Thank you."*

As the afternoon progressed, my mind flooded with memories of the past. I recalled being chief pit steward at a Can Am race in College Station. Mario Andretti and Bruce McClaren were competing. I was in charge of the pits.

I remembered riding a dirt bike/motorcycle 40 miles cross country and finishing the race. Cooking once a month for the hungry in New Iberia, feeding 250 people, popped into my mind. I prepared chicken spaghetti and bread pudding in huge pots. I pulled a horse trailer to competition events with my young daughter. I helped my young son build a remote control airplane and fly it. I became computer literate in my 50's, wrote and published two books, won awards and purchased three ranches. I learned about raising sheep. I nursed a husband with cancer and buried him. I have a cell phone, a digital camera, an IPad, and a Kindle, not bad for a woman in her 70's. I even know how they work. I began public speaking and was invited back, quite an honor. The tears went away. No more self-pity. The party was over.

34 America's West

I have always loved the west, probably because I'm from Texas. That may not make sense, but it's my truth.

When I first traveled west I was in high school, ready to challenge the world. Our destination was Los Angeles to visit my mother's younger sister, Aunt Joyce, and her husband Harlan. Their home, perched on a hill overlooking Los Angeles, was modern, a typical California bungalow.

Aunt Joyce and Uncle Harlan were the best at keeping us entertained. We visited Disney World, Sea World, and Knot's Berry Farm, my first experiences as a tourist. The Los Angeles Farmer's Market furnished giant strawberries and fresh fruits. I saw the footprints in concrete at the famous Grauman's Chinese Theatre. I had fun.

The second time I visited California was as an adult with my first husband. We drank Scorpions out of a punch bowl at Trader Vic's, partied at the Magic Castle, and spent a weekend at the Biltmore in Santa Monica, visiting the beach and dining on fresh abalone at Talk of the Town, a once famous restaurant now closed.

Years later I returned to California with my second husband. We partied as if there was no tomorrow. Something about California caused me to feel wild and free, to turn it all loose. Drugs and alcohol helped.

On the return drive Palm Springs beckoned. The gondola ride to the top of the mountain overlooking the desert frightened me, but the wealthy resort scene entertained us both.

Years later a girlfriend and I drove to Sedona, Arizona. Barbara was a California girl, pretty far out there. She wanted to visit a vortex, be covered in crystals and find some answers.

The red rocks and mountains were beautiful, but learning the town was built on land sacred to Native Americans bummed me out.

The art galleries reminded me of Aspen or Vail, and the prices were comparable. I felt conned. For me the most enjoyable part of the trip was the miles of Texas, across the ranch lands of southern New Mexico, and through the pine forests of Flagstaff.

I never visited the Grand Canyon until years later. Having an inordinate fear of heights, I was terrified standing on the edge of the canyon, my legs trembling. I quickly looked down and backed away.

New Mexico is truly a land of enchantment as the state license plate reads. I first visited Taos and Santa Fe in the early 1970's. Drugs, hippies, and strange people dominated the scene. It was a bit too much for me, though I participated. I fled, afraid of falling into the abyss of addiction.

Today my brother owns a ranch north of Santa Fe, in the Las Vegas, New Mexico, area. I love the rolling grassland and the mountain peaks and the food. My cousin lives in Santa Fe and introduced me to the Santa Fe scene, the opera, the Indian market, the luxurious spas, and the famous food as well as the pricey galleries. In Santa Fe I enjoyed my first massage given by a man. It was very professional.

I found the Zozobra Festival in Santa Fe particularly fascinating. I think it was in September, and a huge bonfire was prepared near the main plaza. People piled on their worries and pain to be burned by the flames. There were wedding dresses, photos, and replicas, all waiting to become smoke and ashes.

I noticed at a luncheon that all the women dressed similarly and looked alike. They were not from New Mexico, not like the people I saw on the plaza in Las Vegas where I enjoyed an ice cream cone and visited a rock shop, not like the Santa Fe natives who yielded their worries and pain to the bonfire.

I've been to Alamagordo, the government installation, Four Corners where four states meet, to Ruidoso next to the Lincoln National Forest, Roswell where the Alien Museum sits on the main street, and Mesa Verde in southern Colorado. Albuquerque and the surrounding Indian Pueblo were more to my liking than the Santa Fe scene. I think it's because more of the people living in Albuquerque are natives. The delicious food does offer some compensation, however.

I viewed the cliff dwellings at Mesa Verde near Cortez, and I've driven through New Mexico many times on journeys to Colorado destined for my mother's lodge high above the town of Silverthorne in Summit County, Colorado. I've motored the rugged and scenic drive from Durango to Grand Junction and Loveland Pass in a blizzard with chains rattling on the tires of my Volvo. I've skied poorly at many of the ski resorts and partied in Aspen with friends of questionable character. I've snowmobiled, sledded, and cross country skied in Colorado and even rode horseback over the Continental Divide, camping overnight in an Alpine meadow. I rafted the Arkansas River with my children. Colorado is a state with a lot of public lands, rugged beauty, and unending recreation. It is also cold there, and I prefer the heat.

I've rafted in Utah, toured the national parks in Idaho, seen the redwoods, the sequoias, and geysers and glaciers. I've driven the scenic coastal highway from Los Angeles to Washington State, enjoying steamed oysters, fresh fruit and berries along the highway, and spent a few days in San Francisco. I loved Chinatown and the John Muir Nature Park.

I can easily understand the lure of the west. The wide open spaces, the absence of a large population, the clear waters, and the gigantic scenery sing to my soul. The folks who cried, "Go west young man, go west," weren't kidding.

35   I Am Angry

I try to avoid watching television except for the news and weather. The weather I can't control. The news I would like to alter. The ineffectiveness of our government is appalling. I complain and I vote in every election. Nothing seems to change. The politicians become richer, and the middle class becomes poorer, waiting for their monthly allotment/entitlement checks.

I know people on disability who work for cash, drive new cars, and purchase expensive phones and computers for their children. The schools don't teach script handwriting. How will future postal employees read script addresses? History and geography are available on the Internet. Cashiers cannot make change, add or subtract, much less multiply or divide without a calculator, which is on their phone.

The costs of groceries and gasoline are outrageous. We buy cheap products from all over the world, only they are not so cheap when we have to pay for them. Repairs are so expensive, it is easier to just buy new.

Unemployment is high. No one wants to work; they would rather live on unemployment benefits as long as possible.

Race is an issue. Everyone desires to be politically correct, even to a fault. Our citizens are apathetic, quietly living desperate lives.

The government quotes statistics without source or verification. The borders are porous. Our military is scattered all over the world. People are starving, living without clean water or food. Nations kill their own.

Violence runs rampant. People are going looney, killing without reason. Our freedoms are vanishing. Often I feel that anarchy is imminent, and the helplessness I feel is aggravating. I prepare for the worst, hoarding supplies and food in anticipation of the country's collapse.

Occasionally something happens to restore faith. The Bundy standoff with the government revealed that not all citizens will lay down their arms. There are still those who will fight for their rights.

Our society is elitist. Political dynasties are created. You must be part of the in-crowd to succeed. Athletes are paid more than Chief Executive Officers. Fans pay $500 to attend a music concert or sporting event. Our dollar has no value.

I thought perhaps the American Dream had died until recently, when two working men won the Kentucky Derby, The Preakness, and came close to winning the Belmont, the Triple Crown of horse racing. Hurrah for them. They risked their savings, retirement, and succeeded. Their story warms my heart. America is not yet lost.

36 An American Beach

America's coastline provides a variety of beaches. My most recent beach adventure occurred at Port Aransas, Texas, on the Gulf Coast. Port Aransas lies on Mustang Island, not far from Corpus Christi, which translates from Spanish to the Body of Christ, an unusual name for a city.

The small island can be reached by ferry or by road. I traveled with my four-year-old grandson and daughter and son-in-law, the occasion being his first visit to a beach before his mother, seven months pregnant, would be confined to shorter trips.

The luxurious home I rented lay on a cul-de-sac a short block from the beach, which was accessible by road or foot. After unloading the pickup, we dined at a local restaurant. As we entered the palm-thatched roof building, a variety of beach accessories and decorator items captured our attention. Stuffed fish of every size and species covered the walls and hung from the ceilings. Theiss (rhymes with nice) exclaimed, "Wow," a most appropriate response.

We splurged. I ordered oysters Rockefeller and a crab salad. We shared fish, crab legs and shrimp. The bill was steep.

Most of Mustang Island is dominated by luxurious homes, condos, hotels, and tourist shops — lots of tourist shops. Needing lightweight chairs for the beach we stopped at the most outrageous shop that boasted a giant walk through a shark. Theiss ran through the shark as I snapped pictures. Beyond the tail of the shark was a man in an open booth with two colorful parrots. Jimmy Buffet's music played in the background. Posters of tourists holding the parrots decorated the sides of his booth. We stopped. This man was an outstanding example of American ingenuity. Before a few moments passed he had Theiss sitting in a chair with a parrot on each arm. The price of the photos was one for $10 or two for $15. Our choice was two. He laid one of the parrots in Theiss' hands as the parrot said, "Hello." He tastefully squirted us all with a squeeze bottle of water, not a gun.

While we were waiting for the pictures to be developed, three middle-aged people strolled past. In a minute or two he had the three of them sitting on a bench with plastic flowers in their hair and parrots on their arms. This man was a master entrepreneur and admitted that he made about $3,000 a week. It was obvious he loved his work.

We finally ventured into the store and purchased some flip flops, a shark beach towel and a hat for Theiss. From the store we returned to our lodging and prepared for a late afternoon jaunt to the beach. The beach was not crowded. Port-O-Cans were placed at intervals as was an open air shower. The beach was clean of litter except for large piles of sand and seaweed. When I realized that the sand dune provided shade, I opened my beach chair and relaxed in the shade while my grandson played in the surf with his parents. He crawled in the shallow waves and let them splash, rubbing his eyes from the saltwater.

Theiss ran back to me and said, "Grandma, this is a nice place. I love the beach." He occupied himself for a short while with the plastic shovel and bucket we purchased, then went back to play in the surf. The sun was setting as we returned to the house and sat on the deck, watching the sea gulls and birds.

We returned to the beach the following morning after a quick trip to another tourist shop, purchasing a small yellow raft. We put Theiss in the raft and pulled him into the surf. He held on tightly to the rope and loved the ride, getting dumped a few times. We never allowed him near the water without his life preserver.

A good thing about beach resorts is that you can dine most anywhere in shorts and flip flops. On the way back from a late lunch where I treated myself to an oyster poorboy, we stopped and over-indulged on Gelato, Italian ice cream made fresh daily, and then purchased some fresh shrimp for our evening meal.

Theiss was eager to return to the beach, but we told him, "The beach is closed because of a shark attack." It worked. A cool breeze and soft sunset entertained as we boiled and grilled shrimp. Theiss slept with Grandma. We snuggled.

Since the beach was closed due to a shark attack, (not true) we went back to town for another seafood lunch after booking a Dolphin Cruise early in the afternoon, the cost about $100 for the four of us. It was worth it. Our group of about 20 tourists included some Mexican nationals who often vacation along the Gulf Coast. Seven children were on the boat, and they gathered on the mid lower deck around a wooden tank, about 3 by 10 feet, filled with small crabs, sea horses, and other swimming creatures.

As we left the harbor and entered the bay we saw dolphins and baby dolphins and then floated by the lighthouse built before the Civil War in the 1850's. And then the first mate announced that we were going to cast a net to dredge the bottom to replenish the tank. He described the process to the wide-eyed children. After lowering the net he held up his fingers, saying, "We're going to drag the net for nine minutes, just as many minutes as I have fingers."

One finger was missing. He explained, "One time we netted a shark who bit off my finger." At first I thought he was joking. He continued, taking off his sunglasses, revealing an empty eye socket. "The shark also took my eye and part of my shoulder." He pulled down his tee shirt to show his scarred shoulder.

He retrieved the net and at first it looked like a big clump of seaweed, but before long he was adding more tiny seahorses, tiny crabs, blowfish, shrimp, and other ocean species, allowing the children to hold them. Theiss was fascinated, holding and watching them swim in the tank. I looked at my daughter, "Looks like we have a marine biologist in the making."

Then the children went to the upper deck where the captain let them hold the steering wheel of the boat, a great photo opportunity, a Kodak moment, or should I say a digital moment. The afternoon was perfect, highlighted by yet another two stops on the way to our house, one for more Gelato and one to purchase two live hermit crabs for Theiss. The crabs were elaborately painted and larger shells were in the plastic home for them to move into when they outgrew their present shells. Theiss named them Michael and Joey. The cost of the two hermit crabs, a small sponge, and some cracker meal was a bargain at less then $20.

Since the beach was still closed for the shark attack (still not true), we spent our last evening on the deck enjoying the ocean breeze. Michael and Joey kept us company and joined us for the ride home.

A trip to the beach is a nice adventure. I heartily recommend it.

37 Magic

Believe in magic? I do. I certainly don't want to live in a world where magicians are replaced by bureaucrats whose only trick is to make time and money disappear. I prefer the magic way; at least it gives pause for wonder.

Wonder is magical. Living on a ranch in the middle of nowhere, I am spellbound by the magic of nature. I see butterflies flitting in pairs after the coldest day of the year and wonder where they were during the night when the temperature dropped to near freezing. I ponder how the agarita bushes know when to bloom their colorful yellow flowers and exude a scent that is so delicate, how the white brush has even a sweeter smell, and how the rock squirrels know I have just filled the bird feeder or that the bird bath has fresh water.

I am amazed that when I book a flight to Boston, planning on staying in a hotel on Commonwealth, I pick up a book to read and the first chapter contains a scene in Boston on Commonwealth Avenue. And if that's not enough of a coincidence, the second book I read that week also mentions the same Boston street. How can that be? Magic, of course.

I email a friend I haven't communicated with in a month and receive an immediate response that he was planning on emailing me that same morning, more magic. Often all three of my brothers call me on the same day, still more magic.

The spinach seeds I planted last week appear as tiny spinach plants. The asparagus roots shoot up four inches overnight. One day the pepper plants have no blooms, the next day they have two. An iris blooms overnight, the yellow flower vibrant against winter's drab colors. The pear tree is loaded with white blooms, and the bees are busy buzzing around them. Who told the bees that the pear tree was flowering, and where were they during the chill days of late winter?

Why do the lambs jump and frolic in the pasture? How do the upper winds arrange the clouds in patterns resembling sand dunes or buffaloes ranging the skies? Do the clouds ever look down and say, "Hey, that one's shaped like an idiot." How do the migrating geese know to fly in a "V" pattern? How does a baby know how to smile?

I walked out the back door yesterday afternoon and three feet away stood a large porcupine in full blown attack mode. When he saw me, he slowly ambled up the rock steps and into the brush.

Later I stepped out of the shower and saw in the persimmon tree out the window two ladder-back woodpeckers, so colorful with their red heads and black and white checkered bodies.

That's what I call magic.

38   **Dumb and Dumber**

No matter how old I am, I still manage to do dumb things every day. Take my latest misadventure.

It all started with an email from my daughter-in-law referring to some magic herbal combination called Garcenia Cambogia that promises effortless weight and body fat loss. I immediately go to the website and sign up for the double order (buy some and get some free).

As I fill in my credit card number and other info I see a box that is checked subscribing me to some email service counseling for $12.95 a month. I try to uncheck the box but the computer refuses to cooperate. I lose patience, not my long suit, and exit the website.

Minutes later I receive an email confirming my order. I am furious. I return to the website and call the toll free number to cancel the order.

I hear the Indian accent and immediately know I am screwed. I explain to him that I wish to cancel the order. He refers to the return policy, says the order is streamlined and cannot be canceled. I am advised that when I receive the product I should call and obtain a Return Merchandise Authorization number (known in the con business as an RMA), pay the return postage and a restocking fee of $5.95 per bottle.

I ask to speak to a supervisor. The answer: *"Not available."*

I reply, *"I'm going to call my credit card company and dispute the charge."*

The Internet is a great information source. I type in the name of the product and read reviews, most of them unkind from dissatisfied customers, affirming that the product does not induce weight loss but rather increases pounds.

This does not diminish my anger and frustration, especially in light of the fact that I am, at most, five pounds above my desired weight. Now I feel foolish and stupid as well as pissed.

After sleeping on it, I call my credit card provider and explain the situation and advise them to dispute the claim. They assure me they will handle the dispute and obtain an RMA.

The following day I receive a phone call from the company fleecing me. A man congratulates me on ordering the product and wishes success. I explain that I wish to cancel the order, and he gives me a phone number for customer service.

I call the number, ask for an RMA, and am informed that their records show that I have disputed the charge and until my credit card provider calls them and the dispute is removed, they cannot give me an RMA.

The credit card people tell me that they do not make calls to Merchant Services, but if I drop the dispute they will advise the merchant, via email, that the dispute has been canceled. This will take up to 30 days.

I am in the 30-day window of return opportunity. The 30 days began with my placing the order. I have not even received the elixir to weight loss.

Ten days later the package is delivered. Another senseless effort to obtain an RMA fails. I tell the man that they can either give me an RMA, or I will reopen the dispute and return the product to the address on the package. I try to reason, telling him that if he gives me the RMA they will receive the product and receive the restocking fee of $5.95 per bottle. There are six bottles in the package that I refuse to open. He declines my offer.

In the meantime my dumb and dumber month drones onward. I order new lithium batteries from Amazon for my weed eater. I order 36 volt. They send 40 volt. There is no return on batteries. I repair my gas operated weed eater and place the rechargeable weed eater in the utility room, now totally dysfunctional.

When I realize that my Reverse Osmosis Unit water filters under the sink need to be changed, I refer to the owner's manual, go to the Internet and order three sets of filters. My ranch handyman arrived to replace the filters and one of them was wrong. I consulted the invoice and read that to return the incorrect filter I had to obtain an RMA and return the product within 30 days of placing the order. Again time worked against me. I emailed the merchant and he emailed back, asking, "Why doesn't the filter work?"

I emailed my response, "It doesn't fit." This issue is still pending.

The automatic gate opener quit working. After careful examination by someone smarter, it was determined that the circuit board was kaput. I obtained the brand and model number from the unit and went to the Internet to find a dealer. The nearest dealer was only 100 miles away. I called, gave him the model number, and he sent the circuit board. Upon opening the package, the number on the circuit board was not 633/634 but 635 but appeared to be the same size. Before I let the ranch handyman remove the old board and install the new one, I called the dealer who assured me that my unit was very old and that the 635 was a replacement that would fit. I am reluctant to try it because I feel there will be a no return policy on circuit boards. Two weeks of feeling dumb and dumber continued as I recalled more recent stupid stuff. A friend emailed me a free offer for old skin rejuvenation. I went to the website and signed up for the free offer. The next thing I knew I received an email thanking me for my subscription to their product on a monthly basis. Thank heavens, they allowed me to cancel with no penalty.

The same thing happened with a hair product my daughter recommended. I ordered some and soon thereafter received a box of hair products, none of which I use. Again I was allowed to cancel without too much of a penalty. Luckily, my daughter loves the products and was happy to receive my gift.

When I downloaded Quick Books, an accounting system, I subscribed to 90 days of technical support, which I never used, thanks to friends with expertise. A credit card statement after the 90-day period showed a charge from Quick Books. I called them and discovered that I had subscribed to automatic renewal of technical support. I canceled with no penalty.

I once read an email that said, "I never make the same mistake twice. I usually make it three or four times so that I get it right." I definitely qualify for that one.

I recently read that only a human stumbles over the same rock twice. I'm right there.

The Summer Reading Program

My pregnant daughter and four-year old grandson, Theiss (ryhmes with nice), came for a week-long visit. Being the doting grandmother I took him to the small town 20 miles distant for a day of the library's summer reading program.

Friends present oohed and aahed over my grandson. One of them asked him, *"You are so handsome, are you married?"*

He replied, *"No, but I have a baby in my mommy's tummy."*

That particular day's agenda took place in the town's park. A lady officer from some agency delivered a lecture on search and rescue dogs, complete with illustrations drawn on an erasable board. The dog sat calmly on the open stage. When the children of all ages became antsy, she demonstrated the dog's skills.

My grandson loudly remarked, *"That dog is old."*

The dog performed some of the commands but not all. My grandson became bored, *"Grandma, I want to leave now."* I brought him back to the ranch.

Why is it that parents believe they should entertain their children all summer long? As children, my three brothers and I enjoyed the summer months, visiting our Grandma on the farm and various cousins.

One summer we attended church camp. I didn't like it that much. The dormitory and bathrooms were dirty, there were too many kids I didn't know, and the food was slop. I was glad when the week ended.

Speaking with friends who have children, I am amazed. They send their children to Boy Scout Camp, Tennis Camp, Cheerleading Camp, and other expensive, exclusive camps in the Texas Hill Country, sometimes for three weeks at a time and a cost of thousands of dollars.

What happened to simple imaginative play. When my children were small I would promise to buy them some boxes at the grocery store if they behaved. The boxes were free. They loved building forts with the boxes. The rest of the time we mowed the yard, visited friends and relatives, fished, swam, and grew a garden. Summer was a time of learning and relaxing.

My four-year old grandson has his own IPad. He demonstrated games, and I managed to achieve the first level. I took him to my garden and showed him how to pull a plant close to the roots. When he did a big orange carrot came out of the ground. He was amazed. The wonder in his eyes made me smile. He said, *"Grandma, it's dirty."* We picked green beans, onions, and peppers and then returned to the house, washed the carrots, grated them, and added crushed pineapple and yogurt.

Later that day we went to the lodge on the ranch where he had lived with his mother until the age of two. I showed him his room and pictures of him as a baby. He admitted that he didn't remember.

On another occasion, my daughter was showing the lodge to friends. Theiss was with her and he remarked, *"This was my room when I was a little baby."*

She later said, *"I was showing the lodge and Theiss remembered his room. I can't believe it."*

I never said a word.

Highway 90

Highway 90 from Bracketville, Texas, to Marfa, Texas, is a familiar path. I've often driven the hundreds of miles to visit my daughter who graduated from Sul Ross State University, named after a former Vice President of the United States.

The journey from Bracketville, a town known for being one of the last civilized outposts in the mid 1800's between San Antonio and El Paso is the home of Fort Clark. Today Fort Clark is a retirement community and the springs are still flourishing, though coveted by San Antonio in the city's thirst for more water.

Outside the town is Alamo Village where many movies and commercials have been filmed. The highway goes south to Del Rio, and intersecting crossroads lead to Quemado, Rocksprings, Sonora, and Carta Valley. On the outskirts of Del Rio lies Laughlin Air Force Base. Del Rio is a bustling border town, across the Rio Grande from Ciudad Acuna. Today the border town is all but deserted due to cartel violence. Age-old restaurants and bars have been shut down, and the Border Patrol maintains a strong presence, their white vehicles with green lettering parked along the highway.

Those of us who are older recall Wolfman Jack broadcasting from Del Rio, Texas, in the 1960's and 1970's. The strength of the radio waves could be heard in northern New Mexico.

Leaving Del Rio, Lake Amistad surrounds the highway. The lake, whose name means friendship, is historically low but a beautiful blue. Resort homes dot the shores, and the bridge over the Pecos River is spectacular. Somewhere out in the middle of the lake is the border between the United States and Mexico.

Comstock is a settlement on the lake about 25 miles out of Del Rio, and after Comstock, the terrain is quite desolate along the deserted highway except for the border checkpoint where I coasted to a stop and was waved through by the uniformed agents after being asked the only question they can legally ask, "Are you a United States citizen?"

Langtry, the home of Judge Roy Bean, self-proclaimed "law west of the Pecos," contains the last remnants of civilization for the next 100 miles, except for the deserted settlement of Dryden and a turnoff to Pandale on the Pecos River.

The speed limit is 80; the Chihuahuan desert flanks the highway. The open spaces, canyons and mesas calm the soul. I try to picture early adventurers or stagecoach travelers journeying through the vast inhospitable terrain. I am thankful for my air-conditioned vehicle. The temperature in July approaches 100 degrees.

Sanderson is a small town dominated by empty storefronts. It was a cattle town when there was grass. The railroad that parallels the highway once hauled cattle to market.

Marathon, now famous for the Gage Hotel, shows signs of life. The road to Big Bend National Park intersects Highway 90. The hotel parking lot is full of cars. The speed limit is reduced from 80 to 35. I slow down and pay attention. Small towns in Texas are notorious for issuing speeding tickets to travelers in transit.

Twenty five miles past Marathon lies Alpine, so named for its Alpine climate. The elevation is near a mile high, and the July temperature is closer to 90 than 100. Sul Ross State University perches on the side of a hill. The town is bustling, even without a Walmart. A few fast food restaurants line the highway that runs through the middle of town. Here the Holland Hotel captures the imagination. The Gage Hotel and the Holland Hotel originated from those named families who owned hundreds of thousands of acres and intermarried to create cattle empires, inspiration for the book and movie, *"Giant."*

Further down the highway is Marfa, known for the mysterious, dancing lights out on the plateau beyond the town. The railroad continues to parallel the highway as I approach the town of 2,500, in past years discovered by non-Texas artists and those with a hankering for the unusual. Marfa is home to a curious mix of inhabitants, two very expensive restaurants, and a stunning resort hotel. The grocery store is less than adequate.

"Giant," a movie about oil, cattle, and Texas was filmed in Marfa. The Judd Foundation displays massive concrete pieces in a barren field. They call this art.

The golf course in Marfa lies at the highest elevation of any golf course in Texas, over a mile high.

From Marfa, the highway flattens with the terrain to the town of Valentine, population several hundred. The town was founded in the late 1800's by a railroad crew on Valentine's Day. Not much remains except for its famous Prada Store.

The last stop before Highway 90 becomes Interstate 10 is Van Horn, and here again a historic hotel, the El Capitan, is the center-piece of town. Van Horn is about the same size as Marfa where its sister hotel, The Paisano, is located.

And here my inspiration to travel Highway 90 from the west to east coast fizzled. The road, now part of the interstate system, has lost most of its singular identity and allure. Most of what can be seen is too familiar to stimulate a challenge.

So I changed my mind and decided to drive north to Canada on Highway 83. Like the poet, I chose the road less traveled.

41 Buying a Vehicle

Buying a new vehicle is not to my liking. I prefer to drive one until the mileage exceeds 100,000 miles and then give it to one of my children before replacing it with a new one. Living on a ranch requires a fleet of vehicles designed for specific purposes.

A Jeep is a necessity. The rugged roads, high hills, rocks, and canyons require a four-wheel drive vehicle. A heavy diesel pickup pulls a stock trailer, as well as a flat bed trailer. A regular pickup provides hauling space as I drive to town to dump garbage, purchase feed and supplies, haul appliances and other large items.

An economic fuel automobile is used for long road trips. Add a diesel tractor for ranch work. I categorize my vehicles by their utility. The Jeep is my mule. The pickups are the quarter horses, and the automobile is my thoroughbred.

The time had come to purchase a new pickup. I drove to the dealership where I had purchased four vehicles over the 20 years I lived in southwest Texas. I checked their inventory and prices on the Internet and knew what I wanted and how much I was prepared to pay.

I entered the dealership in faded jeans and sandals, not wanting to appear too prosperous. The salesman who greeted me at the door was older, and I discerned from his bearing he was macho. Not a good sign.

I told him what I wanted and we went out to the lot in the hot summer sun to look at what was available. He apologized. *"I've been gone for a month and am not familiar with the inventory."* I wondered where he had been. I selected the pickup I wanted. He asked if I wanted to drive it. I declined and asked for a price with 10-ply tires, a grill , and the side bars that enable a short person like me to get in the truck.

We returned to the air-conditioned showroom where he sat me at his desk and went to talk to the sales manager. A few minutes passed. He returned. *"Would you like a cup of coffee or a cold drink?"*

"No, thank you. How long is this going to take?"

"A little while."

"Please call me with the price."

We exchanged cards and I left. The following afternoon he called with the price, several thousand dollars more than I was willing to pay. I offered my bottom dollar and he promised to let me know. They accepted my offer. I agreed to return the following day to close the deal.

Again I entered the cool showroom, was ushered to his desk, and presented with an invoice which added up to the amount I had offered.

As I perused the invoice, I noticed that they were charging me $1,400 for the 10-ply tires. I looked at him and said, *"I don't mean to be rude but you must think I'm stupid to pay $1,400 for the tires when I recently purchased a set of the same tires for $1,200, and what about giving me credit for the tires you will remove from the truck. According to this invoice, I will be paying $1,400 for the tires and an additional $600 to $800 for the tires you'll take off the truck. That adds up to over $2,000 for a set of tires. You're going to have to adjust the price."*

He rose from his chair, *"Let me go talk to my sales manager. Would you like some water or a cup of coffee?"* I arose, *" No, thank you. I have an errand to run. I'll be back in 30 minutes."*

When I returned, the invoice had been adjusted to my satisfaction. I agreed to the corrected invoice and was then asked to sit at the desk and wait while the papers were being drawn. The salesman asked, *"Would you like some coffee or a cold drink?"*

"No, thank you. How long is this going to take?"

"Not long."

I arose, *"I have groceries to buy. I'll be back."*

"If you have ice cream we can put it our refrigerator."

"Thank you."

I purchased my groceries, no ice cream, and returned for the third time. As I walked in the showroom, the staff was waiting. Joe, the salesman greeted me. *"You seem like a busy woman."*

I replied, *"Yes, I am busy and have no patience as I'm sure you discovered."*

Everyone laughed and we all became friends. The papers were ready. I signed, paid, and was asked. *"Would you like for us to deliver the truck when it's ready?"*

I answered, *"Call me when the truck is ready. I'll let you know."*

I was thinking, "I'm not so sure I want them to know where I live."

When the truck was ready with the heavy duty tires, the grill guard, and the sidebars, I hitched a ride to Uvalde with a friend, walked in the showroom, received the papers, and the key and walked out to the parking lot, prepared to drive off in my new pickup. It was then I realized the key was not a key but some type of square module.

I pretended I was cool, got in the pickup, and figured out that the key module fit in a receptacle, started the engine, and looked for a transmission shifter. There was none. I fumbled around, acutely aware that the sales staff in the showroom were watching. After finding the dial-a-shift, I managed to drive away.

Nearly a year has passed and I still haven't bothered to work the computer screen, turn on the radio or connect the blue tooth, whatever that means. I merely drive it. That's adequate.

Intelligence

Why is it that a smart wealthy man with a dumb wife is accepted, whereas a smart wealthy woman with a dumb husband is not? In a couple, one is usually smarter than the other. One is a have, and the other is a have less. There are no equals.

I was married to a man who could barely read or write and possessed little or no comprehension of the written word. Yet he could walk into a room or a bar and command attention, and read the characters and personalities with the genius of an Einstein.

I know people with advanced college degrees who have no clue how to survive in the wilderness, couldn't begin to use a can opener, and would be surprised to learn that turnips grow in the ground.

In the past, dyslexics have been treated like dummies; it is now known that they possess greater intelligence than the average person, whatever average means.

College is not meant to teach a trade but rather to help one become an educated person. You learn a trade by practice, and a college degree does not guarantee success and wealth. Think of the college graduates unable to find employment today.

There is a big difference between street smart and book smart. I prefer the street savvy — people who know the way of the world, know how to read body language, know how to listen and communicate, and have the good sense to know when retreat is necessary. Not all battles are worth fighting. Discernment is key.

Knowing the difference between what's true and false is important. Everyone lies. When asked, "How are you?" most reply, "Great," when in fact they are miserable. We lie to please others or hide our flaws.

Last night I was watching the news. Early in the broadcast the anchor said, "Sixty per cent of Ebola cases are fatal." Later the same broadcaster stated, "Up to 90 percent of Ebola cases are fatal." Up to can mean anything from zero to 90. That is just plain stupid, yet many watch the news and accept what is said without question.

A news commentator remarked, "Russian forces have invaded Ukraine, a small country in central Europe." Switzerland is a small country in central Europe, not Ukraine. No correction was offered. Don't schools teach geography anymore? Does anyone know how to read a map?

Awareness is the key to intelligence. Only when we are aware, alert, and tuned in are we able to differentiate between fact and fiction. Going through life in a numbed state is not smart. Wake up America! Get up off your recliners. Life has no remote. Stand up and change it.

43 **Through**

I'm 72 and I'm through. And no, 70 is not the new 60, 60 is not the new 50, and 50 is not the new 40. Seventy is 70. Period.

One can either dislike or like it. My choice is to like it. I'm through wearing makeup to go to town and dump my garbage. I'm through worrying about how my hair looks or whether my clothes match, at least here at the ranch. In truth, I take pride in the outlandish, mismatched clothes I choose to wear at home.

As for the body beautiful, that is out of my control. The cottage cheese on my upper arms is easily disguised by not going sleeveless. The loose skin on my legs I don't much care about since I can't see it most of the time. The broken blood vessels on my upper legs are faint, and the spots on my hands can be attributed to my being an outdoor person.

I have friends who endure Botox shots to the eyes and lips, who suffer through face-lifts, loose skin neck removal, and liposuction. Pain does not appeal to me, and, to be honest, I can't tell the difference in my friends' body alterations. When they ask me, *"How do I look?"* I truthfully reply. *"You always appear the same because I see you on the inside."*

I'm fortunate to have no aches or pains, no chronic illness or impairment, brain-wise. There are no prescriptions to which I am addicted, and I eat wisely and maintain a size eight. I don't watch much TV and am current on world events. I read non-fiction, as well as fiction.

Life is good, and I hope it stays that way, but whatever comes, I'm ready.

Redemption comes from my grandson, age four. Every time I see him I repeat the same line. *"Your beautiful, famous grandma is here."* His eyes light up in joy. He believes me. Of course, I always bring him a transformer or some Legos, his favorites. And I have backup. His little brother is due in a week, and I'll be beautiful for a few more years.

Sometimes a bit of depression sets in, not about my health or dying, but having to miss out on seeing my grandsons grow to maturity. Believing in the afterlife and no death of the spirit, I plan to observe from the other side, maybe reincarnate.

The garden, the ranch, writing, reading, and cooking occupy most of my time. I visit with friends and family. The social dynamics of most parties don't appeal to me unless I have the opportunity to dance, especially a waltz. I love to dance and occasionally even enjoy a bit of romance.

As for being in my 70's, I plan on enjoying each day of good health and not waste my time worrying about tomorrow. These are the cards I've been dealt, and for now, I'm content to play them.

44 English

In America we speak English. I have a degree in English, not good for much but enough for a love affair with the words, being an avowed wordsmith.

I did not realize how fortunate I was to mature in an English-speaking country until I traveled the world. Often a guide would comment on how difficult and challenging it was to learn the English language. All airports must have an English speaking person in the control tower. English is the universal language, at least on this planet.

But the English spoken is often twisted. Just last night while watching the news, a noted news journalist quoted a press release from Washington D.C. "The air strikes in Iraq will not be over soon but won't continue indefinitely." What the hell does that mean? Okay, they won't be over soon and won't continue indefinitely. I know what soon means but indefinitely means forever. So what the statement says is that the air strikes won't be over tomorrow and they won't go on forever. What a vacuous, meaningless remark.

Later in the broadcast the news anchor reported that America carried out five air strikes in the last 24-hour period. And later, it was reported that Israel conducted 25 air strikes in the past 24-hour period. Sounds to me like we're not serious about our air strikes, and the Israelis are a bit more aggressive.

What is an air strike? One plane, two planes or many planes? Are our air strikes as strong as Israel's or stronger? Does an airplane on an air strike carry bombs, or do they fly within striking distance of an enemy target?

The wordiness of broadcasters insults my intelligence. For instance, they love to say, "the world in which we live." An unembellished "our world" would be simpler and save air-time for more substantive news.

On that same newscast it was reported that a 20-year old driver, a five-year veteran of auto racing, was killed. By my math he was 15 when he began racing cars. Isn't that a bit young?

Our president spoke, saying 99 percent of Muslims are against jihad. If that's true, then there is no problem with jihad, and terrorism does not exist.

Concerning amnesty, I have listened to commentators claim repeatedly that there are 12 million illegal immigrants in the United States. How do they know? Do they keep a head count of those who illegally cross the border? If they do, then why don't they turn them back? Recently I heard the number 20 million. There's a lot of difference between 12 and 20.

English or Swahili, I wish the truth were told, whatever the language.

Stupid and Smart

Every day I do something stupid. I don't know whether it's an age thing or simply loss of focus. Fortunately, on occasion, smart sneaks in.

Last week at a shopping center I attempted to unlock a white pickup that wasn't mine. My first response was to look around to see if anyone observed me being stupid.

One morning I dosed the wrong eye with my prescription drops. The same day I pushed the remote control for the automatic gate, expecting the bump gate to open.

I can't even begin to describe all the stupid actions I initiate on my computer, my iPad, or cell phone. At least no one observes those moments except my son who often rescues me from my stupidity by logging into my device and clearing the issue.

Ranch stupid occurs often. A Jeep necessarily navigates the rough roads on weekly missions to fill feeders and remove memory cards from the surveillance cameras. Usually I ride with someone who works for me, but recently I attempted the chore solo. Since I'm short, my legs don't reach the pedals. I discovered that the seat will move forward but not lock in place. Two years have passed since I purchased the used vehicle, and I still don't know to lock the seat in place. How dumb is that?

Last night I ratcheted up the stupid. In the past, on occasion I've picked up the remote TV control, planning to make a phone call, but never went so far as to punch in numbers. This time I took that last step. Lifting the device to my ear and discovering there was no ring, I quickly put it down. At least I didn't look around to see if anyone was watching.

And then my post office box renewal arrived in the mail. I scanned the envelope to see on which box my rental was due. I saw nothing indicating the number. (I have several boxes.) I called the mail carrier for the information. The following morning as I sat at my desk, preparing to write the check, I noticed a small sticker on the front of the envelope, citing the box number and amount due. Once again, I felt stupid. After 20 years of receiving the notices with handwritten numbers and amounts, I realized I was programmed to look for handwritten information.

Smart prevailed the following day. The butane man arrived to fill my butane tanks while the weather was still hot and the price low. I unlocked the gate on the other part of the ranch and gave him the combination for the automatic gate opener. When he appeared at my house to fill my tank, he said. *"I can't get the gate to close. I checked the battery and the fuses. They were okay, but the gate wouldn't close."*

I told him I would deal with it. Rather than call my handy-man, I drove to the gate, and it closed with my gate opener. I was smart to attempt the fix before calling for help.

Smart continued. When I attempted to print a photo for my Aunt Stella, the printer noted that the ink cartridge needed replacing. I replaced the cartridge, but the printer kept telling me to insert a memory card and print out a blank page. I tried again with no results. I finally went to help and determined that the printer was not linked to the computer and was advised to check the connections, turn everything off and then back on. It worked. Elation followed. Smart was on a roll.

Alas, stupid intruded once again. I called the St. Joseph Indian School in Chamberlain, South Dakota, to arrange for a visit on a planned road trip to Canada. The receptionist informed me that a Pow Wow was being held that weekend and that I was invited to a donor breakfast and banquet. I agreed to attend the banquet. Later that day I realized the plans were to be in Chamberlain on Thursday, not Friday. A phone call back to the school cleared up that stupid.

My housekeeper arrived one Thursday, excited about the garage sale she planned. Ever the packrat, I asked, "What all do you have for sale?"

The list was endless. I zeroed in on cast iron skillets and grills. With six houses, you can never have too many iron skillets. They're my favorite, not the teflon shit that allegedly emits vapors that will kill a bird. A crock-pot and bread-maker piqued my curiosity, especially the bread-maker. I remembered my mother throwing ingredients in a big bowl, and soon there were yeast rolls, bread, or cinnamon rolls. Early in my married life I attempted yeast bread with no success. Either I killed the yeast with water too hot or didn't activate it with water too cool. And when the bread-maker craze began I left it alone, no more appliances sitting on the counter rarely used. But when my friend Eric raved about the homemade bread available at the Country Store in Camp Wood, I thought a bread-maker would make a neat Christmas present for him.

I purchased the bread-maker, the crock-pot and all the cast iron cookware she had for sale. The giant skillet was the prize purchase. I gave Eric the bread maker, and then since the winter months kept me indoors, I thought about purchasing a bread-maker for myself. On the Internet I found one from Sears on sale for $39.95. I ordered it and waited anxiously for delivery.

In the meantime I purchased fast-acting yeast, organic flour, wheat flour, and placed an online order for some rye flour.

My first loaf was heavy as a rock — tasty but not light and fluffy. I used a thermometer to calculate the correct liquid temperature. Whether it was rye, whole wheat, or white bread, all my loaves were rock solid. I gave them all away but still managed to gain a few pounds sampling my failed efforts.

When I decided to once again attempt a loaf of rye bread, I carefully followed the recipe directions, which called for one and three-eighths cups of water. I was so involved in finding three-eighths on my measuring cup that I forgot that it was one cup plus the fraction. The lack of required liquid nearly burned up the bread-maker.

When I went back to the instruction book to reread the instructions, I noticed a sentence that read, "Do not raise the lid while the bread is in the bread-maker. "My impatient self periodically raised the lid numerous times while the bread baked, savoring the smell, reviving fond memories.

Once more I tried, not touching the lid, a good loaf at last. I gave it to Eric since he had yet to use his bread-maker. And then I remembered. My mother would prepare the dough, place it in a bowl to rise, and cover it with a dish towel. She did not periodically lift the dish towel.

Conclusion, I am stupid about baking bread and even stupider about eating it with preserves, peanut butter, molasses, jelly, cheese, lunch meat and, of course, butter.

And John Wayne did not say, "Stupid hurts," or "Stupid should hurt."

46　The Longest Roads

Part 1

The Texas skies provided a spectacular night time electric storm with unfortunately no rain, a great disappointment. I left early the following morning on a road trip, the occasion being a TV interview on KNVO 48, Fox News 2, in McAllen, Texas, to promote my second book.

Texas is a big state and by coincidence I live 60 miles from the crossing of once the two longest highways in America. In Uvalde, Texas, Highway 83 intersects with Highway 90. Even numbered highways run east/west, and odd numbered ones move north/south.

My goal is to travel the distance on them both, from Mexico to Canada and from the east coast to the west coast. On the occasion of the TV interview in McAllen, I consulted the map and discovered that I could travel the southernmost segment of Highway 83, the journey from Uvalde south to the Mexican border.

As I left the city limits of Uvalde on Highway 83, the irrigated fields of corn kept me company, but as I approached La Pryor, the fertile fields vanished and the brush country took charge. Mesquite, cactus, cenizo, huisache, and sage provided a thick cover. In La Pryor, I drove past the People's Cafe where the enchiladas are authentic.

Elaborate entrances advertised large ranches – The Southern Star, Zacateca Ranch, and Myane Ranch.

From La Pryor to Crystal City, the oil boom is obvious. Tall fences enclosed high dollar oil field equipment. RV parks, new motels, and franchise restaurants lined both sides of the highway. The truck traffic was light for a Sunday morning.

As I approached Carrizo Springs, oilfield activity increased. New roads through the thick brush branched off Highway 83. More RV parks, restaurants, and even a Walmart stood newly erected in Carrizo Springs. Asherton was equally bustling, but the activity thinned as I approached Catarina. Only an old pink hotel built hacienda style offered hospitality.

Driving south towards Laredo, palm trees stood as sentinels, advertising the warmer climate. The brush thinned and Highway 83 led me through the streets of Laredo and an older part of town. The outskirts were marked by busy malls and large shopping centers.

After Zapata, road signs guided the traveler to Falcon Dam and Lake, on the Texas/Mexican border. Roma, Rio Grande City, Mission, and McAllen seemed to run together as one big city.

My hotel beckoned on the side of the highway, but instead I drove to the TV station, timing the distance before I checked into my room. As I left the comfort of my cool car I was assailed by blowing wind and a temperature of 100 degrees, similar to a hot hair dryer blowing in my face.

Sleep eluded me and I finally gave up, dressed, and went down to the lobby for my complimentary breakfast. The small dining room was not yet open, but a coffee bar in the lobby beckoned. As I attempted to fill my first cup of coffee, a young lady joined me. After adding the small container of hazelnut coffee creamer, I searched for a stirring stick. Sensing my confusion she asked, *"What are you looking for?"*

"Something to stir my coffee."

She pointed to the styrofoam cup containing the black plastic sticks a few inches from my hand and commented. *"The first cup is the tough one."*

We both laughed, and I knew the day would be a good one.

By then the dining room was open and I selected a bowl of warm oatmeal and added some raisins and a banana before sitting at a table next to a man enjoying a bowl of cereal.

We exchanged hellos and I asked, *"Where are you from?"*

"Wisconsin."

I remarked, *"You're a long way from home. What brings you to McAllen?"*

"A consulting job in Reynosa, across the border in Mexico. What about you?"

"I'm a writer and am scheduled for a TV appearance this morning on Fox News 2."

"You look very nice."

I asked, *"How is the safety in Reynosa?"*

"Not good. We drive the main road through Reynosa to the office building, which has security, do our job, and drive straight back. I have no desire to stop. Just the other day, one of the girls in

the office said her mother was grocery shopping, and a gun fight took place outside the grocery store. Everyone hit the floor, and the store locked down until the police arrived. It's not safe."

He then asked me about my books. We spoke of travel and exchanged cards before I left for my first TV experience.

Morning was dawning as I arrived at the TV station per my instructions to be at the studio by 6:45 A.M. Cars were in the parking lot, but the doors were locked. I panicked as I walked around the building banging and trying every door. I returned to my car, retrieved the contact number and left a message with the host of the Morning Show, then calmly waited at the front door.

Adriana rescued me and led me through the quiet offices to the studio and introduced me to the staff, sat down with me on a sofa, and visited. Everyone was kind and made me feel comfortable. I watched as the show began. I met the other two guests, Cynthia from the Red Cross and Victor from the Job Force. Cynthia was recruiting volunteers for the hurricane season and selling tickets to a fundraising event. Victor furnished information on job availability. The atmosphere was casual and friendly. Everything was done with such ease.

My turn came. Adriana seated me in a comfortable armchair, gave me a small microphone, which I threaded up through my blouse, clipped, and then hid the wire under my leg. The interview went well, I was relaxed and funny and followed Adriana's instructions to look at her and forget the camera. I did. It worked.

Following my segment I remained for the entire show, exchanged cards with the staff, gave Adriana copies of my books, and drove home along the same route.

The interview was enjoyable and I reflected that my apprehensions had been stupid. As I approached Laredo, memories of former visits to that city surfaced.

I recalled the time Raleigh, my second husband, and I returned to Laredo after a road trip to Puerto Vallarta back in the 1970's. Upon entering the United States, we were pulled over at Customs and ordered out of the car and escorted to separate cubicles within the sterile building. I was locked in with a woman who ordered me to remove all my clothes and shoes. While I was doing that she examined the contents of my purse. Then as I was standing buck naked, she ran her fingers through each and every seam of my clothes. Then she examined my arms, fingers, toes, armpits, the back of my neck, and ran her fingers through my long hair. She then left the room, locking me in, still naked. After what seemed a lifetime she returned, told me to get dressed, and said that I was free to leave. I met Raleigh at the car. He, too, had been examined, the event most likely caused by his checkered past. We laughed about the incident and expressed gratitude that they had not examined our personal crevices.

As I smiled with that memory I also remembered getting crabs from a restaurant toilet in Laredo during another visit. My trip down memory lane was interrupted as I approached a border checkpoint where I was asked if I was an American citizen and where I was going. My answer, *"Vance, Texas."*

"Where is Vance?"

"Sixty miles north of Uvalde."

"Have a nice day."

Oilfield trucks dominated the roads as I returned home. The lowest segment of Highway 83 had been navigated. I looked forward to continuing the road north in the coming months.

Part 2

Later that month I drove another short segment of Highway 83. From Uvalde going north, Highway 83 winds through Concan and Garner State Park, one of the most widely visited state parks in Texas. The resort area of Concan boasts cabins for rent, restaurants, a dance hall, and a golf course. Convenience stores along the route offer tube and kayak rentals, as well as ice and beer.

The terrain had changed from flat and thorny brush to trees, hills, and rocks. After passing through the county seat of Leakey, a small town of several hundred, the highway led straight to the Edwards Plateau.

Garven's Store, an old time service station famous for barbecue, biker gear, and jerky, provides a convenient stop. On sale are tee shirts sporting the logo, "I rode the three twisted sisters," referring to the three winding roads that are the source of euphoria and danger for motorcycle riders from all over the world.

The town of Junction, well-named on the crossroads of Highway 83 and Interstate 10, doesn't slow us down, "us" referring to my companion on this third leg of the journey north to the Canadian border.

Susan and I graduated from high school together, lost touch for years, and then reunited when she and her husband moved to Kerrville, Texas, several hours from my ranch.

Susan and I are widows, native Houstonians, both Capricorns born within days of each other, who grew up in the same neighborhood. In addition we're both obsessive/compulsive, which translates as highly intelligent, well organized, and energetic, reminiscent of a great tee shirt logo I once saw in a catalog, "I'm obsessive compulsive and attention deficit. I want everything perfect but not for long."

Our method of travel was simple. Read the GPS on the screen of my diesel Mercedes and keep the giant paper atlas handy. Whoever was not driving was responsible for keeping us on Highway 83. Sounds simple. It wasn't.

We talked our way through the towns of Menard, Eden, Ballinger, Paint Rock, Winters, and north to Abilene. The business route through Abilene kept us off the loop and Interstate as we continued to Anson, Hamlin, and Aspermont.

The thrill of the highway energized us. The wide open spaces, the small towns, and the ripe cotton fields restored our faith in America. The roads were smooth, highways well marked. We smiled. This was our country.

Some of the land was fallow, but dry land farms dominated the landscape. Looking out over the hills, it was easy to imagine the Indians camped along the creeks, cooking over a campfire, roasting a fresh deer or turkey.

From Aspermont, we drove through Guthrie and by the time we reached Paducah, Texas, we were hungry. There was not much of a choice. The steak house was shut down, and Dairy Queen was the only option. A quick hamburger in a deserted Dairy Queen provided fuel for the remainder of the afternoon as we passed through Childress. We were now in the panhandle of Texas, poised to enter the panhandle of Oklahoma.

We stopped in Shamrock, Texas at the junction of Highway 83 and Interstate 40. After checking in a Best Western motel, we scouted the town, stopped at the liquor store for a bottle of white rum and some mojito mix, and visited with the folks in the store. One of the customers, a Missouri Synod Lutheran minister, the same religion of my family, rode off on a bright green motorcycle.

We learned that Route 66 passes through Shamrock and stopped at the visitor center to view the memorabilia and purchase a tee shirt for my grandson. The visitor center was in a restored gas station, one of several restored stations in Shamrock. The town's name was given in 1890 by George Nichols in honor of his homeland when the post office was established in his dugout home. The St. Patrick's Day celebration is a yearly event.

The following morning we traveled the last miles before leaving the panhandle and the state of Texas. The dominance of oil in that area reminded me of a man I met on a trip up the Columbia River. We were visiting over dinner when someone asked him what he did for a living. The question came after he bragged of his airplane and travels, his hometown being Childress.

His answer, "When they struck oil on my ranch, I quit ranching and haven't hit a lick since."

Our first missed turn came at Canadian before reaching the Oklahoma border. We were so busy talking we missed the left turn and drove 35 miles before I noticed on the GPS screen that we were not on Highway 83. Luckily, it was early in the day. I was not tired and did not despair, saying, "If this is the only wrong turn we make, then we're doing just fine." I was wrong.

The open spaces continued to charm. Evidence of fallow land and oil production dominated the landscape. The road was smooth, and there was little traffic except for trailer loads of cattle being moved to feed lots. The price of beef was high.

The drive through the Panhandle of Oklahoma was short. We crossed the border into Kansas at Liberal and continued through a long stretch of no towns, beautiful scenery, farmland, and fields of late summer crops to the town of Garden City. By then we were hungry again and needed gas. Amazingly, we found a full-service gas station. The kind man washed the windshield and filled the tank with diesel. When we asked him to recommend a good place to eat with vegetables, he directed us to a local diner on our route out of town.

We joined the lunch crowd. I ordered a Reuben sandwich, Susan a BLT (bacon, lettuce and tomato). We were discovering that healthy food was not an option. Most everything on the menus was fried with potatoes being the main side dish, along with the germ-laden salad bars.

The highway through Kansas was open with fields of sorghum, ripening corn, and grazing cattle. Oil pump jacks peppered the landscape.

We made our second wrong turn of the day, but were quick enough to catch it after only going one mile. So far that was one for Susan and one for me. More to come.

Along the way we had taken on a third traveling companion, named Howard by Susan. Upon leaving Kerrville, a pesky fly buzzed the front seat. Susan swatted, rolled down windows, and attempted to remove it from the car, to no avail. Her flailing annoyed me a bit. "Susan, that fly is a sentient being. He may be our guardian angel. Leave him alone."

She replied, "He's a what?"

"A sentient being." I spelled the word for her and explained that all living creatures are sentient beings and that I pray for the happiness of all sentient beings every day. I added. "Even dung beetles are sentient beings."

She graciously accepted my explanation, and we continued our trip. That first night Howard joined us in our hotel room. We agreed that he hid in our luggage to remain with us.

With Howard protecting us, we passed through Kansas, crossed the Platte River, and arrived in McCook, Nebraska, a prosperous, somewhat large town with a thriving pipe industry and the familiar John Deere dealership.

Traveling through Nebraska, we encountered more corn fields, irrigated crops, and cattle trucks, along with scenic forested canyons. The speed limit in Kansas and Nebraska was 65 miles per hour, but we were cruising at just under 80. My diesel Mercedes responds well to pressure on the pedal, along with providing great gas mileage. The roads were mostly deserted, which provided the opportunity to pee along the road. Susan was the first. I think it might have been in Oklahoma or Kansas. I pulled over onto a side gravel road with ample brush coverage. Susan managed to fall backward into the ditch. She was unhurt, so we continued on.

In those first few days, we developed a system. Once we consulted the map and determined a destination for the night, the navigator used her cell phone, called the toll free numbers of chain motels and made a reservation. It was my turn and once we had agreed on Valentine, Nebraska, I called the toll free number and spoke with a representative from India. After listening to his canned spiel about no pets, no smoking, no cancellation, and conveying a desired reservation for two, he mentioned that the chain had several properties in Valentine. I settled on the Econolodge.

That particular day was a long one of driving due to the lack of towns. As dark was approaching, we made another pee stop; again it was Susan. Just as soon as she was in full squat, a truck blasted over the hill. I think he waved. Susan said, "Just watch, he'll be back."

Clouds built up and the sunset was amazing. At yet another pee stop, I took pictures after stepping on a cactus. Susan carefully picked the spines from my sandaled foot.

We buzzed into Valentine at dark and I drove past the Econolodge because it was on the wrong highway or so I thought. I was wrong and cranky, my excuse being I was tired. Susan called the motel and received directions not only to the lodge but to the steak restaurant a block away from the motel.

Tired and hungry we stopped first at the steakhouse, went in the bar, ordered a mojito, and dined on a delicious steak salad. As the customers cleared out of the restaurant, the waitress was cleaning the large plastic menus. When we commented, she told us that the owner was very particular about cleanliness.

When we pulled into the motel, the lady at the desk said, "I have been worried about you two. I'm so glad you're here."

Susan said, "I'm Louise, this is Thelma." We laughed. The weather had turned cold and rainy. We wore our coats.

The Thelma and Louise thing had begun on the first day. Our first night in Shamrock, Texas, we had done the same thing. As we entered the lobby of the Best Western, Susan said, "I'm Louise, this is Thelma." I had recently seen a television advertisement when two women in a car had some spare time and the passenger said, "Let's take a cross country trip like those two women in the movie."

The driver replied, "I saw that movie. It didn't end well."

That first night as Susan was surfing movies on the TV, that movie was on. We watched the last half, realizing that I was the one that got raped and Susan was a murderer. The Thelma and Louise thing stayed with us the entire trip.

The temperature was in the low 40's as we shed our sandals and put on shoes with socks. After the complimentary breakfast we headed north, our destination, Chamberlain, South Dakota, and the St. Joseph Lakota Indian School and Museum. Over the years I had contributed to the project and wished to visit the school. Chamberlain was less than 100 miles out of the way. But first we made our last wrong turn of the trip.

There is a saying, "I don't make the same mistake once or twice; I usually make it three or four times before I get it right."

This was the fourth time. The fault was that of our giant atlas. We were between two pages and the plastic spirals hid the highways. I couldn't drive the car through those small plastic spirals. We drove a lot of miles on the wrong highway. It was foggy, and the road was deserted. Susan had a pee stop. Once I realized the GPS screen was telling me we were on the wrong highway, stuck in the atlas spirals, I turned around and then I had to pee. The road was empty, so I just stopped in the middle of the highway, announcing, "I have to pee."

Susan said, "You can't stop in the middle of the highway. You have to pull off the road." I didn't want to but I did.

When I got back behind the driver's wheel, she was laughing hysterically. I couldn't figure out why it was so funny. I do it all the time at my ranch. The sides of the road are full of weeds, chiggers, ticks, and stickers. I always stop in the middle of the road.

We learned our lesson. Watch the screen in the car, as well as consult the atlas. That was our last wrong turn.

The trip to Chamberlain, South Dakota took us over the wide Missouri. There I realized why Lewis and Clark traveled the Missouri. It was much bigger than I had imagined, quite navigable.

After consulting the map, we decided to spend the night in Pierre, South Dakota, the state capitol. Susan called our hotel numbers only to discover that there were no rooms available in Pierre, pronounced "peer," not "pee air."

Susan came up with a brilliant idea. "Stop at a McDonalds; they have WiFi. I'll get on my IPad and find a room in Pierre."

She booked a room across from the hospital in Pierre, presumably the last room available. The rate was $60. We had our doubts.

We were hungry. The town of Chamberlain was charming. The light poles were tree trunks.

There was a Mexican restaurant in Chamberlain, and tacos appeared on most of the menus from Texas through Kansas, Nebraska, and now South Dakota.

We ate lunch at the Anchor Grill. I ordered the jalapeño pretzel burger, Susan the soup and sandwich.

St Joseph Indian School rested on the edge of town. From the grounds of the campus we could see the wide Missouri. The grounds were impeccable, not a branch or leaf out of place. The museum was interesting and well-done, the gift shop a buyer's delight. I was very impressed and left them a donation. I also made some nice purchases, including two bracelets for my grandsons, some porcupine quill earrings for myself and a picture, now hanging in my bedroom. I will continue to donate to the school.

Upon arrival in Pierre late in the afternoon we found the motel. It wasn't too bad and had WiFi. We felt safe. Susan got on her IPad and found a restaurant not far away, in the downtown area. The grilled salmon was delicious, and the dark, quiet restaurant was the first on our trip to have actual atmosphere.

We returned to the room, Susan barricaded the door with furniture, and we slept well except for noises from the floor above.

We couldn't wait to leave Pierre, declined the free breakfast, and drove on, determined to eat breakfast somewhere else for a change. The free breakfasts were becoming quite boring.

We drove over an hour before we came to a very small town, Selby, South Dakota.

There was a coffee and breakfast shop, charming, with designer coffee. I ordered an egg and sausage wrap. At the last minute Susan changed her order from a croissant to a wrap like mine. The waitress never heard her. She ate the croissant. Before berating the waitress we agreed she must have a rough life. Negativity was not on our agenda.

We passed through a tiny town of 12, saw fields stacked with round hay bales, old farm homesteads, fields of ripening corn, silos, cattle, and sunflowers in full bloom.

We drove through a county seat with a population of 89. And I thought Real County had a tiny population.

We bypassed Bismark, the capital of North Dakota with a population of 659,000. The temperature was cold, in the 40's all day. Minot, North Dakota, was our destination. Susan's brother lived there with his wife and son. He was a developer, building hotels and housing for the oil field workers exploring the Bakken Shale Formation of over a million acres reaching into Canada, not very far to the north.

Minot, pronounced "my not," is a town of 60,000, appearing brand new with a mall and every chain restaurant imaginable. Our reservations were for two nights at the Best Western, next to the mall. Susan's brother and wife lived in a small apartment, not far from our motel.

Early that evening they picked us up and took us to a Japanese restaurant, a chain that served dinner at a grill table. Our personal chef was a young Japanese man newly arrived in Minot. He entertained us with his knives and chatter and prepared some outstanding steak. Speaking with him I discovered he had an agent, had worked in New York City, Orange, Texas, and only in the last two weeks had arrived in Minot.

Being from the south, loving warm temperatures, I could only sympathize what he would be enduring for the winter where weeks passed with the temperature never rising above zero. Perhaps he was from northern Japan and able to endure the cold.

I was grateful for my faithful Navajo coat. The temperature was near freezing, and it was only early September. Being a bit road weary, we returned to the motel early, anticipating a full day ahead. Ernest, Susan's brother, picked us up and drove us to their apartment, cooked a great country breakfast complete with homemade biscuits, and enlightened us on the Bakken shale development. He told us there were thousands of oil companies drilling and that most of the land was owned by three Indian tribes, retribution I suppose for the shabby way the Indians have been treated.

Ernest and his wife showed us the gear they wear in the winter, a coat and mask that covered every bit of skin. While we discovered it doesn't snow that much, the ice and sheer cold are brutal. Ernest admitted getting frostbite just walking to the garage where their car is housed, a few hundred feet from the apartment complex. I said, "If I lived here, I wouldn't leave my house the entire winter."

They told us there was a complex not far from their apartment where they swam, exercised, and socialized during the cold months.

Ernest shared a funny story. When they first moved to Minot from California, they ordered furniture for their apartment, specifically a bed and mattress. The furniture was delivered, the bed set up, and to their dismay the mattress was hard as a rock. They complained to the company that the mattress was not the one they ordered, only to be informed that it was frozen and would thaw to its original softness.

Susan and I returned to the motel and drove to the mall, a few blocks away. It was simply too cold to walk. The mall contained every store imaginable to satisfy a shopper. We walked through Target, purchased some colorful socks, and strolled through the mall, enjoying the warmth. I was bundled in my Navajo coat and at some point discovered that I had lost one of the porcupine quill earrings purchased at St. Joseph's Indian School.

Susan insisted we backtrack to find the earring. I accepted the fact that it was lost but agreed. We found the earring on the floor in Target. From there we went to a small jewelry store where I purchased plastic backings for the earrings.

We had a light lunch, and that afternoon Ernest picked us up and took us to a museum park to see replicas of a 1500's Norwegian church and other historic structures. There was a granary and an original house from the 1800's. Three rooms with low ceilings didn't appear to provide much warmth other than basic protection from the elements. I don't know how those people survived. I couldn't even tolerate the September cold that afternoon. Our visit was hurried.

We visited a gift shop and purchased some souvenirs and returned to our motel for a short nap before dining at Minot's latest new restaurant, which happened to be Mexican. The facility was crowded and obviously popular with the locals. The food was not the Tex-Mex quality we enjoy in Texas.

The road trip on Highway 83 was over. We had reached the Canadian border.

Part 3

Two nights in one location were a welcome relief but the road beckoned, the long journey home lay before us. We left in the early morning cold, going west on Highway 21, planning on driving through the Bakken field. We observed motels, truck traffic, and small towns with familiar franchise restaurants. A small town of several thousand boasted a Fuddruckers. We stopped at a truck stop for coffee and a bathroom break. Everyone in the place was from somewhere else, including foreign countries. Workers migrate to high-paying jobs.

The road led us through Stanley and Tioga. The smooth roads of Highway 83 were a distant memory. We made slow time due to a lot of road construction, turning south from Williston and driving through Teddy Roosevelt National Park. The beautiful scenery was a welcome diversion from the rough highway.

We crossed into South Dakota where I was stopped for speeding in a small town. As usual, we had been talking, and I had not noticed that the speed limit dropped from 55 to 35. The highway patrol lady was cordial, issued my ticket, and instructed me to pay the $25 fine and mail it in the postage paid envelope she provided. What a break! I imagined the fine would be at least $150.

Our guardian fly, Howard, was still with us but had been joined by a friend we named Harold. Most of the time they were content to guard us from their vantage point in the back seat.

We took an easy route through Rapid City, following the obvious signs to Mt. Rushmore. Our reservations were at the Best Western in Keystone, South Dakota, and we arrived before dark, hungry and tired.

Following the advice of the hotel clerk, we drove a short distance to a restaurant and ordered buffalo and elk. The meal was mediocre, the salad fresh.

The next morning surprised us with snow on the ground. We both commented that we had made the right decision in not driving into Montana and Wyoming. South Dakota was cold enough.

Our free breakfast consisted of oatmeal and fruit. The coffee helped as we left to view Mt. Rushmore, driving through the picturesque town of Keystone with lots of shopping and dining available. The snow-patched pine tree forests on the surrounding hills and mountains were a pretty sight.

As we rounded a turn there was Mt. Rushmore waiting for us with the carved heads of Washington, Jefferson, Lincoln, and Teddy Roosevelt. I pulled over on a scenic overlook, and we took pictures of ourselves with Mt. Rushmore in the background, choosing to pass on a visit to the tourist center. The parking garage was full, and there were gates and an entrance fee. Seeing the monument was sufficient.

Only a few miles beyond Mt. Rushmore lies the Crazy Horse Memorial, the world's largest mountain carving. Still in progress, the memorial is one of the most fabulous monuments I have ever seen, and I have seen many: the Taj Mahal, Machu Pichhu, palaces, cathedrals, the pyramids and such all over the world. Crazy Horse ranks right beside them.

We entered the visitor center and watched a movie depicting the history of Crazy Horse. I'm relating this information because I was so impressed.

South Dakota is home to the Dakota, Lakota and Nakota. Nine tribes, representing approximately 62,000 people, make up these three dialects. The nine tribes are the Cheyenne River Sioux, Crow Creek Sioux , Flandreau Santee Sioux, Lower Brule Sioux, Oglala Sioux, Rosebud Sioux, Sisseton-Wahpeton Oyate, Standing Rock Sioux, and Yankton Sioux.

Sculptor Korczak Ziolkowski worked on Mt. Rushmore before beginning the Crazy Horse Memorial. The first blast took place in 1948, taking off just 10 tons. In May of 1949, Korczak wrote the following.

"Crazy Horse was born in Rapid Creek in the Black Hills of South Dakota in about 1842. While at Fort Robinson, Nebraska, under a flag of truce, he was stabbed in the back by an American soldier and died September 6, 1877, at about the age of 35.

"Crazy Horse defended his people and their way of life in the only manner he knew, but only after the Treaty of 1868 was broken. The treaty, signed by the President of the United States, said, in effect: As long as rivers run and grass grows and trees bear leaves, Puha Sapa - The Black Hills of South Dakota - will forever be the sacred land of the Sioux Indians.

"Only after he saw his leader, Conquering Bear, exterminated by treachery. Only after he saw the failure of the government agents to bring required treaty guarantees, such as meat, clothing, tents and necessities for existence which they were to receive for having given up their lands and gone to live on the reservations. Only after he saw his people's lives and their way of life ravaged and destroyed.

"Crazy Horse has never been known to have signed a treaty or touched the pen. Crazy Horse, as far as the scale model is concerned, is to be carved not so much as a lineal likeness but more as a memorial to the spirit of Crazy Horse - to his people. With his left hand thrown out pointing in answer to the derisive question asked by a white man, 'Where are your lands now?' he replied, 'My lands are where my dead are buried.'"

Having told the abridged story of Crazy Horse, I also have to tell about the sculptor who designed the monument. Korczak Ziolkowski of Polish descent was born September 6, 1908, in Boston. Orphaned at age one, he grew up in foster homes. He was completely self-taught and never took a formal lesson in art, sculpture, architecture, or engineering.

Lakota Chief Henry Standing Bear learned of the sculptor when Korczak's "Paderewski: Study of an Immortal," won first prize, by popular vote, at the 1939 New York World's Fair.

"My fellow chiefs and I would like the white man to know the red man has great heroes, also," wrote Standing Bear when he invited Korczak to the Black Hills to carve Crazy Horse.

Korczak accepted the invitation and arrived in the Black Hills on May 3, 1947. When he started work on the mountain in 1948, he was almost 40 and had only $174 left to his name. Over the years he battled financial hardship, racial prejudice, injuries, and advancing age.

A strong believer in the free enterprise system, he felt Crazy Horse should be built by the interested public, not the taxpayer. Twice he turned down offers of federal funding. He also knew that the project was larger than any one person's lifetime and left detailed plans to be used with his scale models to continue the project.

Since his death in 1982, his wife Ruth, with seven of their children, together with the Crazy Horse Memorial Foundation Board of Directors, have directed the work, which continues to see exciting progress being made with each passing year.

The mission of the Crazy Horse Memorial Foundation is to protect and preserve the culture, tradition, and living heritage of the North American Indians. The Foundation has demonstrated its commitment to this endeavor by continuing the progress on the world's largest sculptural undertaking, the memorial to Crazy Horse; providing educational and cultural programming by acting as a repository for American Indian artifacts, arts and crafts through the Indian Museum of North

126

America and the Native American Educational and Cultural Center; and by establishing and operating the Indian University of North America and a medical training center for American Indians. The Indian University of North America was opened in June, 2010.

Unfortunately, I will never live to see the completion of the monument. Seventy-five years have passed since the beginning of the sculpture, and I suspect that another 75 years will pass before its completion. It is the most awe-inspiring endeavor I have ever witnessed and has been financed entirely by private donations. When finished it will be the largest sculpture in the world.

As a footnote of sorts, I returned home and sent a generous donation to the Crazy Horse Memorial. Several weeks later I received a small box, large enough to contain a baseball. The package was heavy. Inside was a piece of rock blasted from the memorial. I will continue to contribute to the project, mainly because of the university and medical school. I believe in education.

After spending the heart of the day at the Crazy Horse Memorial, we returned to Keystone, had a buffalo burger for lunch, and then shopped the main street for souvenirs.

We stayed in town for a few drinks at Ruby's and later dined on buffalo ribs in the dining room. They were good.

An early evening retirement was welcome before hitting the road the next morning, going south — destination, Burlington, Colorado.

Our guardian angel flies Howard and Harold continued the journey with us. The cold weather kept them either in our suitcases or in the back seat of the Mercedes. We passed through a small town in South Dakota, Boise City, where Susan spotted a deli. I enjoyed a cabbage burger and checked out the predominant John Deere tractor dealership.

Susan and I were children of the 60's. During those years she was busy having three daughters. I was not yet a mother and participated lightly in the drug scene.

Since we chose our destination south through Colorado, Susan said she would like to go to a marijuana store and smoke one toke over the line. Sweet Jesus! We vacillated, discussed it back and forth. Then Susan found a town not too far off the route that advertised a marijuana store.

Sedgewick is a small town of several thousand, but the portable building with a green leaf sign outside led us to believe we had found our destination.

I pulled up to the building and we walked up the ramp to the front door. Susan had to pee. I went to the young lady at the desk, showed her my identification, and was ushered into the main room, not very big.

I asked the young lady, *"What do you have?"*

She replied, *"You are from out of state. You can purchase 1/4 of an ounce."*

"How much is 1/4 of an ounce?"

"One hundred and forty dollars."

"Okay, I want to buy 1/4 ounce."

"How do you want to feel?"

"I want to feel mellow and not hungry."

"Then you want lemon skunk."

I paid for my marijuana as Susan entered the room and asked, *"What's the deal here?"*

"I'll let her tell you."

Meanwhile, I ventured to the other side of the small room where another lady stood behind a counter. I was told to not enter that part of the room because it was only for medical prescriptions.

Susan purchased a peanut butter candy bar for $25. We had no pipe or papers to roll or smoke a joint.

Susan ate two squares of the candy. I declined. I was driving.

To summarize the situation, we were two women over 70, driving through Colorado. Susan was stoned though she continued to deny it. When she became paranoid, I knew she was stoned. She said, *"We have to eat this candy before we leave Colorado; otherwise they will catch us at the checkpoint."*

Driving through the grasslands of eastern Colorado, I said, *"Susan, was there a checkpoint going in to Colorado?"*

"No, but there will be as we leave the state."

"Susan, there were no checkpoints going into or leaving any of the states we have traveled through."

"Yes, but there will be leaving Colorado because of the legal marijuana."

"Okay, if that's what you believe, just in case, I will put the 1/4 ounce in my bra. You put your candy bar in your bra. If we get stopped, they will have to call a female officer to search us. If we get caught, it's my car. They'll take me away and impound my car. You will be okay."

With that decision, we continued through eastern Colorado to Burlington. With impunity and possessing legal marijuana, we ate some more squares of the candy bar in our motel room and dined on steak and chicken salad in the restaurant next door.

As we journeyed south, the end of the trip was in sight. At one point, earlier on the trip, lying in bed, and pondering the day ahead, I thought to myself, "Self, this is crazy, driving over 3,000 miles. You'll never make it home."

Reason prevailed. I smothered my anxiety and continued on. Perhaps it was a crazy idea. We had fun, bonded like high school girls, and peed beside and in the middle of the road. What else is there?

After leaving Burlington, we passed no checkpoint and stopped at a Best Western in Childress, Texas. We dined at an Italian restaurant not far from the motel. The food and service were excellent. Howard and Harold continued to protect us.

We found Highway 83 once again and from Childress retraced our steps through Abilene to Kerrville and Susan's home. After unloading I continued another 75 miles to my ranch. The hum of the road kept me awake, and it was days before I could retrieve parts of myself from the long journey, much less write about the adventure. The marijuana I saved for special occasions.

That trip through the heartland was exhilarating and made me love this country even more. The cultivated fields, small towns and roadside cafés restored my faith. The open road fed my soul.

Susan and I bonded in a way that has encouraged us to continue our adventures. We'll leave surrendering to old age, TV, and rocking chairs to others.

The Crazy Horse Memorial was the highlight of the trip and understanding the shale extraction process for oil renewed my faith in America's obtaining full fuel independence.

How ironic that the Bakken field is at the north end of Highway 83, and the Eagle Ford shale is at the south end of Highway 83. Explain that.

47 **Skunked**

Skunked means you lose. Playing cards or dominoes, skunked means a shut-out, a score of zero.

As Thanksgiving approached I prepared the ranch for 12 visitors, not including dogs. Three of the guesthouses needed a bit of a shine and supplies. My ranch foreman informed me earlier in the week that the front door of the main lodge was open and that a varmint had left signs on the living room floor. He shut the door and removed the paper scraps from the floor.

When I drove over to replenish the refrigerator, the door was closed, but there was more debris, a sure sign that the intruder was still in the house.

Being overstressed, described by my brother as a small car with a big engine, having no brakes or steering and only two speeds - wide open or dead stop - I made a conscious decision to not investigate, that whatever was in there would be too much to deal with, that my daughter and her husband could handle it. One thing for sure, I would not call for help. In the canyon lands, that's a sign of weakness. I shut the door.

The fall Texas weather was unseasonably warm. I pushed the button to lower the window on my new pickup. Nothing. I pushed all the buttons, including the child lock. Nothing. I shrugged, dreading a 60-mile trip to the dealership in Uvalde and waiting for the repair, wasted time, incompetent products, the demise of American manufacturing, Congress, bureaucracy, regulation, immigration, terrorism, and the economy.

I returned home and went to bed early, my first guests due later that evening. The phone never rang, so I assumed the guests had arrived safely. I was right and I was wrong.

The ringing phone interrupted my third cup of coffee. My daughter informed me that there was a skunk under the bed in the master bedroom. The skunk sprayed the room as they fled, leaving the door open for the skunk's retreat. They moved to the other house, but not before discovering a leak under the skunk-occupied house's kitchen sink.

More guests were due the following day. According to my daughter, the house was uninhabitable. I assured her we could fix it. The skunk fled during the night.

We stripped the room, bedding and all, put comforter, sheets, everything we could in the washing machine, and began to spray the room with air fresheners. I sprinkled baking soda on the carpet. We turned on the ceiling fan, closed the door, and her husband fixed the leak under the kitchen sink.

I returned to my house and went online. The solution to the skunk smell was a bowl of vinegar. Sounds too simple, but in 12 hours, there was no trace of a skunk smell. Unbelievable. I resolved to buy a few gallons of vinegar for my emergency stash when the grid goes down and chaos rules.

My daughter insisted that the room would remain toxic, that the chemicals the skunk emitted would reside in the sheer window coverings, the mattress, the carpet, and the walls, that her children could not go into the room, and the odor caused her eyes to burn.

The guests arrived, bunked in the skunk room, and no odor could be detected. The truck windows were still frozen shut, until a 10-year-old pushed a button.

The guests hiked, hunted, fished, and wondered why no animals were spotted. Three dogs running loose might have had something to do with it. I said nothing. The truck windows were working.

We cooked in three kitchens on Thanksgiving day. I baked the turkey, made the dressing, prepared a vegetable salad, and baked two pecan pies. The guests and my daughter prepared sweet potatoes, broccoli and cheese, mashed potatoes and gravy, and a cherry pie. Honey ham was heated from the previous day.

Warm weather kept us all outdoors. Two tables were set up, complete with tablecloths, anchored by some of the abundant rocks on the ranch. After the blessing we feasted, followed by a sluggish afternoon nap time.

The lodge from that Thanksgiving Day would be forever called the skunk lodge. And while we might have been skunked, we were also blessed.

48 **I Give Up**

My motto has always been, "Never, never, never give up." But I confess there are days when I think, "Time to give up, sell the ranch and move to a retirement community, spend my days playing cards and weaving baskets with old people."

Then the spirit makes a come-back. "I can do this. I love my ranch and will continue as long as the mind and body remain functional."

Dealing with 850 acres of land, six houses, three barns, and assorted equipment can be a challenge. Since purchasing the farm, I've had to replace the pump on the well, the heating system in the skunk lodge, the ice maker and various ceiling fans, light fixtures, and a refrigerator or two.

The coyotes, bobcats, and mountain lions wreak havoc on the lamb crop. I trap skunks, coons, foxes, opossums, shoot porcupines that kill my fruit trees, and fight the insects and weeds that invade my garden.

Equipment repair on two trucks, a tractor, a Jeep, a ranch electric buggy, and three trailers, as well as the renewals for licenses and inspection stickers, occupy much of my time. Keeping records for income tax, paying property taxes make for a full filing cabinet.

Nothing occurs in a timely manner. Breakdowns always come in threes, and the logistics of living 60 miles from anywhere adds to the difficulty.

So far there are eight blinds and feeders and cameras on the ranch. Filling them with corn, putting out mineral and salt blocks, and maintaining them takes more than a full day a week.

The wild hog problem requires putting fences around the feeders. The aoudad dominate the feeders and need to be trapped or shot in order to encourage the native animals. Exotic game should not be allowed to interfere with the native species.

Trees fall down, fences need repair, firewood should be cut. With something always needing to be done, I often forget to have fun, go fishing, or just loaf. Being German I have a bad habit of being driven, wanting everything to be perfect and in working order.

In that respect I have given up. I can't control everything. I'm fortunate to have competent helpers. I can depend on them, not necessarily in my time frame, but soon enough.

At my age, it would be easy to sell the ranch to move to a more comfortable, more social life, but that's not me. As long as I can write, view the cliffs, and be energized by nature, observe orange and yellow sunsets, the full moon rising, and the storms on the horizon, I'll be here. God willing, I'll never, never, never give up.

49   **Guns and Signs**

When I purchased the ranch in southwest Texas, among the canyons, rocks, creeks, and springs, I relished the isolation in sparsely populated Real County, so much that I often boasted that if I called 911, it would most likely take an hour or more for emergency responders to arrive. When I spotted a crude wooden board with the words, "We don't call 911," and a plastic pistol hanging below, I bought it and hung it on the gate to my house up on the hill.

I love to laugh. Over 20 years here, I'm still purchasing funny signs, placing them discretely in strange places on my ranch and in my houses.

Over my stove is the sign, "Don't make me come down there. God." On the refrigerator or, as we call it, the icebox, is a sign that reads, "Live your life in such a way that when your feet hit the floor in the morning, Satan shudders and says, 'Oh Shit, she's awake.' "

In the living room a plaque reads, "Aha, I see the screwup fairy was here."

On the gate to one of the lodges an old faded board shows arrows pointing opposite directions, "Rock, Hard Place."

In the bathroom of the hunter's cabin hangs a black and white drawing of a frowning pioneer woman. Below is the caption, "I don't like the cold and I don't like the snow and I don't like you either."

Guns are visible in most rooms. A loaded pistol lies on the bar, a rifle is propped by the back door, a shotgun stands guard beside my bed. While that might sound like overkill, a bobcat sniffed my shoes on the front porch, a wild hog climbed under the fence, a fox passed through outside the sun room door, and porcupines, skunks, and coons appear within a few feet of the house. Two-legged critters are much rarer.

A doormat outside the front door reads, "Come back with a warrant."

I do not believe that our government will ever take away the right to bear arms or even attempt to confiscate the millions of guns owned by American citizens, legal or illegal. Gun and ammunition sales continue to skyrocket. Millions of Americans possess hunting licenses; thus they own guns. The American Rifle Association is a powerful institution, and no, I don't have any of those signs about my guns.

I do have a sign in a lodge that reads, "Life is about how you handle Plan B." Another reads, "Last night I danced as though no one was watching. My court date is Tuesday."

On a whimsical note, a kitchen sign says, "If someone says you live in a fantasy world, don't fall off your unicorn."

Gate signs leading to various parts of the ranch direct "Wits End," "Psycho Path," and "Path of Least Resistance." A brass plaque on the barn below my house reads, "On this site in 1897 nothing happened."

A sign on the mantle above the fireplace reads, "What happens at Grandma's never happened."

My advice: keep your guns, plenty of ammunition, and, above all, a good sense of humor.

50 Conversations

Recently some first-time visitors came to the ranch. We were sitting in the living room where a large picture window frames the sheer limestone cliff across the canyon and creek below. Outside the picture window is a rocked-in flower bed. Winter is not kind to the flower beds. I watched one of the visitor's eyes dart from the distant cliff view to the flower bed a few feet away.

She asked, *"What are you trying to achieve with the flower bed?"*

"Obviously not very much."

"I see the irises. What are the tall green things?"

"Some native plant that blooms purple. There are also salvia, some trumpet vines and Turk's cap, native and drought resistant."

"Very interesting."

I thought the conversation strange but the communication successful.

Later that week, a ranch hand and I were working in the garden, the garden that has cost thousands but repaid in millions by the satisfaction of eating beets, carrots, green beans, and other veggies and herbs that I've grown there.

He looked at me and said, *"I see you planted some onions among the mustard greens and cabbage."*

"Yeah, there was some empty space."

"I can't understand why you are so obsessive/compulsive about the houses and barn on the ranch, and yet in the garden you plant randomly and mix everything together."

"That's a good question. I have to think about it."

Within the hour I figured it out. I can be obsessive about the houses, the furnishings, the decorator items, the pictures, the kitchens, the bathrooms, and my vehicles because I can control them. Mother Nature I cannot control and definitely cannot best. She reigns supreme. She does her thing and I do my thing, so I plant some seeds randomly in the garden, and Mother Nature takes it from there.

The following week I drove to Vance, nine miles away, to meet the husband of a lady who makes wonderful desserts. The occasion was my boyfriend's sister's birthday, and I had invited his family to the ranch for a late afternoon meal.

The dessert of choice was a pineapple coconut cake, the best cake I have ever eaten except maybe a scratch red velvet cake. I prepared the meal except for the dessert. I'm not good at desserts.

We both arrived in time and climbed out of our pickups for the exchange. This man is in his 80's and active. He wore starched jeans and an ironed cowboy shirt. After I paid him the $20 and carefully placed the cake in my truck, I turned. He was still standing outside his truck and asked, *"Do you get massages?"*

I hesitated, *"Why?"*

"Well, you know Mary Ellen died. Her massages kept me moving all these years."

"Yeah, I know."

"I found a lady in Leakey that does massages. She's really good. If you know anyone that needs a massage, I'll give you her name."

"Thanks, so far I don't have any aches and pains, but I'll keep it in mind."

That said he got in his pickup and drove off, headed not back home but on the road to Leakey.

One of the strangest conversations began in a somewhat adversarial manner. I was on a trip and a lady asked me, "Have you ever thought about how you might feel if you weren't so smart, what your life would be like if you were average or less?"

I paused as I felt her negativity, something I try to avoid when traveling. My answer, "No, I can't imagine not being who I am." The moment was diffused, but over the years that question often comes to mind. My three brothers are brilliant, and I confess competing with them is rather enjoyable. My children are smart. But being smarter than someone else has never been my goal. My goal is learning.

51 Gambling

Gambling holds no thrill for me. In fact, gambling makes me nervous. Back in the days when I was married to a Louisiana man, we often frequented the horse races. My budget was $40 for 10 races. I bet $4 per race and chalked it off to entertainment. I wasn't there to make money.

In Louisiana they bet on anything and everything. Every bar has a bookie or a back room or both. There's alway a card or domino game, and, believe me, they cheat.

When I attended cock fights and dog fights, the betting was spirited and vicious.

My mother had a boyfriend who was a serious gambler. He once purchased a new Mercedes convertible and lost it in a card game the next night. In Las Vegas he lost $40,000 or more in one evening. When he died, his tombstone read, "He was dealt a good hand." Engraved on the granite was a royal flush.

I am acquainted with some ladies, all seniors, who drive to the casino in Eagle Pass on the Kickapoo Reservation. They love the food and the slots.

I know several women — all Baptists — who have even ridden a bus all night to gamble all day at casinos in Louisiana. My son attended a bachelor party at a casino in Louisiana. I had never heard of such a thing.

A man in nearby Camp Wood gambles incessantly. He drives to San Angelo, boards a charter flight to Nevada, and gambles and dines lavishly for a few days before returning home. He also bets on sports. He drives to Uvalde and wires money outside the country and gambles against his account. When he wins, they deposit the money in his account; when he loses, they take it out. Since he is a senior and not very mobile, gambling is pretty much his life.

I prefer to take my chances on living and loving. The rewards are surer and better.

52 Homeaway

Life flowed smoothly...too smoothly. When plateaus and rest stops occur, boredom sneaks in and I create chaos. The result is always a learning experience, one that often comes with emotional and financial costs.

On this occasion, after purchasing the adjoining ranch and tuning the three homes to perfection, the flat line appeared. Now what do I do?

A friend owned a home in the Virgin Islands and told me that they listed the property with Homeaway, a world-wide vacation rental service for home owners. According to her, it was a good decision.

Since guided game hunts are difficult to market and entail filling feeders and installing blinds and cameras, something I had already tried with little success, I decided that non-hunting guests would be easier. Paying guests could fish, hike, swim, take pictures, and view the game from blinds without firing a gun. I would only have to fill feeders within walking distance and set the timers to go off in the late afternoon and not at daylight, my reasoning being that no vacationers desired to get up before daylight and walk in the dark. It also meant less corn to buy.

I went online and decided to list the first home, a lodge that slept 16 but with a septic system that most likely wouldn't handle that large a crowd. The first part was easy, filling in the information and rates, but downloading pictures turned into a nightmare. The photos on my Mac were excellent, but the website specified the pixel size. I had no idea what a pixel was, but the pixels in my pictures weren't sufficient. Whether they were too big or too little remains a mystery to me.

I called my son, the computer wizard. He was at work. I experimented exporting the pictures to my desktop and specifying a custom size. After more than a few tries I succeeded, but downloading them one by one took quite a bit of time and patience, not exactly my long suit.

After killing most of an afternoon, pictures were downloaded and I continued with the listing process. Then I waited after receiving an email that they were reviewing my application. I chose the option of paying them a 10 percent commission on all rentals booked online and having them wire the money to my bank account, but being a worrier and not wanting to allow anyone access to that account, I opened a free checking account at the local bank with a $100 deposit. The other options were a flat contract fee, ranging from silver to gold, based on the program selected by the homeowner.

The next email asked for confirmation that I owned the property, a utility bill, a deed, a mortgage or property tax bill, any two. I emailed back saying that the deed did not list an address. The property tax bill was actually 11 statements, none of which showed an address. There was no mortgage, but the utility bills only displayed two addresses.

Aggravation set in. I was ready to trash the idea, but after leaving the computer, going outside, and gathering my thoughts while working in the garden, I calmed down and returned to the task, scanning the utility bills, all six of them, and then emailing them, one by one. Since the deed was in my safety deposit box 20 miles away, I then retrieved, scanned, and e-mailed my 11 property tax bills. There was no property address on any of them. They read parcel, survey, acreage, and so forth.

Not long after, I received an email, confirming I was accepted and my listing would be online within a few days. The assigned account manager, Cody, emailed his contact information, and the listing went live.

I waited, checking my emails on a daily basis, and only two days after the listing went live, I had my first hit. A man in Austin wanted to book for three days the next month. There were 13 in his party, six adults and seven children under 17, including an infant. At first I was excited. Someone liked my lodge. Then the realization of all those people and children running around stopping up the septic system hit me. I remembered that on the listing I had specified a maximum of eight and not suitable for children. I emailed the man back that even though the lodge slept 16, the septic might be too fragile for all those folks. His return email said that most of the group were males and that they would go outside.

After a restless night I replied, saying that I would not be able to accommodate his group but would welcome the adults, that the ranch was not suitable for small children.

After all, it is my ranch. I felt so good about rejecting his reservation that I listed two of the other houses with Homeaway. This time I had no trouble downloading the pictures, and they accepted proof of ownership from the first listing. I had only one more house to list and resolved to choose my guests carefully, thus avoiding train wrecks otherwise known as cluster fucks.

And then to add some spice, I called my travel agent and asked her to find a trip to Venice, Croatia, and Montenegro for June and a trip to Japan in October. Time to do some traveling and leave the administration of the ranch rentals to my IPad.

The next request came from a lady in San Antonio, inquiring if her husband's fence building company could lease the barn quarters for a month for their laborers constructing fences in Leakey 45 miles distant. I responded that I would not lease the quarters for a month, the cost would be prohibitive, and the one-way trip to Leakey would be an hour.

Not long after that request, another one appeared for leasing the barn quarters for three months while a retired couple and their two dogs waited for their home to be built. This was an easy polite "No."

A bright lady, formerly the morning Fox News anchor I met in a television interview down in the Texas Valley, emailed and asked how much I would charge for her and her girlfriend to celebrate a birthday weekend at the ranch. This request didn't come through Homeaway. I quoted half price and told her I expected some referrals.

Their visit and company provided some much needed intelligent conversation and refreshing company. They showered me with a boutique bottle of tequila, a basket of fruit, and some home-made cookies. I thought to myself, "This is more like it."

I drove them to the back of the ranch, invited them to my home for dinner, and they responded with a reciprocal invitation. The girl-friend booked the log cabin Memorial Day weekend for her and a boyfriend. I discounted the price.

Next I received a booking in July for two couples from Dallas for the lodge at the farm, full price, no dogs or children. My efforts were finally paying off. I installed cable TV at three of my listings and decided to build a stone barbecue pavilion on the site of a home that burned down many years ago. Some of the rock work remained in place. I also engaged a local fence builder to close off a portion of the farm so that I could stock some sheep, certifying my agricultural exemption for the newly acquired property.

Another booking request came from an Austin attorney, asking for the lodge for three nights for three adults. His father was flying in from El Paso, a friend was driving from Dallas, and they planned on meeting in San Antonio. He called, inquiring if the property was large enough for hiking. I gave him my sales pitch. He agreed and then said. *"I prefer to pay cash when we arrive."*

I accepted his terms, but it didn't end there. He called, saying they would be arriving late on Thursday night, and since his father preferred to cut costs, they would stay in nearby Barksdale in a reasonably priced motel and arrive on Friday morning after breakfast. What could I say? Again, I became the affable hostess/hotelier.

Mother Nature interfered. The previous week brought rain, lots of rain. The ground was saturated. A low pressure area perched over southwest Texas, drawing rain from Mexico. The weather forecast predicted rain. If Bullhead Creek came down, the crossing at the farm would be obliterated. Guests would be stranded. The only alternative would be to house them at the lodge below my house, thus assuring departure once the rise receded.

I waited all morning. The attorney finally called at 9:30 saying, *"We're running late and will meet you at the gate at 11. Give me the directions again."*

A thunderstorm erupted, dropping more rain. I debated canceling the reservation when the storm moved east. The attorney called again, saying it would be 11:30.

Since the first call I drove down to the lodge, cleaned the toilets, emptied the garbage, wiped out the refrigerator, and shined it up a bit.

They were waiting at the gate and followed me onto the property. I stopped at the lodge and introduced myself. The father and his friend were comfortable and seasoned. The attorney was a bit uptight, a perfect example of what I refer to as "Austintatious." When I pointed to the crossing we just drove over, they immediately understood that another inch of rain might wash it away. They followed me to the other part of the ranch. I showed them the lodge; they were impressed. The attorney said, "We'll pay you for one night and see what the weather brings."

Not losing my cool and convinced the beauty would seduce them, I replied, "The price for this lodge is normally $400 a night, but since you wanted the other lodge for $300 and I can't safely put you there, the price for this will be $300. You're getting a free upgrade."

Unsmiling, he handed me $100, and the other two men each handed me their $100.

I pointed to the hill above the lodge. *"I live up over that hill. If you need anything call me."*

Later that evening I returned down the hill to close the gate over at the farm. The three of them were sitting in lawn chairs by the creek, their chairs inches apart, fishing rods in hand. I stopped. The water was silty from the rains. "How is the fishing? Are you catching anything?"

The attorney stood, *"It's hard to not catch anything. We've been catching bass, catfish, and perch."*

"Great, I'm going over to the other place to close the gate." I gave them the combination and encouraged them to explore.

When I returned home, I had another booking for that lodge, three nights, four adults, in June. I accepted the reservation. The lady called, asked if they could bring their dog. *"No,"* I answered. *"The ranch is not safe for pets, and I have livestock."* She agreed and then added, *"That was my grandfather's ranch. My sister saw it on the Internet. We are so excited to come."*

Their visit that June was not that exciting. They appeared pulling a trailer with a four wheeler, something I don't allow on the ranch due to the rugged terrain and liability. Her father rode it up to my house, intruding on my privacy and asking permission to drive it on the ranch roads, citing his knowledge of the ranch and experience running a bulldozer at the age of 86.

"I'm sorry, I don't allow four-wheelers on the ranch and I prefer that you load that vehicle on the trailer and leave it there." He unhappily complied.

I was excited to have another booking and went to my property owner's site and checked the analytics. Since the end of February I had over 140 hits on all four of my listed properties. My vacation was on hold. Being a hotelier proved a bit more stressful and complicated than raking in the dollars.

The jet stream and low pressure continued to conspire. A flash flood watch with heavy rains dominated the evening news. The sun had not set. I drove down to the lodge to alert my guests but found only the old Toyota pickup. I drove over to the farm, wondering why they would have driven the shiny SUV there, then surmised they drove to town for dinner or supplies.

After returning to the lodge and leaving a note, alerting them of the weather forecast, I waited for their call. When they called and said they had decided to leave for safety and convenience sake, I drove down to return their money. The attorney said, *"At least keep $100. We were here all day."*

"No, I'm refunding it all, hoping you will return."

"We'll certainly be back."

What a relief they were leaving. I would be able to sleep through the storm instead of worrying about them being stranded by the expected rising water.

The storm blew through in the early morning hours, didn't stall, kept going. The day dawned bright and clear, clouds to the south promising more rain. My dams were intact. The guests gone. The day would be good.

When my ranch worker called to ask about the storm, I told him my visitors left as a precautionary measure. He said, *"That's funny, I saw the white SUV parked at the motel in Barksdale with the hatchback open and a small pet carrier."*

"Aha, that's where they were when I went down to give them the weather advisory, checking on the pet. I can't believe they rented a room at the motel for a dog. Does Mrs. Conner allow pets?"

"Only in pet carriers."

"The dog had to be the attorney's. His father flew in from El Paso and the other man drove from Dallas. The pet carrier was in the attorney's SUV. That sneaky bastard, telling me they had to leave so they could be sure and find a room for the night. He lied. Just wait until he calls for a return visit. I'll ask him if he plans on renting a room in Barksdale for his dog. Kennel boarding is cheaper than a motel room. People are weird."

"I'll get the story from Mrs. Conner."

"For sure there are no secrets in the canyon."

The only secrets are in the excesses of my imagination. After I went on all sorts of mind flights, my ranch worker called to say, "I made a mistake. The white SUV was a friend of Mrs. Conner and had a small pet. It wasn't your guys."

How much energy did I waste on those senseless thoughts? How many hours did I squander on negative emotions. In retrospect I recall some law that says your first instinct is usually the correct one. They probably went into town for a meal or supplies as I originally suspected.

The next guests were a couple renting the log cabin for Memorial Day weekend. The weather forecast predicted more rain for the next seven days. So far the flooding hovered to the west. This time I most likely would not escape a catastrophe.

The roads flooded, the crossing washed away, and my guests canceled. Just another day in paradise.

That first year, I grossed about $7,000 and during that time spent money on cleaning out the septic tank, replacing a sump pump, repairing toilets and water leaks and keeping the grounds mowed and the flower beds manicured.

My goal for the second year was modest, $10,000. I was learning that people did not always tell the truth about how many were coming, their ages, or their aspirations, whether they planned to hunt, fish, swim, hike or just vegetate. Twice guests were asked to leave. In the first case, 14 people appeared on a booking for four. They received a full refund before they unpacked. The second case is a controversy still unsettled.

That booking was for two adults for two nights in the lodge below my house with three bedrooms, three baths, and three beds – two queen-sized and one king-sized – capacity of six.

The morning after their arrival I drove down to the house, saw four vehicles, and counted 12 people. I asked them to leave. They did so reluctantly asking for a full refund. They had paid for two nights, and 12 people stayed one night. The dispute remains unresolved. The money was taken out of my account and is under investigation. Either way I was screwed.

I've had some great visitors this year, couples who took their garbage with them and those who stayed two nights and left eight neatly tied bags of garbage. I have a printed list of ranch rules in each house. The visitors are good about following the rules, I think mainly because of the $100 security deposit I require. They will spend $1,200 for the lodging but insist on that $100 refund. If it works for them, it works for me. I check out the house and refund the deposit before they arrive home.

I have learned the hard way to remove the keys from the Jeep. On one occasion I found guests driving the ranch Jeep and politely explained, *"The use of the Jeep does not come with the rental of the lodge."*

"How much is the firewood to burn in the fire pit?" "Is it okay if we bring our guns to shoot at targets?" "Can we bring our dog? He is old." No one has ever claimed, "Our dog is young."

Dealing with the public has always been a learning experience from the time I was a young teenager working in a grocery store and later as owner of a motorcycle dealership. I've come to the conclusion that you can't please all of the public all of the time,

Playing bridge one month, one of my fellow players asked, "Have you had any more experiences with your rentals? I wouldn't do that in a million years."

"I don't mind. There's not much else left to do. At least I'm journeying outside my comfort zone, and that's pretty stimulating for an older woman. So might as well try being a hotelier."

53   On The Road Again

After two years of relative lethargy, I put on my traveling shoes again. While I was not tempted to leave the country, I did manage one short adventure, flying to Portland and boarding a small ship for a cruise up the Columbia and Snake Rivers. A bumpy jet boat ride up the far reaches of the Snake River left me with a torn retina in my good eye. The laser surgery to repair the tear was painful and frightening, especially considering my bad eye was already foggy, at best.

Then I purchased the adjoining ranch and spent most of the year fine-tuning the two homes, barn with living quarters, and a greenhouse. My writing suffered. A little romance interfered, and a road trip in August satisfied the wanderlust. The drive through the heartland of America to Canada restored my faith in mankind and my country. Seeing Mt. Rushmore with the presidents carved in stone and the memorial to Crazy Horse proved as exciting as seeing the Taj Mahal.

The rest of the year was spent with preparations for Thanksgiving, Christmas, New Year, and income tax time. A blue funk set in, but I managed an extensive garden do-over, listed the new homes on Homeaway for vacation rentals, cleaned out drawers and closets, and completed the necessary accounting procedures to send the information to my accountant.

All this done, I reminisced on past journeys, wondering if there were a few left. My writing continued to suffer. I nearly abandoned it, thinking two books were enough and finding no compelling reason to write another. But then I thought perhaps three would be better. After all, more than half the book was written.

I scheduled a trip to the Great Lakes in August, called my travel agent and committed to a trip to Venice, Croatia, and Montenegro; and alerted my travel agent that I was interested in going to Japan in October.

I was on the road again.

54 The Screwup Fairy

Usually I blame mechanical, technical, or emotional failures on the screwup fairy. The screwup fairy usually visits for a week until the magic number of three fuck ups is complete and then moves on to other venues.

This time the mini disasters appeared to be magnetic or charged. My son and his wife arrived at the ranch for a visit. Advancing years dictated that I show him where files, titles, papers, passwords, spare keys, and associated folderol are located.

All was proceeding smoothly. We drove over to the farm (the other half of the ranch), but on the way I stopped at the hog trap to throw in some scraps. Somehow I managed to stick the pickup between two ledges. Son Joe powered the truck out of the situation, and I resumed control of the wheel.

We then passed by one of my coon traps. The coon was alive. Joe attempted to shoot the coon with a pistol. Alas, it was loaded with empty shells. The second coon trap held a dead coon. Joe lectured me, *"Mother, if you are going to trap varmints, you must kill them, not let them cruelly die for lack of water. Why do you trap coons anyway? What harm can they do?"*

On the defensive, I replied, *"They chew up the wires on the deer feeders and eat the corn. There are too many of them. No one traps anymore. The predators and critters are taking over - skunks, porcupines, coons, foxes, bobcats, possums, armadillos. They're everywhere."*

"What do they hurt, Mother?"

I changed the subject, not fooling anyone. My daughter-in-law, Carla, wisely said nothing.

I drove to the back of a large field at the farm where an aluminum gate faced us. The road through the gate led through an abandoned Girl Scout Camp, an easement that allowed access when floods washed away my crossing.

The combination lock on the gate would not release with the four numbers I gave Joe. One of those numbers worked last May. I was positive. This was an easy solve as the bolt cutters would cut the lock, and I had several other locks for which I knew the combination.

Next stop was the safe at one of the houses on the ranch. For some silly reason that I can't recall, I wanted to change the combination. I opened the lock, handed Joe the instructions, and went into the kitchen with Carla to show her some china I had purchased.

Joe returned to the kitchen and said, *"I changed the combination and checked it, but now it won't open and has locked me out."*

I wanted to scream, *"What the fuck have you done to my safe? I just opened it."* Instead I calmly asked, "What happened?"

He shook his head, *"I don't know. I thought I did it right."*

Keeping my cool was difficult. We returned to the house, and Joe opened a beer and sat down at his laptop.

I asked, *"Are you looking up what to do about the safe?"*

"No, I'm checking my emails."

I wanted to scream and then scream some more.

Later he told me that he went to the website and learned I would have to download a form to be notarized, obtain a letter from law enforcement that the safe was not stolen, and forward the documentation to the manufacturer at which time they would give me an override combination.

The coon was shot, the toilet that ran all the time was fixed, and we returned to the safe to replace the nine-volt battery in the keypad. The safe would still not open and continued to lock us out. I downloaded the form to send the safe company.

As we watched TV that evening, the satellite went out, the signal crackling and showing distorted images. I turned off the TV, and we all retired to do some bedtime reading.

Joe and Carla left the next morning. I followed closely behind, destined for the dentist and what I thought was to be a routine teeth cleaning. I was obsessed, thinking of the locked safe. The idea of not being able to open it bugged the shit out of me.

The dentist wanted to pull a tooth instead of cleaning my teeth. I rescheduled, too worried about the safe. On an impulse I stopped at the farm, walked up to the safe with confidence, punched in the new combination, turned the wheel, and the safe opened. What a relief.

Serenity was restored, temporarily of course.

55   **Rain**

In Texas weather dominates the conversation. *"How much rain did you get?"*

"I had 1.2 inches. How about you?"

"My gage read 1.6."

I knew the spring of 2015 would be a wet one. My roof leaked in January. I called the best builder in the area and asked to be put on his list. He told me, "It'll be about three months before I can get to you."

Almost six months passed before construction began, building a roof over the 60-year old flat tar and gravel roof that I had coated twice in the 21 years I lived at the ranch.

And then the rains came – over nine inches. April was wet, but May was a wooly bugger. Bullhead Creek, which runs through my ranch, came down twice with an untimely vengeance. I had paying guests booked in one of my lodges. I upgraded their accommodations to the lodge below my house due to the threat of flooding. And then I advised them to leave after one night. For once I made the right decision.

All three of the low water crossings at the ranch washed out, meaning they were impassable. When the water receded, I was able to drive off the ranch, but only in my big four-wheel drive diesel ranch truck, and after my boyfriend removed the debris with the tractor. Eventually two of the crossings were passable, but the third required a couple of days of bull-dozer work before I could drive over to the lodges on the other side of the ranch. I was on yet another waiting list for the repair.

I could get to the lodges but only with four-wheel drive and through an easement with two gates. This weather event handicapped progress on the fence I was having built, as well as the rock barbecue pavilion. The submersible pump in the creek washed away, too.

Most of the county roads were closed so I had to cancel guests Memorial Day weekend, but did manage to book a successful axis hunt, using the easement and driving the jeep.

The rains blessed my garden. Soon I was picking several pounds of green beans every other day. The peppers produced prolifically along with the onions, carrots, herbs, and lettuce. The grass grew beyond the ability to mow. The ground was mush. Weeds and this-tles flourished.

I canceled a dental appointment, an eye doctor appointment, and my housekeeper, as well as a ranch worker. Nothing to do but wait for the weather pattern to change.

A trip to the Dalmatian coast had been planned for months. With mixed emotions I left the ranch for Venice.

56 **Rejuvenated**

Approaching age 70, I decided after two published books I would either quit or write a book about America. Since three is a good number, I chose to continue writing and limit my travel to America, concluding I was too old for any more world adventures. As usual, I was wrong.

In the three years since that awful birthday, I managed two trips in America — one with a boyfriend to the northwest, cruising the Columbia and Snake Rivers, and the other on a road trip with a girlfriend from high school, recently widowed, through the heartland of America to Canada. Somewhere along the way I had foolishly lost my courage for solo travel.

My writing suffered miserably and so did I. I had purchased the adjoining ranch with three very nice homes and occupied my time decorating and fine-tuning the property for friends and guests in my usual obsessive/compulsive way, finally listing four of the homes on my now larger ranch with Homeaway/Vacation Rentals by Owners.

The presumptive hotelier, I became obsessed with ice machines, a rock barbecue pavilion, new fencing, a roof leak, a failing heating system, propane tanks, and water filtration, pretending to be a hotelier. My garden prospered, and I succumbed to being a homebody, never desiring to leave the ranch except for much needed supplies.

I cracked a molar, endured minor eye surgery, and at 73 asked myself, *"Is this it?"*

For a while it was. I considered quitting, giving in to depression and fear. I drank too much, ate too much, and wallowed in creating perfection, micromanaging not much of anything. At my lowest point I decided, *"Fuck it; I'm not going down that easy."*

I called my travel agent and booked a trip to Venice and the Dalmatian coast, thinking, *"Where is that fearless world traveler who slept on a plywood slat across Siberia and road a camel into the Sahara desert?"*

And then the old lady intruded. *"What if the plane crashes or I get sick or fall down?"*

All the reasons to cancel came to mind until it was too late to ask for a refund.

The spring rains came, the ranch crossings washed away, my roof leaked, the barbecue pavilion was unfinished, the fence builder could not get his equipment to the site, the road up the hill to my house was damn near impassable except for four-wheel drive, and half the county was banging away on my roof.

I drove away in my pickup before daylight, left the truck at airport security parking, and caught a plane to Atlanta. Then it happened, that sense of acute awareness, the freedom one feels when fleeing the comfort zone. I was alive again, not plodding through the predictable.

I chatted with a lady attorney on the flight to Atlanta and at the Atlanta airport with a couple also destined for Venice. I think it was the airport in Atlanta when I realized I still had it - the adventurous spirit that has driven me for so many years. It was good to know I wasn't dead, after all.

The grilled shrimp with roasted corn salsa and the spinach manicotti served with an argula salad with goat cheese and beets, accompanied by Italian red wine, provided the perfect accompaniment to the nine-hour flight. A comfortable nap was interrupted with coffee, quiche, and fresh fruit. Venice was mine as I immersed myself into being where I was, having no choice in the matter.

The plane landed on time. My luggage was not lost, and I was met by an arranged guide for a tour of Venice before boarding the small cruise ship with less than 300 people.

A short vehicle ride delivered us to the dock where I boarded a lovely teak boat. The trip to the island of Murano followed a buoy marked channel, busy with boat traffic. The guide led me to a large building where I was comfortably seated to watch a basketball-sized ball of orange glass made into a $5,000 vase. Three handsome Italian men worked in the extreme heat. The process was fascinating, but not as fascinating as the glass art that was displayed in the galleries — all art, a life-sized Harley motorcycle, vases, glasses, everything imaginable in beautiful vivid colors.

I was told the Murano glass factory dated back to five generations of the family, and the glass works were only classified as Murano if at least one step of the process was completed on the island of Murano. The prices were exorbitant, but I purchased one wine glass for $100 and two small bowls for $30 each.

From the island we journeyed to the island of Burano, famous for its lace. The lace pieces required seven separate stitches, sewn or tatted by seven different women. The lace ladies ranged in age from 65 to 99, the art currently dying due to lack of government funding for the lace school. One of the ladies added that the government was corrupt. Nothing new about that. Again, the prices were outrageous, but I purchased a pair of white lace earrings for $80. The island was not crowded, and some neat shops beckoned. A nice stroll was welcome after all the hours on the plane.

From Burano we followed the channel to the Grand Canal of Venice, passing the Guggenheim Museum. The Grand Canal was filled with boat traffic, and the sidewalks were crowded with tourists.

My guide informed me that Venice on the mainland of Italy is sinking. The population is about 56,000, with the surrounding islands hosting 20,000 and the greater area about 100,000. She showed me a picture from her phone of St. Mark's Plaza flooded with water, something that occurs fairly often.

Early afternoon left me at the dock to board the ship. While going through security I visited with a couple from St. Louis. He was a doctor who had practiced in San Antonio and moonlighted in Uvalde, coincidentally only 60 miles from home.

After settling in my suite I enjoyed dinner with a couple from Australia, home to the world's most intrepid travelers. We discussed books and politics. Their politics were quite liberal.

Breakfast in my room consisted of simple fare - oatmeal, coffee and fresh fruit, followed by a day of touring in Venice. St Mark's cathedral and the Doge Palace, located in the heart of the city known as *"La Serenissima,"* dominated the morning. The crowds were oppressive.

The Ducal or Doge's Palace joins St. Mark's Basilica, and both are showy with an abundance of gold mosaics. The June temperature was unseasonably warm, and tourists milled everywhere. A girl from the ship accompanied the tour. Her name was Irina and she was from Kazakhstan. I stuck with her, knowing she would lead me back to the ship.

The tour guide explained every painting, naming the artist and period as well as the architecture. After an hour I was bored with information overload.

I asked, *"Why do some of the men wear their collars up-turned?"*

"It's the style."
"Do you like it?"
"Not really."
I agreed.

After returning to the ship I enjoyed lunch with a British lady and her friends, tea time with Australians, a nap and dinner with two Australian couples. The Australians rule. They are very friendly, heavy drinkers, and globally well informed.

Normally, Americans dominate the cruise line I was enjoying, but this time the Americans were the minority. I prefer my company international.

As usual I was in bed early, rising with the dawn, my doors open to the Adriatic breeze, waiting for the ship to come alive.

I enjoyed the view from my balcony as the ship docked in Koper, Slovenia. Just half the size of Switzerland, Slovenia is often overlooked and bypassed in favor of more well-known countries along the Dalmatian coast, the country's relative obscurity owed to its history. From Roman times to almost present day, Slovenian territory was incorporated in far larger territories, relegating it to its rustic role.

Backed by hills planted with olive groves and vineyards, Slovenia's small strip of Adriatic coastline is only 29 miles long. Following centuries of Venetian rule, the coast remains connected to Italy, and Italian is still widely spoken.

My arranged tour of the day included a tour of the countryside and a visit to some small villages in the interior. My guide was a charming surprise. He had earned a doctorate in literature and worked for a publishing company. His wife is a gynecologist. His English was superb, having studied at Harvard. He admitted that he refused a promotion because it would result in higher taxes, more responsibility, and the same pay after the tax increase.

He proudly stated that Slovenia is the only country with love in its name, and the population of Kopor is about 57,000. Slovenia formerly existed as part of Yugoslavia, and the total population is close to two million.

The guide told us that persimmons are grown in Slovenia, that after the bombing of Hiroshima and Nagasaki, some of the only trees left standing were persimmons, and that one year later the fruit showed no evidence of radiation. He added that the police only fire an average of two bullets a year, there has not been a bank robbery in 10 years and that white collar crime is the only crime committed in Slovenia. Corruption is prevalent, and he admitted that it often takes six months and a bribe to obtain a permit to install a window air-conditioner.

Historically Venice protected this area known for its salt pans or flats. Salaries were paid in salt because it was precious, needed to preserve food.

Since the day was warm he encouraged us to find the shadows, meaning stay in the shade.

We traveled through the small villages of Izola, Piran, and Porto-roz, walking the narrow streets. In Istrian, a town of 50, we enjoyed fresh local foods from stalls. Proscuitto, local cheese, sausage, vege-table lasagna, served with home-baked bread and olive oil, accompa-nied by wine refreshed our spirits as we made the return trip through the hills and orchards to Kotor.

A walking tour of Kotor revealed a 14th century tower, a palace, and a cathedral but the best part was a visit to a salt store on the main plaza. There I learned that the salt in Slovenia is known as sun-flower salt because the crystals look like sunflowers. I also learned Slovenian salt does not increase blood pressure, that it is exported to 20 countries, and is 10 times more expensive than regular salt. Over 40,000 tons are exported each year.

Naturally, I purchased salt and salted chocolate bars to give friends.

Michael, the guide, said that the primary social ills are bank-ruptcy, mental problems, alcohol, and a high suicide rate. After 40 years of living under socialism, when everyone had a job and job security, unemployment is a problem. He added that under socialism there are many rules, but nobody follows them.

His endearing manner made me feel the same way about his country.

After returning to the ship, I joined a Trivia team, mostly British and Australian and one lady from Scotland. We won.

The lobster dinner with a couple from South Africa, the guest lec-turer from Britain, and a couple from Florida provided lively conversa-tion, stimulating and intellectual.

The following morning the ship docked in Trogir, a Croatian island city which dates back 4,000 years and is among the oldest cit-ies on the Mediterranean.

As we entered the harbor I noticed wind generators on the hill-tops with the white-washed houses trailing down the slopes over-looking the town of Split.

I learned that the Greeks colonized Croatia over 2,000 years ago. When the Romans came, the area became known as Dalmatia. And, yes, that's where the spotted fire truck dogs originated. That part of the Adriatic coast is known as the Dalmatian coast. Croatia is also one of the countries that made up former Yugoslavia.

After the fall of Rome, the Christians arrived. Today Croatia is a republic where tuna from the Adriatic, figs, cherries, olives, grapes, peaches, and apricots are exported. The cherries were delicious.

A scenic drive through the countryside took us to Salona and the remains of the ancient Roman city, where we walked among the ruins of temples, amphitheaters, early Christian churches, burial grounds and baths, which have been excavated. The city 2,000 years ago housed a population of 16,000. The site was quiet and not crowded, on a sloping hill dotted with giant Italian cypress trees, those tall sentinels we call cemetery trees.

From Salona, the next destination was Split, the product of 17 centuries of building. At the core of the city is the spectacular Roman palace, built by Emperor Diocletian at the turn of the 4th century. What began as an imperial residence and fortified camp is today an intriguing warren of narrow cobblestone streets.

Today the population of Split is about 200,000. It is the second largest city in Croatia, the largest being the capital of Zagreb.

The palace complex was large and the tour boring — too long, too much information, and too many tourists. The ship, a nap and a second place with the Trivia team completed the day.

The ship docked in Dubrovnik, a beautiful fortified city with mas-sive stone ramparts and fortress towers that curve around a tiny har-bor. In the 7th century Romans fled from the Slavs of the north and founded the city, later named Ragusa. In the 12th century the chan-nel separating the settlements of Ragusa and Dubrovnik was filled in, and the two cities became one. Today the city is a UNESCO World Heritage Site. During the war for independence, the city came under heavy siege. Today few traces of the damage remain.

The main industry of Croatia is tourism, and 1,240 islands lie along the coastline. The beaches are beautiful. Off one island, according to the historians, Richard the Lionhearted, returning from the crusades, was shipwrecked and later had a small chapel erected on the small island in thanksgiving. The chapel remains to this day.

Dubrovnik is a celebrity destination for the likes of visitors such as Eva Longoria, Sir Roger Moore, Beyonce, and John Malkovich. Parts of the TV series *"Game of Thrones"* are filmed in Croatia.

I spent the better part of the day visiting the Konavle Valley, viewing the orchards and visiting a flour mill powered by a clear fast-running stream. The host offered sugar-coated almonds and home-made brandy, quite a morning buzz.

After a scenic drive, we stopped at a local artist's home in Gruda Village. There we were treated to cake and wine while observing the silk worms that the artist raises for the thread to sew traditional collars that women wear to identify their status – married, single, or widowed. She was delightful.

Returning to Dubrovnik, a city of about 40,000, a walking tour of the city exhausted my attention span. The city was crowded with summer tourists.

During the walking tour the guide reminded us that the Adriatic coast was conquered by the Greeks, the Romans, the Turks, the Venetians, Napoleon, the Austro-Hungarians, and became a part of Yugoslavia before gaining independence, thus the reason for the coastal cities being walled and fortified.

I was happy to return to the ship, but not happy that our Trivia team came in dead last. I learned that Amman, Jordan, was once named Philadelphia, that after America and India, the country that produces the third most movies is Nigeria and that the largest desert in the world is the Sahara. Our team voted for the Gobi desert. I voted for Sahara. That evening I dined outside on the upper deck, enjoying a grilled steak and stimulating conversation with a couple from Florida.

As the ship docked in Kotor, Montenegro I learned that Montenegro was once the smallest of the republics of Yugoslavia and the former primary port of Serbia. The six republics that composed Yugoslavia are Montenegro, Slovenia, Croatia, Serbia, Bosnia-Herzegovina, and Macedonia. Montenegro achieved independence in 2006. The fortified old walled city is now a UNESCO World Heritage Site. The rugged mountainous country boasts a population of over 600,000 and covers 14,000 square kilometers. Tourism is the main industry, the town of Kotor drawing 250,000 visitors last year.

I signed up for a day-long tour of the country, expecting a serene panoramic drive through the mountains to the interior.

The panoramic drive included 25 hairpin turns on a one-lane road that was designed and built by the Austrians from 1879 to 1884. Owing to the rugged terrain it was said to have been the most difficult project in Austria at the time. I believe it. When we met another vehicle the drivers cooperated, each backing up until passing was possible. Our driver appeared to be between 12- and 14-years-old.

Having an inordinate fear of heights, I could not look down and successfully fought off a panic attack, carefully counting each switchback until the final one. And then I recalled trekking through the Himalayas in Bhutan and silently mocked myself for being such a sissy.

We arrived in the small village of Njegusi where we sampled some of the local ham, bread, and cheese as well as wine and brandy. I ate as though I was starving.

From the small village we continued on a less – but not much less – mountainous road to Cetinje, the former capital of Montenegro. In this lovely clean city, we toured the National Museum, which once served as the palace of King Nikola Petrovic I, who ruled from 1860 to 1918.

Leaving the museum we proceeded to lunch at a local restaurant. Still full from the anxiety eating binge, I passed on the meal, which began with sweet donuts, then salad, soup, another salad, and lamb with vegetables, and sweet cake for dessert, along with wine, of course.

And then to my surprise, we returned to Kotor via a modern highway, a great relief. I walked through the Medieval Old Town, visiting the cathedral of St. Triphun and the 17th century Grgurina Palace, which today houses the Maritime Museum. The day had been a long one, and I was sick of cathedrals, palaces, museums, and old walled cities, not to mention the overbearing crowds of tourists.

Our Trivia team bounced back to second place, and I went to bed with no supper, still full from lunch.

The island of Corfu, Greece greeted the ship the following morning. I left for a tour of the island, the second largest, yet most densely populated of the Greek islands. Corfu's reputation as the greenest and quite possibly the prettiest of the Greek islands with its emerald mountains, ocher and pink buildings, olive, lemon, orange, and fig orchards is well deserved.

The town hosts a population of 40,000, the island 120,000. The main industry is tourism.

The scenic drive took us to the palace dedicated to the god, Achilles, built by Empress Elizabeth of Austria in the late 1800's. Kaiser Wilhelm later purchased the palace, and one of the James Bond movies was filmed there when the palace was a casino. Today the gardens and rooms have been somewhat restored. I enjoyed the pictures of Empress Elizabeth and her family.

As far as palaces go, this one was lovely, modest in scale, and appeared to be quite livable, not overtly ostentatious. The gardens sloped steeply to the blue waters below. So far most of the places visited were straight up and down, steep cliffs dotted with colorful homes on the hillsides, actually more like mountainsides to this Texan.

Leaving the palace, we continued through the countryside to the Byzantine Monastery of the Virgins, fairly modest with a spectacular view of Paleokastritsa Bay, that is, if you like heights. Offshore I saw the purportedly famous Mouse Island. I don't know the island's claim to fame.

From the monastery, we proceeded uphill to the Castellino Restaurant high on the hills above the traditional village of Lakones.

After a tasty meal of veal and a fruit dessert, I returned to the town square and strolled the streets before catching a shuttle down the steep hillside to the pier where I then waited for a tender to ferry me to the ship.

While waiting for the shuttle I visited with a woman from Nebraska, suffering from the humidity and heat. She arrived on a cruise ship with 3,000 passengers and claimed to be having a great time. When I asked her opinion on the presidential hopefuls, she replied, *"I suppose Obama is going to run again."* She didn't know that he was currently serving his second and last allowed term of office.

I gave two correct answers for the Trivia match. Moses stuttered, and Nicaragua is joined on its borders by Costa Rica and Honduras.

A splendid meal of grilled prawns and spinach with gorgonzola cheese served on the deck was enhanced by stimulating conversation with a lively Australian couple. Love those Australians.

The introduction to the Italian coastline appeared when the ship docked off the town of Amalfi. Amalfi was an important maritime republic in the Middle Ages. Today it is a popular resort along the coastal drive. Crusaders sailed from Amalfi, and the Spanish conquest of the area in the 1500's left its apparent influence on the architecture.

On the cruise to Amalfi we passed through the Straits of Messina with a pilot on board, the straits being quite hazardous.

From the pier I traveled to the small town of Ravello, perched high on a cliff, overlooking the Gulf of Naples. There I visited the Villa Rufolo, a palatial Moorish-style estate built in 1270 for the Rudolfo family and the garden that inspired the German composer, Richard Wagner, to write the second act of his final opera, *"Parsifal."*

I strolled through the village, visiting the ornate cathedral built in 1086. In the shops I purchased a colorful salt and pepper set, some lemon liqueur, and a tee shirt for my grandson. Returning to Amalfi, I hurriedly visited another cathedral and cloister, pretty sick by that time of church sightseeing. The Greek Orthodox churches I visited contained relics, a thorn from Jesus' head, a splinter of the cross, the bones of St. Mark, and skulls of various saints. These relics are much revered; the more relics the edifice houses, the more holy its reputation.

One last day aboard remained. The Trivia team continued to do well, but the food and ship were fast becoming tiresome. I had seen as many cliffs plunging into the sea, small boats in sandy coves, blue waters, white villages dripping in bright flowers, terraced hills with orchards, and fat tourists as I could bear. The ship docked in Sorrento where I began the 43-mile drive through two tunnels to the ruins of Pompeii, a city frozen in time under the dust of 25 centuries until it was discovered in 1748.

The site, designated a UNESCO World Heritage Site, was crowded. Over two million visitors come here each year. The temperature was in the 80's as we walked through the ruins of the Forum, theaters, the Sabian Baths, mansions, shops, and even a brothel.

The guide was extremely knowledgeable, giving us, once again, too much information. I learned that the city of about 20,000 was destroyed by the eruption of Mount Vesuvius in 79 A.D., burying the town under 20 feet of ash and pumice stone, yet preserving an entire city.

Many of the inhabitants were suffocated by the fumes. Today Mount Vesuvius lies only eight miles from the ruins and the distance between the ruins and the volcano is filled with businesses and residences. The last eruption was in the 1940's, and the guide informed me that an eruption is long overdue.

She also commented that over 600,000 people now live in what is called the red zone and that an evacuation plan has been put in place. The evacuation plan is titled *"Run Like Hell."*

The last afternoon of Trivia gained more points, and I redeemed my hard-earned points for two fountain pens. Both of them work well.

I disembarked in Rome, the beginning of a nightmare journey. The previous day, attempting to print out a boarding pass, I discovered that my flight time had been changed to leave six hours later, meaning that I would miss my connection in New York.

I changed my flight to one leaving earlier, making a connection in Atlanta with a four-hour layover in Atlanta and arriving in San Antonio late that night. That was only the beginning.

The drive to the airport in Rome lasted an hour and a half. By then it was 10 a.m. The flight left at noon. And little did I know that a terminal had recently burned and that three of the five terminals were closed at one of the busiest airports in Europe at the height of the tourist season.

As I was dropped off at the terminal, hundreds of people carrying and dragging baggage crowded around the terminal doors. It took nearly 30 minutes just to enter the terminal. The horror continued — long lines, no signs, and multiple security checks.

The flight lasted 10 miserable hours, only to be followed by four hours in a freezing Atlanta airport. Custom procedures had changed. You go to a kiosk and follow instructions, have your passport scanned, and collect your baggage, after showing your printed receipt.

Never have I been happier to be an American on American soil. I promised myself, this is it. I proved I can still travel solo but I have had enough of museums, ruins, beautiful scenery, palaces and cathedrals.

My instincts proved right. This book is about America, about the beauty of the place I choose to live, the United States. Honestly, there is no place in the world I would rather be.

While waiting in Rome to board the plane I sent an email to a friend. *"Enough is enough. Beam me home, Scotty."*

One last defining moment hit home. I had noticed few to none solo travelers. Most of the passengers traveled in pairs. And as I saw them take care of each other, whether their limitations were mental or physical, an arrow of loneliness struck me with regret over my failure to maintain relationships.

Perhaps that is why I write, living through words and thoughts, rather than relationships with others. I really don't know why and probably never will. That's just the way it is.

Funny thing though, when I returned home, the roof was still being built, the fence was not finished, the barbecue pavilion was still under construction, my garden was full of weeds, and the Texas skies were as beautiful as ever. Nothing had changed — least of all me.

57 **Reassured**

A rejuvenating trip to Venice and the former Yugoslavian republics reassured me that I was not ready to give up, grow old, or abandon my dreams. I would continue to travel in America, manage the ranch, finish the third book, garden, raise sheep, and host guests. Altogether, not an easy task.

The summer rains continued, and by the end of June I received more than the annual rainfall, delaying the completion of projects started in May.

As the weeks passed, the fence was completed, the roof finished, the rock barbecue pit, fireplace, and pavilion nearly finished, and the garden prospering. I kept up with my chores, renewing licenses and having four vehicles inspected, maintaining filtration systems, septic systems, and attempting to keep up with the grass mowing.

In the meantime, I traveled to San Antonio for an eye appointment with my retina specialist. Leaving the ranch at dawn forced a detour the long way due to the recent floods damaging the caliche road in back of the ranch.

Arriving on time at 10 a.m., I waited for the usual eye test, the measurement of pressure on the bad eye, before being ushered to the room where eyes are dilated and pictures are taken of the damaged eye. The picture taking failed due to clouding in the eye, and I returned to the dilation room to wait and wait. After an hour and a half I asked the man sitting next to me, *"When was your appointment?"*

"My appointment was at 9:45."

I asked the lady in the corner, "When was your appointment?"

"Mine was at 10."

I asked another man, *"When was your appointment?"*

"Mine was at 9:45."

I stood. *"I'm leaving."*

One of the men said, *"I think that's the best thing you can do."*

I returned to the front desk and politely asked to be rescheduled. The next appointment available was a month away. I accepted it and drove to Kerrville to have lunch with a girlfriend and fellow traveler.

When I arrived at the Mexican restaurant, she had a friend with her. As I shared my experience at the eye doctor's office, her friend asked the name of the doctor. I learned she had been a patient of that same group of doctors, and when she revealed her eye issues, I felt blessed. Her eye problems were monumental in comparison to mine. She revealed that she was now a patient of a retina specialist who came to Kerrville once a week and that he was very good. I obtained his number. Another opinion seemed prudent. The conversation and spinach enchiladas were refreshing. The stop at Walmart was not.

I hired a new man to maintain the grounds, had the new ice maker repaired with an additional filtration system, replaced the Italian tiles in the hallway that were coming loose due to a leak in my hot water heater, replaced the hot water heater, and then my air-conditioning system quit. First thought was compressor. Wrong again. It was fire ants in the contact points.

The rains returned, again washing out the crossing on the new part of the ranch, rendering access impossible. I used the easement through a neighbor's property, four-wheel drive only.

The crossing was repaired, but the phone cable under the creek was cut; thus, no phones or WiFi. Paying guests were expected in five days. In addition, the automatic gate to the lodge quit working. The game feeders needed filling, and to top it off, it was July 4th weekend.

I longed for a day with no one coming to fix something and a day with no ranch chores and everything working. That day seemed a distant fantasy.

My one remaining peach tree was loaded with peaches. As they turned pink and the limbs sagged, I picked some to ripen on the kitchen counter. I checked every day until a storm blew through and knocked many of them in the mud. Some of the peaches displayed small bites. My first suspicion was coons and birds until I observed a grey fox mid-morning under the tree. My yelling didn't phase him. I salvaged about a bushel and a half and made peach cobblers as the peaches on my counter ripened. Most of the cobblers I ate myself, but I did give some to the postman.

In addition, I was picking several pounds of green beans every other day. Those too I gave to friends, eating as many as possible. The same was true of my peppers. Then one morning I looked out my window and saw that same fox under my bird feeder, 20 feet from the front porch. The bird feeder was in pieces on the ground.

The hummingbird feeder was also on the ground. I fixed the bird feeder, but the hummingbird feeder was beyond repair.

With three hummingbird feeders and three bird feeders at my house, I was forever cooking nectar. Also at the other homes on the ranch I had feeders that I only filled when guests were coming.

When there were only three houses to maintain, I prided myself on knowing where everything was placed. Now with six houses and another barn and a greenhouse, it's a different story, keeping track of toilet bowl cleaner, RidX for the septic system, toilet paper, light bulbs, paper towels, soap, ant poison, rat poison, trash bags, coffee filters, and all the rest. Clean and uncluttered vehicles became a thing of the past. I now drive around like a janitor with supplies in the back seat of my truck. Here there are no completions, only lists and chores.

The good news is that I have a good plumber who knows where the ranch is located, an ice maker and air-conditioning repair service, a bulldozer operator who repairs the crossing and the roads, an electrician, a yard man, a handy man, a well man, and a housekeeper. I know how to order the filters for the various systems on the Internet and remain determined to keep it all going, as well as travel America and finish the book, except for one small fact.

Yet, my daughter talks as if I am too old to listen or make intelligent decisions. My son wonders why I choose to remain isolated when I am such a social animal. And my friend, the postman, sympathizes. He isn't as old but his daughter thinks the same of him and says that she is glad to know that we are friends who can keep each other company and not be lonely. Isolation and being in this nature's paradise are our choice. Lonely is our preference. Cities, crowds, and traffic drain energy and are not an option.

I plan on staying here to the end.

58 Terminology

On a trip to the east coast of South America, the first stop was Rio de Janeiro. Our tour guide referred to the country as Latin America and the people as Latin Americans. I liked that..

Living near the Mexican border in south Texas, I'm stumped at what to call the illegals. Are they Mexicans, illegal immigrants, Hispanics, Latinos or just plain undocumented? Not all of the illegals are from Mexico. Many come from Guatemala, Salvador, Honduras, Nicaragua, China, Africa, the Middle East, and Far East, more than I expect our government reveals.

I propose calling all the immigrants from the American continent as Latin Americans. That seems more practical than labeling them Mexicans or Hispanics. They are from America, mostly of Latin heritage, often with native American or American Indian origins.

And why are blacks called Afro Americans? I am German American. What about Irish Americans, Italian Americans, Chinese Americans, and so forth? We are all Americans. Why not just say, "I am an American." Does it matter whether one is black, white, caramel, yellow, or red. We are human beings, all created equal. We should treat everyone the same until given a reason to act otherwise.

This politically correct bullshit is ridiculous. Take the Confederate Flag. It should fly wherever anyone chooses to fly the banner. That is part of our history and freedom of choice.

The American Civil War was not about slavery, but about state's rights. The Texas Revolution was not about freedom from Mexico, but about freedom to own slaves and operate the plantations in Texas.

The need to rewrite our history is about appeasing idiots, not telling the truth. Most history, anyway, is written by those with an agenda.

Look at the travesties that befell the American Indians, the natives of this great country. And yet, Andrew Jackson, a man who ordered the extermination of the native Indian population, is considered a hero. I guess the monuments in his honor will be torn down along with the Confederate generals honored in the south.

Why not tear down the monument to Custer and rename Custer National Park? And since the war for Texas independence was about slaves, perhaps the Alamo should be given to UNESCO as a World Heritage Site and renamed Monument to the Failure of Freedom. I think that transfer has already occurred.

Where I live in southwest Texas, we have a saying, "If it's not broken, why fix it?"

Leave history to the historians, not the politicians, pundits, or journalists looking to create sensationalism or a distracting story.

And by the way, I am sick of seeing documentaries and movies with Texas settings where the scenery does not jive with the area portrayed. I have seen movies about the King Ranch with a landscape of mountains, spring fed creeks, and large trees. Movies about the Texas Revolution portray mountains, deserts, and rocks in southeast Texas.

I'm relieved when reviewers share my observations.

Wake up, America! Pay attention. My roots may be Texas German American, but above all, I am an American.

59 **Visitors**

With six houses on the ranch, I often have visitors. I'd like to think that they come primarily to be one with nature and not just to visit me. Usually the paying visitors come for the solitude, isolation, and a chance to get away from the hustle and bustle of their ordinary, busy lives.

Knowing someone else is on the ranch is a bit of a distraction for me. I try to stay out of their way, leaving them free to do whatever they wish, within the ranch rules, which I display in writing at all the houses. I don't allow pets or noisy four-wheelers. The minimum stay is three nights, the premise being that it takes at least three nights to fully absorb the beauty and moment of the surroundings.

When paying visitors call, referred by Homeaway/Vacation Rentals by Owners, I can usually tell if they are craving the quiet or if they really want to be close to Garner State Park or the Frio River where there are crowds, restaurants, entertainment, and noise. Most of them do not call back when I tell them I am an hour and a half from that resort area, but the few that reserve accommodations are elated that cell phones don't work and that they are at the end of the road.

Some of them argue that their pets are well trained, that they wear helmets when they ride their four-wheelers. They ask why I don't allow four-wheelers, why I won't accept small children. I don't answer except to repeat my restrictions, sometimes saying that there are stinging insects, rocks, cactus plants, and all sorts of critters.

When they arrive, I show them around, have them sign a release, and leave them alone. After they leave I go to clean. So far, everyone has left the premises spotless, beyond my expectations.

My nephew, his wife and five children recently came for a visit. The children hiked, swam, fished, and spent most of their time outdoors. No IPads, IPhones, texting, or TV. And when they left the house was clean. The linens were washed, the beds made, the trash carried off. I invited them for dinner one evening, and when the children brought their plates into the kitchen, every plate was clean. That's what I was taught as a child — you eat what you put on your plate.

In contrast, I had visitors with a 13-year-old who stayed in the house, slept till noon, and texted and watched TV. They left the house clean but didn't change the beds.

Five adults came for a visit. The 86-year-old father towed a trailer, carrying a four-wheeler behind his pickup, unloaded it, and rode it up the hill, asking, *"Can I ride the roads on the ranch?"*

I replied, *"I don't allow four-wheelers on the ranch. The roads are treacherous, rocky, and just plain dangerous. You can ride it on the county road and hope the deputy sheriff doesn't come through, but not on my ranch."*

His answer*: "I drive a bulldozer four hours a day. I know what I'm doing."*

I repeated, *"I don't allow four-wheelers on my ranch."*

He accepted my answer but wasn't happy about it. Slowly, I'm learning how to say no, make no exceptions, and accept the fact it is my ranch, after all.

The experience of paying visitors so far has mostly been good. I'm learning a lot about city folk who come to experience nature. One group of four couples was mesmerized by the stars and clear water. They plan to come back.

Another group who visited during a full moon could not believe it was so bright it cast shadows. The noise of the axis deer seeking a mate frightened them. I have heard visitors comment about large moths they mistook for hummingbirds, the noises of deer in the brush and the various bird calls, including the screech of a red-tailed hawk. I know then that they've experienced the best of a vacation in the wild – the liberation that comes from the absolute beauty and wonder of nature.

The Great Lakes

The flight to Chicago passed quickly, due to my seat companion, an Oriental man who got on the plane with his extended family. He took the seat beside me, while his family dispersed elsewhere on the plane. When I asked, *"Where are you from?"* he answered,

"From Ireland." His accent was unmistakenly Irish.

During an extended conversation I learned he was Malaysian, had lived most of his life in Dublin, and had attained the highest degree of mastery in Tai Kwan Do in Ireland. He would soon be traveling to Croatia to be inducted into the International Hall of Fame for Tai Kwan Do.

He proudly displayed pictures of his daughters, dogs, wife, and home on his telephone. His daughters are also masters in the martial arts discipline. He was an interesting, admirable man.

After retrieving my baggage I caught the shuttle to the Palmer Hilton in downtown Chicago.

The trip was courtesy of Road Scholar, a non-profit organization I had journeyed with over the years. Road Scholar arranged the trip; I paid for it.

The evening dinner consisted of a buffet, chicken and some nice veggies. As I surveyed the group of about 150 fellow travelers and group leaders, I wondered about the logistics of managing that many elderly people. The average age of the Road Scholar traveler is 72, close to my age, though I hate to admit it.

We were divided by color into five groups. I was an orange, a nice fiery color, and the orange group leader was a likable and knowledgeable lady attorney from Wisconsin. Her life story was an interesting one, having adopted four children from the Philippine Islands.

A tour of the historic Palmer Hilton hotel started our morning on an interesting note. The hotel was built in 1871 and burned in the Chicago fire two weeks later. The Palmer has hosted many presidents, as well as presidential nominating conventions. Brass peacock doors designed by Tiffany grace the front entrance.

From the hotel we coached to the Pritzker Pavilion, a nice park built over the still functioning railroad on the shores of Lake Michigan. The Clown Fountain with 999 faces was interesting and refreshing in the August heat. Most of us hugged the shade before walking across the street to the Art Institute of Chicago for a guided tour of the museum's highlights.

The cafeteria in the Institute provided a nice lunch of baked salmon and vegetables before we continued on to the Chicago River to board a boat for an architectural tour. There were over a hundred of us as well as other tourists on the boat. The guide was an extremely knowledgeable young man. He continued to enlighten us through a heavy rainstorm that drenched the boat, sent some running to covered decks, and the rest of us donning disposable rain parkas furnished by the crew. At least the rain dispelled the summer heat.

From the guide I learned that the 1893 World's Fair introduced the Ferris wheel, electricity, Pabst Blue Ribbon Beer, Cracker Jacks, and Aunt Jemima's pancakes, and that four of the last nine governors of Illinois have been imprisoned.

As the boat moved along the river I learned more about architecture than ever imagined, the contrast between the old and the new, structure and design. The tour was memorable.

I could go on about the Chicago fire in 1871 that burned most of the city and other facts, but rather than boring you, if you're interested, check out the information on your phone or other device.

At last we embarked the St. Laurent, a ship owned by Haimark Cruise Lines and chartered exclusively by Road Scholar for the tour of the Great Lakes. The ship, recently remodeled, held a capacity of 200 passengers. My very comfortable stateroom contained a large picture window.

That first evening I enjoyed canapés and champagne and dined on lamb and vegetables with two sisters from Illinois. The ship's movement provided a gentle night's sleep.

We cruised the first day aboard, and I attended a lecture, learning that Lake Michigan is the only Great Lake located entirely within the United States, that it has a surface area of more than 22,000 square miles, is the fifth largest lake in the world, and that the name Michigan is believed to come from the native Ojibwe word meaning "great water." I will not bore you with other facts and details. Look them up.

After a lunch of veggie wraps, fruit, and salad I attended another lecture about Mackinac Island and the excursion for the following day.

I awakened in the Straits of Mackinac, which connect Lake Michigan to Lake Huron, as we docked at Mackinac Island.

Mackinac Island is a tourist destination for travelers from the Midwest and can also be reached by ferry. As I disembarked the ship, I observed hundreds of bicycles available for rent. No cars are allowed on the island, which hosts about 492 residents. Horse-drawn carriages convey as many as 35 people per carriage, and the entire island smells like horse manure, accounting for the lovely flowers and lush plants. There are even carriages equipped only for the handicapped. And carriage drivers are happy to share the names of the large Belgian horses.

The carriage was comfortable as we toured Fort Mackinac, built by the British in 1780, conquered by the Americans in 1796, and reclaimed by the British at the start of the War of 1812. We took it back in that war. Several movies have been filmed on the island.

We visited Arch Rock with its nice view and heard a typical Indian love story about how the hole in the rock was created by the tears of an Indian princess.

The carriage stopped at the Grand Hotel, a magnificent Victorian structure, where an optional buffet lunch was offered for $48. Many of the people signed up for the heavy lunch. I declined and instead toured the lobby and took in an art exhibit. The decor was colorful and fascinating and when I inquired as to the cost of the rooms, I was given a figure ranging from $300 to $500 per night. The hotel lives up to its grand name.

I learned that today the Grand Hotel has 390 rooms and was built in 93 days, a tale in itself. I doubted it until I later learned the story to be true.

John Jacob Astor, the fur trader and namesake of Astor House on the island was never on the island himself. He was afraid of the water. Eighty percent of the island is state park, and the hotel is shut down in the winter because the lake freezes.

When I returned to the center of town, I realized that ferries had dropped off hundreds of more tourists. The streets were crowded, which made shopping difficult. Most of the shops sold fudge, and the sweet smell was tempting. I returned to the ship and enjoyed a hamburger.

That evening the concierge from the Grand Hotel spoke about the hotel. His passion for the subject and love of the hotel resonated in his words.

I learned that the last luxury steamships sailed in 1966, that there are only 11 left, and that four generations of private ownership have controlled the hotel.

According to the lecturer, in the late 1800's, a small group of capitalists made fortunes and created a social class with their children in which it was acceptable to display their wealth.

In 1887, the hotel boasted 200 rooms, a fountain for canoeing, and sponsored all sorts of events, the purpose being to create a resort that supplied more than food and rooms, a resort with heart, soul, and spirit that sold memories and created experiences. To this day that purpose has never changed. I was impressed.

Currently the hotel employs 720 people, one-third of them being foreign nationals, legal, of course.

Following a wonderful meal of prime rib, snails, and oysters, I enjoyed a game of bridge and when the duo that provided music played some great dance music, several of the ladies got up to dance, asking me to join them. I replied, *"I don't dance with women and I don't dance alone."*

My orange group leader said, *"Okay, I'll find you a man to dance."* She did, one of the other group leaders. While he was not the best dancer in the world, he had rhythm. After two dances, the other women stole him away, and I returned to my game of bridge.

The following day we left Lake Huron via the St. Mary River and entered Lake Superior floating through the Sault Sainte Marie Locks and docking on the American side, the town appropriately called Sault Sainte Marie. The Canadian town across the lake boasts a population of 70,000 and is also named Sault Sainte Marie, whereas the American side hosts about 14,000 residents.

Instead of participating in a tour of the locks, many of which I have traveled through on other trips, I chose to do a bit of shopping along the main street where I purchased tee shirts for my grandsons and a beaded lanyard for my daughter.

The locks are per tonnage the busiest in the world, 10,000 ships passing through yearly carrying iron ore, salt and grain. The locks are closed January through March and can accommodate vessels of

1,000 feet by 105 feet. Most of these vessels remain on the Great Lakes for their useful life and are called lakers.

Lake Superior, the largest of the Great Lakes with depths ranging from 400 to 1,300 feet deep, contains the most water and presents the most danger.

During a city tour I learned that Sault Sainte Marie is the oldest city in Michigan, originally established by Jesuit missionaries. The tour stopped at the river history museum where ample time was provided to explore a lake freighter and the museum inside. It was huge, difficult to imagine loading and unloading cargo, but the guide explained the process, which turned out to be quite interesting.

The evening meal was among my favorites, prime rib steak, clams, and florentine spinach. I skipped dessert.

After leaving Lake Superior, we returned to Lake Huron and docked on Manitoulin Island, disembarking in Little Current, Ontario, Canada. After driving through the agricultural countryside, we arrived at the Immaculate Conception Church, the spiritual focal point of the native community that brings together the beliefs and customs of both the native Ojibwe culture and the Catholic Church. The church, which smelled of cedar, was round, simple in design, and emanated a quiet spirituality.

We then walked across the street to visit the Ojibwe Cultural Foundation for a welcome ceremony and an interpretive tour of the heritage museum and art gallery where we participated in a smudging, a purification ceremony calling on the spirits of sacred plants to drive away negative energies and restore balance. The smell and smoke were calming and reminiscent of the woodsmoke smell when the weather in the Texas Hill Country begins to cool.

Behind the cultural foundation we were seated in an open-air amphitheater and treated to a traditional dance and drum presentation. The costumes were magnificent, the narration entertaining, and while I did not join in the dance at the end of the presentation, many of the other guests enjoyed the exercise.

Manitoulin Island is 110 miles long, contains about 13,500 residents, one-third of them being members of the First Nations, the term Canada uses to describe their native population. Because of the maritime climate, the population swells to about 40,000 during the summer months.

175

The following morning the ship docked for the first time ever in Midland, Sainte Marie, Canada. The town welcomed us with bagpipes and miniature pecan pies, which were sugary sweet.

Prior to the arrival of Europeans, the town of Midland was home to the Huron Wendat First Nations people. The first Europeans, the French Jesuits, arrived in the early 1600's. The site we visited, Sainte Marie Among the Hurons, is a re-creation of their mission, a beautiful project. Again, the smell of woodsmoke made me a bit homesick.

The SS Keewatin, an Edwardian steamship built in 1907 in Scotland, was our next stop. The ship served with the Canadian Pacific Steamship Company, sailing the entire length of the Great Lakes until she was retired in 1966. The ship has been restored to its past splendor with authentically furnished cabins. In my opinion, luxury cruising during the time of the ship's life was not very luxurious. We are spoiled.

The population of the area swells to over 100,000 during the summer months because the area is less then two hours from Toronto by car.

After a quick hamburger aboard ship, I returned to the town for exercise and shopping. Being a nut about cute signs I found one for the guest lodge at the ranch that reads, "Unattended children will be given an espresso and a kitten."

The sign I purchased for my house reads, "I have no Bucket list but my Fucket list is a mile long." It hangs in my living room unless I have young guests.

The next day was spent on board, cruising Lake Huron, the second largest of the Great Lakes, a welcome rest for me on this supposed vacation. I require myself to take notes and write observations, though I managed to play some bridge before attending yet another lecture.

That evening I enjoyed the current rage, a hot rock dining, where some extremely hot lava rocks and raw meat and veggies are provided and each person cooks dinner to his or her own preference. The evening breeze, colorful sunset, and some wine enhanced the experience.

Sailing from Lake Huron to Lake Erie, the ship docked the following morning in Windsor, Ontario, Canada. After passing through customs we crossed the bridge that connects Windsor to Detroit, Michigan, and visited the Henry Ford Museum where I saw the limousine that carried President John Kennedy, the bus that made Rosa Parks famous, Abraham Lincoln's chair from the Ford Theater, and other fascinating displays.

My favorite was a set of cushions designed to resemble a hot dog bun. I lay down in the bun, pulled mustard and ketchup pillows around me, and had a friend take a photo, very funny.

After returning to the ship, I attended a lecture, learning that Windsor, Ontario, was settled in 1749 by the French and has a population of about 200,000. Detroit, across the river, lies in the middle of the Great Lakes, and to reach Lake Erie, the ship must go down the Detroit River to reach Lake Erie, the St. Lawrence Seaway, and the Atlantic Ocean. The Erie Canal, constructed in 1825, made Michigan accessible to and from the east coast.

Today Detroit is still losing inhabitants; 50 percent have left since 1950. The city declared bankruptcy in 2013, but hope prevails, and the city is moving forward.

The following morning we disembarked the ship at Port Colborne on the southern end of the Welland Canal. The original canal was opened in 1829 and was extended to reach Lake Erie in 1833. As the ship awaited its turn to transit the locks we left the ship and rode by coach to Niagara Falls and through the Niagara Wine Region.

The view from the Canadian side of the falls was fantastic, the volume of water unbelievable. I boarded a boat and cruised into the misty spray of Horseshoe Falls along with hundreds of tourists all wearing complimentary orange waterproof ponchos. Within the Niagara Great Gorge we journeyed past the American Falls, Bridal Veil Falls and into the heart of Horseshoe Falls. It was a bit scary, but I survived.

After the cruise we continued through Niagara's beautiful wine region, which possesses a unique microclimate that lends itself to the care and tending of premium grapes. The scenery was lovely with magnificent homes and miles of vineyards.

Lunch was served at a winery with complimentary wine tasting. Lunch was tasty, the usual chicken, but I found the wines bitter and earthy. At the winery I learned about ice wine, wine made from frozen grapes. A sample tasted like nectar of the gods. The price for a very small bottle was over $20, and the guide explained that a frozen grape produces one drop of juice. I bought a small bottle that remains in the refrigerator for a special occasion. Ice wine is a dessert wine.

We rejoined the ship after spending a nice day ashore rather than suffering through the passage of the locks.

A sumptuous dinner was served for the farewell evening, steak and oysters, and the following morning before leaving the ship I splurged on vanilla French toast, complimenting the German chef for some of the best meals enjoyed on a cruise.

Toronto, the capital of Ontario, Canada, lies on the northwest coast of Lake Ontario and hosts a population between two and three million. Toronto is the cultural and financial center of Canada. Ten provinces and three territories comprise the country, and the locals claim there are only two seasons in Canada - winter and construction.

Following a tour of the city, we dined high in a revolving tower. I tried not to look down as I dined on – you guessed it – chicken. After checking in a downtown hotel, I took a taxi to a shopping area. The driver was from Bangladesh. Fortunately, I found nothing to buy and returned via taxi with a driver from Pakistan.

As I walked the area around the hotel, looking for a frothing iced coffee, I noticed the various races and foreign languages spoken. I was a minority here. Like New York City, Toronto is an international metropolis.

After a final goodbye meal and farewells, I was ready to return home. I left the following morning in a rainstorm, arriving safely in San Antonio, and driving home before dark. As usual I kissed the ground, thankful for yet another safe and enjoyable trip.

On that journey I had discovered another source of pride in my country – the big and great Great Lakes. As a center of commerce and shipping of natural resources, the Great Lakes are as much a symbol of the vitality of America as the center of America, the heartland, is for agricultural products. Once more I am ambushed by my country.

61 Changes

Twenty one years have passed since I purchased my ranch in Real County. Actually, it seems like yesterday, and I don't have a clue where all that time went. Supposedly out there in the ether or wherever it is that time goes.

While the small town of Camp Wood, 20 miles from the ranch with a population about 600, has changed, the trees, cactus plants, thorny shrubs, and rocks on the ranch remain constant.

Camp Wood now has a Family Dollar Store, a bar, two beverage barns, a second Church of Christ, and soon another bar and even an auto inspection station.

When I first purchased the ranch, there were few concrete bridges. The bridge over the east prong of the Nueces River at Vance was gravel, covering culverts. The bridge over the Nueces at Barksdale and another at Williams Crossing were similar. When it rained profusely, several times a year, the crossings were washed out, and there was nothing to do but wait until the river receded and the county could restore the culverts. The isolation was exhilarating except when the power failed. Then life was a bit rougher. The bridges are all now well above the water and constructed of concrete except for those on the county roads. Three crossings on my ranch are still gravel, and the yearly floods still isolate me, cause for small consolation and big expense.

In the last two years, a private crossing on my ranch has washed out three times, requiring a bulldozer and bobcat, as well as lots of material to render it passable again. Such is the cost of living in paradise, though some people find it spooky and scary to live in the middle of nowhere. I tell them, "The reason I am here is that I am not all there."

Today Fed Ex and UPS deliver to the ranch. Internet is provided via the telephone system. No more dial up modems. I even have wireless, but cell phones still don't work here at the ranch, and some servers don't even work in Camp Wood.

I still have to drive 60 miles for groceries and a visit to Walmart. Good medical facilities and an international airport are in San Antonio, about a three hour drive. Still it is not as bad as living in far West Texas where conveniences are even harder and more distant to find.

179

Repair services - plumbing, electric problems, air-conditioning and heating, appliances - are expensive.

The few neighbors that I had are diminishing, moving into towns nearer medical facilities or locating closer to family. Properties are for sale; owners live far away.

An Italian restaurant has opened on the main drag, open only one day a week by reservation only and a fixed menu for $30 per person, maximum seating for 20. I recently read in the free paper that it has closed.

One constant around here is the hunters. Every year, beginning Labor Day in September, the hunters converge on Real County, bringing their four-wheelers, blinds, feeders, and trailers loaded with corn and pellets, most purchased elsewhere. The local feed store has closed. No one knows why. It has since opened under new management with a diminished inventory.

The roar of motorcycles in great numbers continues even though there are deaths every year caused by bad judgment and animals roaming the winding roads.

Other constants are the nursing home and the schools, probably the biggest employers in the area. There's not much of a labor force or opportunities to make a living. This is hard scrabble country. I wouldn't have it otherwise.

Accidents

Famous last words: "I haven't had an accident or insurance claim in years."

The husband of one of my bridge player friends died and was cremated. After some time passed, she hosted a memorial service for him at her home in a lovely setting on the banks of the Nueces River.

That second Saturday of the month was also the day of the farmer's market at the city park in Camp Wood. I arranged to pick up another of the bridge ladies at the post office, make a quick stop at the farmer's market, and attend the memorial service. We diddled around a bit too long at the market and arrived a few minutes late for the service.

Cars lined the narrow road, the guitar player had begun playing *"Amazing Grace,"* the mourners were singing. I found a spot under a large oak tree and pulled my pickup under the spreading limbs. There was a very loud screech as the limb scraped the roof of my truck. The music and singing stopped. Fifty heads turned in my direction. I turned off the engine and nonchalantly reached into the bed of the pickup for the two lawn chairs we had been instructed to bring.

We joined the others, and the service resumed.

The next morning I noticed my windshield sported cracks, which grew as the week progressed. Most of them were on the passenger side, not interfering with my vision. I ignored the windshield and chalked it off to a ranch ding, taking no action until the hassle factor intruded.

The following week I met with an outfitter to show him the ranch, on the premise he would bring hunters to stay in my lodges and pay me to hunt native and exotic animals.

When he arrived we got in my diesel pickup with four-wheel drive and drove around the ranch. The first stop was a 40-acre tract in an overgrown, brushy canyon. I missed the road and ended up in the brush. No problem, I backed up, a bit chagrined and continued to another part of the ranch where I managed to drive my right rear wheel off the creek crossing. I knew immediately that I was in trouble and let loose a loud, "Oh fuck."

He laughed as I put the truck in four-wheel drive but left it in neutral. All I could think was that the truck would fall over into 12 feet of spring water and we would drown. Reverse put me back on the narrow crossing and we were able to continue. The rest of the tour went smoothly at least on the outside. I figured he thought I was some crazy old lady, even though he appeared unflustered by my mishaps. At the end of the day I remarked, "I bet you're a great hunter. You seem very patient, not prone to overexcitement."

He later called and we came to an agreement that would be beneficial to us both. Every time I drive across that spot, I recall that awful sinking feeling. To this day, I can't forget.

While I traveled the Great Lakes, a storm passed through the canyon and blew three chinaberry berry trees onto the rock hunting lodge and adjoining patio. The damage to the lodge was minimal; the cedar stairs to the upper bedroom kept the trees from bashing into the lodge.

Removing the 60-foot trees from the house and patio proved a problem. The insurance adjuster reminded me that my deductible was $2,790. Every time the wind blew, the tree trunks squeaked against the staircase.

My boyfriend, the local tree expert, assured me that he could remove the trees, that his ex-brother-in-law had a Sky Track, whatever that is, and that if they could get it in place, he could get the trees off the house.

Arrangements were made, and the Sky Track arrived on a huge flat bed trailer pulled by a large truck. They had to unload it by the road because the crossing I fell off was too narrow and the curve too severe for the truck and trailer.

Once the job was complete, the trees removed from the house and patio, the crew gathered at the road to load the Sky Track and talk. Since I was no longer needed I backed up to leave and unfortunately backed into the post that held the keypad for the automatic gate. The post was stout, so stout that it trashed the driver's side mounted mirror. The loud crash stopped the conversation. The mirror hung like a limp dishrag.

All heads turned. "Are you okay?"

"I'm fine. No problem."

I acted as though it was nothing and drove home. A friend later duct-taped it in place. The mirror was splintered.

A month passed before I reported the windshield claim and the side mirror claim. My deductible failed to cover the repairs. The combined cost was $845, less than I expected.

Soon after that I nicked a concrete post with my left front bumper, little to no damage, and backed into a tiny compact car at the gas pump, putting a small pimple on the front of the car. The noise of the contact sounded like a train wreck, and even worse, it occurred in front of the whole town, most of whom I knew. The owner of the car graciously said she would not file a claim, which provided some relief.

I scheduled cataract surgery and could not believe the improvement in my eyesight. I'm still afraid to drive, back up, or park, but realize I just have to get over it. Meanwhile, I'm hoping for no more accidents.

63 Health and Happiness

I am not a doctor. I have no medical expertise, but I can read. That's not to say I believe every word in print.

As I've grown older, I've noticed that many friends my age take various prescribed medicines, as well as over-the-counter supplements. They live lives defined by their maladies and scheduled visits to an array of physicians.

Horror stories abound about people dying in hospitals from botched elective tests and procedures. A friend, now deceased, shared a story that I think began with bunion surgery. She claimed all the years of wearing pointed toe cowboy boots caused her problem. Foot surgery on both feet left her in a wheelchair with casts for six weeks.

A clamp on her leg during the surgery permanently constricted blood flow to her foot. A colonoscopy test perforated her colon. Rotor cuff surgery left her shoulder damaged and was a painful, unnecessary procedure.

Prescribed cholesterol medication, blood pressure medicine, thyroid pills, blood thinners, pain pills, and an antidepressant were taken daily under various doctors' orders. She then developed asthma and a lung infection for which she consumed more pills. When diabetes was detected, additional medication was added to her regimen.

Never did she receive advice concerning altering her diet. She dutifully took her pills, having one of those plastic pill cases where you put a weeks worth of medication in the little squares. She died of gangrene in a nursing home way before her time.

A cousin undergoing heart surgery suffered a broken blood vessel, almost bled to death, and is now confined to a wheel chair.

I don't know all the details, but the husband of a friend developed pneumonia, spent two suffering weeks in a hospital with a collapsed lung, and died.

Another friend suffered through knee replacement surgery. The operation was successful, but he then developed back problems and was sent to another doctor. The new doctor said the knee surgery was unnecessary, he needed back surgery. He suffered until he died of colon cancer, refusing to live with a bag outside his body. I don't blame him.

My Aunt Stella who is 99 was told 30 years ago that her cholesterol was off the charts. The cholesterol medication she has taken never changed the numbers. She is sharp, mobile, and lives alone at 99.

My experiences are similar. Simple cataract surgery eight years ago resulted in the lens being placed anterior to the cornea. Within six months the retina detached. A buckle and gas bubble were placed in the eye. I spent two weeks lying face down. Vision was partially restored. A film grew over the eye; it was removed. Vision deteriorated; I was given corticosteroid drops, shots, and advised that no other procedures would be available, too much of a risk, that blood flow to the eye was restricted.

For several years, I faithfully visited the retina specialist. Finally, on the occasion of a routine visit for which I had an appointment scheduled a month prior, I walked out of the office after waiting an hour and a half. Patience is not one of my virtues.

Through a friend I found another retina specialist who prescribed stronger eye drops and mentioned that I might be a candidate for an eye transplant, but in the meantime I had been taking lots of Vitamin D, because a routine yearly blood test revealed my body was dangerously low in that nutrient. Stupid me continued to take the pills until the bad eye hurt so bad I couldn't stand the pain, the constant discomfort of grains of sand in my eye. The new retina doctor sent me to a cornea specialist who sanded the deposits off the cornea. He also performed cataract surgery on the good eye.

I questioned him on the status of the bad eye. He recommended that an ultrasound be done on the eye to determine the status. They couldn't look into my eye if I couldn't look out. In the eight years after the retina detachment, no doctor had recommended that test.

The doctor who performed the test said that the eye looked good. I was shocked. No one had ever told me the eye looked good. He said I might have a good chance of restored vision with a cornea transplant.

I said, *"Every doctor that has treated the bad eye said that there was not enough blood flowing to the eye to sustain healing from a cornea transplant."*

He asked, *"Blood flowing to what part of the eye?"*

I answered, *"I don't remember, but I was told that the chronic inflammation is due to lack of blood."* And then I felt silly and angry. Three years ago I walked into a glass door and the eye was filled with blood. I had an emergency trip for a shot to the eye, and then just two weeks ago I woke up with a red eye, having ruptured a blood vessel. Obviously, there was blood somewhere in the eye.

The doctor said, *"The inflammation in that eye is caused by the anterior lens rubbing against the cornea."* A consult with the cornea surgeon was scheduled.

Driving home I reflected. Different doctors, different opinions. The original doctor messed up the eye, the retina doctors just kept me visiting, doing nothing, the new doctor increased the strength of the drops, and the cornea specialist said something else. Where was the truth? I thought I was pro-active, informed, and yet I knew so little. Second, third, and fourth opinions are important, but even more so the realization that the medical profession is in bed with the pharmaceutical industry and the insurance companies.

To the doctors, the patient is an annuity. Every visit is followed with a return visit. The truth is hidden, pills are prescribed and appointments are scheduled, referrals are made, and another annuity is created. The patient is the victim.

I went online and researched cornea transplants. While the odds are good, I am not sure I will continue, at least not until I have some more answers and more opinions. When I consulted my cornea specialist concerning the transplant, his advice coincided with my research.

"You have excellent vision with your good eye. Let's leave things alone unless your vision in the good eye worsens."

I totally agree. My advice: *"Let the patient beware and aware. Ask questions and never be intimidated. It's your body; the doctor is the mechanic working for you."*

64 **Charge It**

One fine fall morning I put on the coffee and sat down at the computer to read emails. As I turned on the lights over my computer, a light bulb popped. Since the overhead light was too far above for easy replacement, I continued my morning ritual.

When the coffee kicked in I went to turn on the bathroom light. Another bulb popped and before noon, yet another bulb failure. No problem as I kept a year's supply of bulbs for the houses on the ranch.

The following day, Bobby and Ed drove out to the ranch to help with needed chores, mainly filling the game feeders and building a new blind from which to observe or harvest animals. The battery on one of the feeders failed to toss the corn. They removed the battery and placed it on the charger in the barn. As they drove to another part of the ranch, the automatic gate refused to open with the remote control. This battery they also removed for testing or charging before they began work on construction of the blind.

When the screw gun failed to operate due to a low battery, Bobby lost his patience — not that he has much to spare. While Ed placed that battery on another charger, Bobby walked out of the barn to the tractor. *"If the tractor doesn't start, I'm going to quit for the day."*

The tractor started, but Bobby still wasn't sure. *"I think I'll go try the Jeep."* The Jeep started.

Bobby remarked, *"I think we should go into town to the auto parts house and buy every fucking battery in the store, or we could go try the ranch buggy. Maybe it won't start and then we'll try the riding mower, maybe a weed eater, and the chain saw. That way we can buy all the batteries in town and maybe an extra charger or two."* Ed and I remained silent.

While waiting for the screw gun to charge, they retrieved the memory cards from five of the cameras placed at the blinds to view the animals that come to the feeders. While looking at the memory cards with my IPad, two of the memory cards contained no pictures, translated dead batteries. Chalk it up to another day in paradise.

65 Fitbit

Among my first visitors to the ranch rental additions were the lady from Fox News in McAllen and her girlfriend, two young attractive career-minded women from extreme south Texas.

I so enjoyed engaging in intelligent conversation with the younger generation. They restore my faith in humanity and the country's future.

Cocktail hour loosened inhibitions; I asked them, *"What are those purple things on your wrists?"*

"This is a Fitbit. It records our heart rate, steps taken, stairs climbed, hours of deep sleep and calories burned."

I was amazed and asked, *"How much does it cost?"*

"About $100."

"That's not bad."

When Christmas approached, I ordered one for myself and one for my daughter, both purple. Once they arrived, I opened mine immediately and quickly scanned the instructions. There was a little black thing in the package that I ignored, that is until I couldn't get my Fitbit to do anything. Then I read the instructions more carefully. It was a boogle or doogle or some such device and had to be plugged in to my computer for the Fitbit to work.

Now, months later, I still love the stupid thing. One of the best features is the button on the side. I can push it and see the time, day or night, whereas my wrist watch does not illuminate in the dark.

My grandson also loves the thing. When he comes to the ranch for a visit or I go to Alpine to visit him, we sleep together. (He's only six and this is not weird.) He awakens about 5:15 every morning, having to catch the school bus to Marathon at 7. Even on holidays and weekends, he is awake well before dawn.

He reaches over, grabs my left wrist, and pushes the button and tells me what time it is, forcing me to be grandmotherly at not a nice hour. He's quite fascinated by the Fitbit but still too young to trust with a $100 device.

Since I acquired my Fitbit my brother, sister-in-law, and other friends and family are wearing them, too. The Internet tells me that the Fitbit is now available in other colors. A designer Fitbit, more attractive than the current plastic model, is also on the market.

I am now averaging about 8,000 steps per day. Some days I surpass 12,000 steps. When my heart rate is over 100, I rest until it goes down. When the battery weakens, I dutifully charge it.

I am quite satisfied with my modest purple Fitbit. In fact, I recently purchased a snazzy high-powered pistol with a purple grip to match my Fitbit. This grandma is armed, fit, and dangerous.

66 **Movies**

I can't remember the last time I entered a movie theater. The movies I watch are on television, courtesy of Direct TV, but recently the *"Star Wars"* phenomenon attracted my attention, thanks to my six-year-old grandson.

Christmas approached. I happily purchased a stuffed Yoda and R2D2 for both grandsons, even though the younger is only 15-months-old. I then realized that three prequel movies had been released since I viewed the original three.

Not being a science fiction fan, I watched the first three years ago at the insistence of my children and quickly became enamored, loving the strange, diverse characters and falling in love with Han Solo, the young Harrison Ford.

So for Christmas I bought the set of six for my daughter and family, and when I went to Alpine for a visit, we watched one of the prequels I had missed. I loved it, realizing the *"Star Wars"* series is a strong allegory, religious and political, and couldn't wait to see the other two movies.

The visit was not long enough, and I returned home with a whetted appetite, stopping at Walmart to buy the entire series as a Christmas present for myself. The weather cooperated, turning rainy and cold, providing the perfect excuse to binge and watch all six in sequence.

Again I caught the subtle messages, proud of my discernment and planned to drive 60 miles to the nearest theater in Uvalde on my birthday, January 2, and watch the long-awaited release of number seven.

Second thoughts took hold – cold and rainy weather, germs in a nasty theater, pitiful old lady alone on her birthday, calorie-laden, unhealthy popcorn. So I came up with a better plan. For a few dollars, I downloaded the book on my Kindle and read the latest *"Star Wars"* edition lying snuggled in a blanket on the sofa with a cozy fire burning in the fireplace, and created my own movie.

The nasty weather persisted and while surfing the television for a movie one evening I found the complete series of Lonesome Dove being shown, my all-time favorite except for *"The Searchers"* with John Wayne, who supposedly said something like, "Life is hard, especially if you are stupid." I do love John Wayne.

"Lonesome Dove" began. Several years had passed since I last watched those two Texas rangers, and I had forgotten a line that Tommy Lee Jones said as he and Robert Duval were riding into San Antonio to hire a replacement cook for the trail drive. Jones remarked that the town had changed, not to his liking, and Duval responded in effect, "What do you expect? You killed all the people that made Texas interesting."

As the trail drive progressed through south Texas, the landscape was so familiar — the Nueces River and the brush country and rocks — that I realized that what I was seeing on the TV screen was home. A warm, fuzzy feeling came over me. After living here for over 20 years, this was truly my home. I wonder when that happened.

67   The Shepherd

I had never been near a sheep until I purchased the ranch 22 years ago, and then it was almost a year after that. I was 52.

My fourth husband was from a family of West Texas ranchers – sheep, goats, cattle – and he grew up working livestock.

Because we needed to run livestock on the ranch to qualify for the agricultural exemption to avoid excessive property taxes, he chose sheep, having a close old family friend in Paint Rock who raised Columbia/Rambouillet sheep. Being an English major I could spell Columbia, but the other, I had no clue.

Before long, we had a nice herd of sheep. We wormed them, docked tails, castrated, bottle-fed rejected babies, and cared for our sheep. I love the taste of home-raised lamb, being an avid meat eater, and had no qualms about butchering and processing the lambs for the freezer.

Later we added a few Spanish/Boer goats, enjoyed eating the meat, but did not enjoy their bad habits, namely escaping from any enclosure and roaming the countryside, only to return to have their babies on the home turf.

When John died I became the shepherd, committed to keeping the blood-line and herd viable. I managed to have them sheared twice a year, keep them healthy and within the boundaries of the ranch.

As time passed the predators increased due to the absence of neighbors who raised livestock and trapped and killed predators to protect their animals. It wasn't long before I was the only one left, and the predators, namely bobcats, feral hogs, mountain lions, and coyotes, prevailed. There were years when I did not raise one lamb and my herd saw no increase.

I resorted to penning the new lambs and their mothers in confined areas, having to feed them for months, not a winning situation.

Ten miles down the road I observed a large herd of Dorper sheep raising lots of babies. A donkey shepherded the sheep. Inquiries and research indicated that a single female donkey could protect a herd of sheep.

When I purchased the adjoining ranch and was forced once again to run livestock, I chose Dorper sheep because they did not have to be sheared, and the meat was supposedly tastier. Less trouble all the way around.

Purchasing sheep at the weekly auction in Uvalde was an iffy situation. There was always the chance that I would buy someone's culls or problem animals, and one thing I had learned was that I did not want any problem animals.

I had once been given a free donkey that chased and bit people and animals. I once bottle- fed a male lamb that upon maturity attacked me.

Fortunately, my boyfriend's ex-brother-in-law's nephew had some Dorper sheep, which he delivered for a reasonable price after I built over a half of a mile of fence at $5 a foot and a small pen with a water trough and float within the confines of about 50 acres.

The Dorper sheep were young and sweet, mixed colors, some of them resembling Oreo cookies, great color combinations. Three days later I went to feed them and found only two, one in shell shock and the other with half her intestines hanging out. I figured the culprit was a hog, not coyotes who go for the legs or a mountain lion who attacks the neck.

Of the many exercises I enjoy, jumping to conclusions is my favorite. I immediately assumed the entire herd of 16 was dead and looked out for buzzards, also known as turkey vultures.

Three days later the remaining 14 sheep appeared. I was relieved but wary. I emailed an ad to the local free paper requesting two female donkeys wanted to guard sheep.

For two weeks, no results. I saw an ad in the Uvalde paper for a wild mustang and wild burro adoption sale sponsored by the BLM, that government agency often under fire for land rights abuse, the price per animal $50 if the buyer passed the adoption criteria. I called the toll free number only to discover that no burros were included in the sale.

Then someone I knew called and said he had two young female donkeys, price $100 each. I asked if they would be penned and easy to load. When he answered, *"Yes,"* I said, *"Sold. When can I pick them up?"*

The day and time were arranged. Another call offered two free females, but they were wild, unconfined, and there were no pens or chutes. Free is not worth a rodeo. I declined.

My trailer accommodated the two sister donkeys, and I unloaded each of them with a herd of sheep.

The donkey with the herd of Columbia/Rambouillet protected the four lambs I had kept confined once I turned them loose with the herd. When a new lamb was born, she kept it alive even though something ate half its tail. I named her Alice, and when two additional lambs were born, she added them to her babysitting duties.

I watched Alice carefully. During the day she stayed under a large oak tree while the babies were lying in the grass at her feet. The mothers grazed quite a distance away. When a lamb's mother called, the donkey would push the baby to the mother who then allowed the lamb to nurse.

While I have raised sheep for over 20 years and by no means consider myself an expert, I have never seen anything like a donkey with sheep.

On another occasion, a lamb became confused and could not find its way out of the pen where the sheep drink water. The donkey came and herded the lamb out of the pen and back to its mother.

In the evening, the sheep travel up the rocky hill and bed down behind my house. The donkey brings up the rear. During a recent stormy week, I was sitting outdoors. The sheep remained up on the hill as thunderstorms threatened. Early in the afternoon the herd came down the hill, the donkey trailing. I realized that it would not rain; otherwise, the sheep would have stayed up on the hill. I was right. The storm passed to the east of the ranch.

As for the herd of Dorpers, I have not lost another sheep, and babies are due soon. The donkey stays with the herd. I named this donkey Fanny. I am amazed with the donkey/sheep relationship and have been told that the guardian must be a female donkey or a castrated male, and that there can only be one with the herd.

My duty as shepherd of the flocks is now in the hands of two sweet young female donkeys. They're doing a much better job.

68 Twenty Miles

When I leave the ranch, I drive 20 miles to the unincorporated town of Barksdale, perched on the banks of the Nueces River, population 80, three churches, a high school, chicken restaurant, post office, and motel.

Even after 21 years, the journey is never boring or tiresome. As I leave my home on top of a hill, I ease down the caliche road, pass between the barn, hunter's cabin, lodge, and garden, and turn onto the unpaved county road, cross Bullhead Creek below the dam, and approach the bump gate with caution, never forgetting the scars on my vehicles from past carelessness.

As I drive through the abandoned Girl Scout Camp, I remember the years when the camp was active, teaching young girls horsemanship and archery, and providing the setting for other Girl Scout activities. Today the derelict property has been repossessed by the heirs of the original donors, according to the gift deed that required use of the facilities. The 195-acre parcel has been on the market for over two years, the price $10,000 per acre.

A bank of mailboxes, including mine, sits beside the entrance, and a county road splits off to the left, going through the flat area of the camp to properties once owned by early settlers, now possessed by absentee owners with no intention of occupying the land, except for one home with a swimming pool several miles deep into the canyon and one other section of land owned by a southeast Texas couple who have a weekend dwelling.

After passing through my bump gate, the road becomes paved and maintained by the state. There is a large parcel of land owned by a couple from Dallas, trust fund babies who 20 years ago lived on their property, but when the wetback murders occurred on their property, they abandoned their home and moved to the luxury of Hunt and a home on the Guadalupe River. They rarely visit their property.

The next property is a section of land, 640 acres, owned many years by a family from San Angelo. The two sons recently listed the property at $10,000 per acre.

Joining that ranch is a nice property of several thousand acres, now in a family trust. One of the trustees built a lovely rock home with a tennis court on several acres owned individually, but age and health dictated a move to Austin to be near family. They visit monthly.

The Double C ranch changed hands about 10 years ago. A man from Houston purchased it from an attorney who picked up the property in the RTC meltdown in the 1980's.

Back in the old days, those ranches were owned by original settlers who raised sheep and goats and eked out a hard scrabble living until taxes and nature destroyed their livelihood.

When I drive into town with my boyfriend, he tells me their stories. "There was once an irrigated peach orchard down in that field. My cousin once owned that place. Vercia Lee was born in that old rock house. The Welch family lived over there in a log cabin until it burned down."

The man from Houston who purchased the Double C dredged Bullhead Creek, bulldozed much of the land, and planted trees in the riparian areas, trapping water and preventing it from flowing downstream, ruining the swimming and fishing holes below him.

Beyond him is a white brick home built by a couple from Holland. They didn't last long, and the property has changed hands several times since they left.

As I approach Vance, game proof fences appear, more properties purchased with oil money from Midland. Sheep, shepherded by a donkey to deter predators, graze behind the fences. Another ranch hosts exotic animals.

At Vance, population 4, there is a Baptist church, cemetery, and an abandoned house and filling station. The cemetery is old and displays a state historical marker. One tombstone reads, "Mexican Name Unknown."

Vance was once the county seat with a school and courthouse. The records were stolen by some folks from Leakey, the courthouse burned down, the school house was moved, and Leakey became the county seat.

The west prong of the Nueces runs through Vance, and it is here that Bullhead Creek used to run into the river, but no longer, only when it floods.

Just before the river at Vance rests the Flying Bull Ranch, owned by a wealthy family from Corpus Christi. There the Texas Rangers qualify for arms and Robert Duval from the movie *"Lonesome Dove"* visits. They have homes and a nice elk herd.

After passing through the river bottom, the land rises to one of the best exotic game ranches in Texas. The owner in absentia raises giraffes, zebras, sable, lemurs, and assorted hoof stock from over the world. The ranch is immaculate.

Joining that ranch is an even larger one with eight homes, one on the tax rolls at over four million dollars. At one time my boyfriend's grandfather owned the place. Eventually it was sold to, coincidentally, an old Houston oil family heir who had an Arabian horse farm down the road from my family home in north Houston. Some of my relatives, skilled carpenters, built the many improvements on the property. When the owners died, the ranch was left in trust to one of the sons who died and left it to his son who sold it to one of the owners of the Flying Bull. What he plans to do with the ranch is pure conjecture.

The remaining miles are vacant landscape until one reaches the outskirts of Barksdale and the site of an abandoned Boy Scout Camp and a small, semi-failed subdivision on the banks of the Nueces.

The first 10 miles from my ranch to Vance are inhabited by only myself and the couple that live behind the Girl Scout Camp. In the 21 years I have been at Ambush Hill, the few neighbors I once had have dwindled to three, and while the isolation is not like Wyoming or Montana or some other western states, it's good enough for me.

The current terror, chaos, political uncertainty, and economic roller coaster somehow don't seem so threatening when the land remains relatively untouched by the hands of time or altered by the march of civilization. Obviously I am content to be here and ambushed by this part of America.

69 Romance

Romance with Billy faded over the last year. Though we were friends, exchanged a few hugs and swift lip kisses, the flames of passion diminished, but the coals continued to hold heat.

Difficulties with his landlord and roommate caused a change of lodging. Billy moved into the hunter's cabin at the ranch, and while the accommodations were modest, he had no complaints. The price was right.

The distance from the top of the hill to the bottom afforded sufficient privacy. Our friendship had progressed so that his presence caused no intrusion into my eccentric ways. Several times a week we enjoyed a few beers and a grilled meal.

When I tired of the conversation, I simply went to bed and he returned to the cabin below the hill. If I left to visit family or friends, he kept an eye on the ranch. He knew the rules and the routine.

If he stepped out of the prescribed boundaries, I let him know, and we kept our distance until we could resume our normal friendship.

His tree work kept him busy, but his helpers provided relief. He managed to save some money and talked of buying a travel trailer and parking it at a nearby campground.

Spring came in profuse bloom. I hired a part-time worker to build some blinds and maintain the feeders, another part-time man to help with mowing and ground maintenance, and a great housekeeper to clean the houses on the ranch.

In short, with all that help my life had become easier. It had also become very boring. What was left? I had the garden, the sheep, the rental lodgings, the occasional hunters, an unfinished book. But where was the excitement?

Travel became a hassle, no place left I wanted to see. My children were approaching 40, the grandsons a joy. What was left? Ranch work and management and maintenance.

I thought about pampering myself for a change. A cruise on a small luxury ship with a lot of days at sea to play bridge, have a manicure, a pedicure, a massage, a facial, some gourmet food would provide an opportunity to dress up and swap lies with fellow travelers.

I could always finish harvesting my mustard seeds and make homemade mustard, or weed eat the grounds at my house, or replace my filthy window coverings, or finish the book I had put off with delay after delay.

The spring weather turned wet, damp, and misty. I downloaded some mindless mysteries on my Kindle, cooked some spinach and kale from the garden with some German sausage, and settled on the sofa to read.

Billy called, asked if he could drive up the hill for a visit. "Of course," I replied.

We sat facing each other in front of the picture window, viewing the cliff and various shades of green foliage across the canyon and catching up on the local gossip. Billy brought his beer; I was not drinking, having just eaten a bowl of sausage and greens.

Billy gave me that sly look, the sexy grin I hadn't seen in nearly a year, made some remark about not being lonely or horny down in the hunter's cabin, and I knew he was thinking about sex. I wasn't, hadn't in a while, and gave him no encouragement.

The conversation turned to us, to our relationship. After repeating what my brother David always says, "Sonja, you are a small car with a big engine, no brakes and no steering," Billy looked me dead in the eye and continued, "Sonja, being with you every day is like being in a fireworks stand with everything going off."

Shortly after that remark, I went to bed but couldn't sleep. Maybe it wasn't over; I still had a bit of life left, along with a remaining small allotment of craziness.

The following day I went online, called my travel agent, and booked a trip to Alaska via Japan and Siberia, across the northern Pacific and the Bering Sea. I always wanted to visit the Aleutian Islands.

70 The Holy Grail

I was washing some greens from the garden. The phone rang. *"Hello."*

"Hi, it's Eric."

"What's going on this fine morning?"

"You won't believe. I just saw on the Internet that lonely is the new lung cancer."

"What? You're joking!" That's crazy, but you know I can believe it. I never get lonely, but I miss caring."

"Caring about what?"

"Caring about people, friends, children, family, boyfriends."

The conversation moved to other subjects, and when the call ended I went back to washing garden vegetables, reflecting on lonely and caring.

Being a woman growing to adulthood in the 1950's, I was taught to care/do for others, whether it was my brothers, classmates, neighbors, or complete strangers. That was what we did. We cared.

Today I miss caring – for me translated cooking, washing, picking up, cleaning, running errands.

When I travel to Uvalde, I ask acquaintances if they need anything. Most of the time they politely say no. This week was a bonus. I was asked to purchase two jalapeño pepper plants; another friend asked for an oil filter for his mower; and another requested that I pick up a tree pruner that had been repaired. Last week it was just some coffee creamer.

I love to cook and enjoy cooking for others, nothing more fun than a day of cooking and preparing for company.

And then there's caring for the land. My brother David in a recent phone conversation asked, *"Do you know what the Holy Grail is?"*

"I have a concept. Tell me yours."

David explained that after King Arthur sent the knights on the quest for the Holy Grail, only Sir Percival returned, revealing the simple truth that the Holy Grail was the land and the king. He said, *"You have the Holy Grail with your ranch."*

I agreed, *"Yes, the land heals and awakes passion."*

He added, *"When the land suffers, you suffer."*

When the conversation ended, I smiled, thankful for another beautiful spring day. The Holy Grail, indeed.

Alaska, the Long Way Around

Anyone who knows me or who has read my books knows I don't like traveling the beaten path. That's why to explore more of Alaska than on a previous trip to the southern part and inside passage, I flew to Tokyo, Japan.

The decision to venture from the ranch was precipitated by the humdrum/aggravation of maintaining the ranch and six houses. I was just plain sick and tired of fixing everything. Life had become boring and not very rewarding. Wanderlust prevailed.

With only a two-week interval before departure I had booked a repositioning cruise with a small luxury line. The ship would be sailing from Tokyo, north to the Siberian peninsula of Kamchatka, and then across the northern Pacific Ocean and Bering Sea to the Aleutian Islands and mainland Alaska to cruise the Alaskan coast for the summer months. Five or six days at sea would be a welcome vacation. I envisioned days of playing bridge, competing at Trivial Pursuit, sumptuous meals, massages, a manicure, pedicure, pampering and meeting interesting fellow travelers. As usual, my expectations exceeded reality.

Since I had been given an almost expired generous voucher on a previous canceled flight from Delta Airlines, I booked with them; accepting that the flights from the west coast, the obvious route, were full, I agreed to fly to Atlanta and take a 14-hour nonstop to Tokyo. However, the flight from San Antonio to Atlanta left at 6:00 a.m.

Not comfortable with driving three hours in the dark, I booked a room at the Marriott next to the airport and drove to San Antonio the afternoon before, not realizing that three Marriott Hotels were located within a mile of the airport. I found the two wrong ones before finally checking into the one with my reservation.

By then I was flustered and aggravated, more so when I couldn't figure out where to slide the plastic card that would allow me to park my pickup in the secure parking lot. The desk clerk came outside in the summer heat and showed me the slot. I left a wakeup call for 3:30 a.m., read on my Kindle, and went to bed, sleeping fitfully, awaiting the phone call that never came. Fortunately, I awoke at 4:00 a.m., rushed from the hotel in the dark to the parking lot, and started the engine, only to see a flashing low tire icon on the dashboard. My blood pressure must have been on dangerous by the time I drove to Security Parking a mile away and parked the pickup, knowing full well I would return in over two weeks, dead tired from flying, to deal with a flat tire.

The airport was crowded as I passed through security and waited 15 minutes in line for a Starbucks small latte that cost $5.61 and ended up mostly on the crotch and upper legs of my linen slacks. Fortunately, I was not burned and merely covered the disaster with my Navajo coat of many colors until the coffee dried and faded into the natural color of my pants. Ever the optimist, I was thankful I had the good sense to not wear white while traveling.

When they called my name to come to the desk at the boarding gate, I was given the opportunity to change seats so a couple could sit together. I readily agreed and was heartily thanked by the couple who were flying to Atlanta for their anniversary. I knew the tide had turned. The trip would be a good one.

The walk through customs in Tokyo was just that, and I engaged a taxi for the ride to the hotel, which lasted over an hour. When I asked the taxi driver if he spoke English, he pointed to his watch.

Traffic was heavy but moved smoothly as I looked out the taxi window and observed tall buildings, parks, and the biggest ferris wheel I'd ever seen. As I entered the lobby of the immense hotel, the atmosphere was quiet, sedate, and behaved, same as the staff.

After being shown to my room, I used the bathroom where I discovered a heated toilet seat. Returning to the lobby, I changed money, located the concierge and the ship's hospitality desk with the help of a beautiful, young English-fluent lady. She refused a tip, and I returned to my room for a shower and sleep. I had left Atlanta at noon, flown 14 hours, and arrived in Tokyo at 3 p.m. Compared to the night spent near the San Antonio airport, the silence in my high Tokyo hotel room was heaven.

Early the next morning I was caffeine deprived and finding no coffee pot in my room, descended to the lobby in search of a fix, only to discover that the restaurant would not open for another 20 minutes. However, the polite Japanese allowed me to enter and served me coffee while I enjoyed a park-like setting two stories below with a waterfall, pond with bright orange koi, and lovely greenery. The towering skyscrapers surrounding the serenity presented an interesting dichotomy.

Since I was given a free voucher for the breakfast buffet priced at $48, I indulged, saving room for some raw fish at the fish market. More Japanese were dining than foreigners, none of them texting or using cell phones.

The guide/taxi driver parked a short distance from the fish market. As we walked the blocks to the market I learned that he was a cancer survivor in his mid-50's, and that his wife was a photographer. He had two sons and had learned English while studying in Fort Collins, Colorado.

Tokyo consists of an area of 228 square miles that houses 34 million people and will be hosting the 2020 Summer Olympics. Much construction was in evidence, and the crowds at the Tsukiji fish market were oppressive. I discovered that the city was in the midst of a big holiday weekend called Golden Week, having something to do with the Japanese and the English. Tourists from China, Korea, and Thailand crowded the fish market's narrow lanes.

My guide, Yoshi, led me to a booth where I purchased a platter of raw salmon and tuna which I shared with him. The crowd was so thick I was carried along, taking in the truly foreign fruits and vegetables and noticing that there were no smokers or, for that matter, fat people. I asked Yoshi about the Japanese and smoking.

"I've read that the Japanese are heavy smokers but have the lowest incidence of lung cancer due to their fish diet."

He replied, *"That is not true. We are not heavy smokers, and lung cancer is common among smokers."*

From the fish market Yoshi drove around the Imperial Park and the moat surrounding the Imperial Palace. The traffic was light as we arrived at the Sengaku Temple and strolled the pavilion flanked with souvenir shops. I purchased tee shirts for my two grandsons and returned to the hotel for transportation to the ship. I was anxious to settle in for a relaxing cruise and leave the driving to the ship's captain.

Once aboard the ship and several glasses of champagne later I was escorted to my room and unpacked before the safety drill where I met another widow traveling alone. We dined that evening outside by the swimming pool, grilling steaks and lamb chops on hot rocks while wrapped in warm blankets.

The following morning the ship docked in Kushiro, Japan, known as the "town of mist," situated in the southeastern part of Hokkaido, the second largest of the four islands of Japan, with about 200,000 inhabitants. Hokkaido is the least populated island and is known for its brutal winters, volcanos, and mountains, as well as Japan's largest marshland, the Kushiro Shitsugen, designated as a national park and considered one of the greatest treasure houses of flora and fauna in Japan.

The Ainu were the earliest inhabitants but were defeated by the Japanese in the 15th century. Not many of them remain. Timber, fishing, and tourism are the main industries, and the port is busy due to its being a warm water port. The water may be warm, but the temperature on deck was in the low 40's.

I exited the ship for a drive to the emerald waters of Lake Mashu and then to the active Iozan Volcano. I didn't stroll too close to the smelly, steaming, and smoking sulfur springs at the base of the mountain.

A Japanese lunch was served at a local restaurant, and the presentation was lovely. I learned that the Japanese believe that food must be as pleasing to the eye as to the palate. Following lunch we stopped at the nearby town of Kawaya Onsen for a relaxing foot bath in the warm, therapeutic waters of one of the town's many hot springs and returned to the ship via a ride through the countryside, observing dairy cattle and fields where sugar beets, potatoes, and onions are grown.

Vehicles drive on the left side of the road in Japan. Knowing there was no early British influence in Japan, I questioned why and was told the Japanese warriors rode on the left side so the hand wielding the sword was on the right side. I suppose there were no left-handed warriors.

After returning to the ship, I joined a Trivia team with seven Brits and the American widow. We won first place not due to my intelligence but to that of the Brits. The passenger list on the ship consisted mostly of non-Americans, less than 50 of my fellow citizens, and I dined with the Brits on steak and lobster, remembering to set my clock forward one hour, the first of eight nights that the clock would be set forward. Losing an hour each day was confusing, and the constant daylight added to the disorientation, one of the vagaries of travel.

Since I didn't know how to change the time on my Fitbit, I left it on Texas time, delighted that I was mischievously confusing the device with my sleep patterns.

204

The ship continued north along the Kuril Islands, beautiful snow-covered volcanic islands rising from the Pacific Ocean. Over 50 of the Kuril Islands lie along the coastline of Asia, the four southern-most being claimed by Japan and disputed by Russia. About 20,000 inhabitants live on the islands. After a day of cruising along the scenic islands the ship arrived at the Kamchatka Peninsula, part of the eastern frontier of Russia, and the Siberian Russian city of Petropavlovsk, accessible only by air or ship.

Due to its close proximity to America, the territory was closed for many years to foreigners and Russians alike. Fortunately, the region's isolated position played a significant role in preserving its unique wilderness and rich biodiversity.

The Kamchatka landscape is dotted with 150 fuming volcanoes, 29 of which are active, and is inhabited by the world's largest brown bear population, estimated at over 10,000. The largest eagle in the world, the Steller's sea eagle, of which there are an estimated only 4500, is also found in the region.

The peninsula, founded in 1741 by Vitus Bering, the Danish-born Russian captain who discovered the straits that bear his name, developed slowly. Bering named the town for his two ships, the Svyatoy Pyotr, St. Peter, and the Svyatoy Pavel, St. Paul, hence the name, Petropavlovsk. In the years to follow, it became the Tsar's major Pacific seaport and was used as base for explorations that resulted in the discovery of the Aleutian Islands and Alaska.

Before disembarking I had learned in a lecture that the city of Petropavlovsk and the peninsula hosted a population of about 300,000.

I learned the different varieties of salmon, that Petropavlovsk endured a maritime climate, the temperature rarely dips below 10 degrees of zero, that the snow melts in June, that the average apartment contains 500 square feet, the trees were not budding, there was a Gold's Gym, and that the native population suffered from addiction and alcoholism. The lecturer added that the native Siberians believed that death was not bad, just another stage of life.

The temperature was 39 degrees when we anchored off the city of Petropavlovsk. The ship's captain chose to anchor away from the crumbling concrete pier and tender the passengers into port, the excuse being the poor condition of the docks.

I had signed for a guided tour of a native Koryak village but was told the tour was canceled. The only remaining excursion that left the drab city of Petropavlovsk led to the Siberian canine kennels, allegedly located less than an hour from the city.

I knew I screwed up when I noticed the six-wheeled Russian vehicles that would be transporting me outside the city. Fortunately, the Navajo coat and fur-lined boots provided protection from the follies of Siberia, not my first time on the Russian eastern frontier.

Following a short tour of the city, the ponderously slow vehicle left the paved road and traveled a trail, the terrain become more difficult as we progressed through the Siberian snow and ice covered forest. As the vehicle slid and slowed, I feared I would die in Siberia, missing out on my wish to be cremated in Texas.

An hour and a half later the vehicle stopped and as I disembarked, thankful to be alive, I slid on the ice, mud and snow only to hear the barking of dogs, lots of dogs, chained in the Siberian forest, their ribs displayed, teeth discolored, smelly, and pitiful. How could I not feel pity for these poor, sweet, blue-eyed creatures, after leaving a luxury ship - warm, well -fed, comfortable, pampered?

I failed to follow the guide who introduced everyone to each animal and rather chose to sit on a hard bench in the cold, wrapped in the Navajo coat, preferring to endure my dismal situation in solitude.

When the native dancers and drummers appeared, I knew the day was coasting downhill. After traveling the world I have seen enough native-dressed dancers, musicians, singers, and story tellers. These were young, enthusiastic, and talented, and after an hour when they encouraged audience participation, I felt the end was near. I was wrong. Questions were invited and answered through an interpreter. The bench grew colder.

Finally we entered the primitive lodge for lunch - seaweed, fish smoked grilled and dried, dried green beans, and assorted dishes. We adjourned to a circular dirt-floored building with a large fire pit in the middle and enjoyed light, thin pancakes served with strawberry syrup and hot tea.

The return trip seemed less scary. I entered the lounge for Trivial Pursuit barely on time. We retained our first place lead, and I agreed to dine with the widow from Washington State.

Life is about people, not about things, and I travel to learn about other cultures and lands. Often I meet fellow travelers who reveal more than is necessary. Ellen was one of those.

She was only 63, bit looked older due to her style and dress, even though her eyes were young. She was a recent widow and I met her playing duplicate bridge on one of the early days of the cruise. I was her partner. She played with intelligence but I noticed a short delay in her words and sentences as though she was composing her thoughts before speaking. After that first afternoon of bridge, she followed me to the lounge for the first day of Trivia, and we joined a team of Brits who needed some American expertise. Ellen was shy but able to contribute her share of right answers, and the team cemented. We won first place that day in the lounge, and when the scores were tallied for duplicate bridge, Ellen and I won first place. She was hooked.

This was her first trip solo. Her husband had died less than a year ago. We continued to play bridge and Trivia on the days the ship was at sea and dined together. One evening we entered the formal dining room and were ushered to a table with another couple. We had requested to dine with others.

Natalie was a bridge player. We had played opposite her in the card room. She introduced her other whatever, Charles, a three-time divorced attorney from San Diego. She was an attorney, also — younger and not very feminine. They were a strangely matched couple.

As always, the food was delicious and the wine flowed. Charles spoke politics, knowing in advance that I was a conservative Texan. He asked, *"What five things do you expect Trump to do for you?"*

I answered intelligently and asked him, *"What do you expect Hillary to do for you?"*

He answered, *"That's irrelevant. Do you know what the Civil War was about?"*

I replied, *"About states' rights."*

Three voices rose in unison, *"No, about slavery."*

Ellen asked, *"Do you know that between Bush Junior and Cheney they had nine DUI's and nothing was ever done?"*

"So what? My boyfriend has had seven and never gone to prison. Big deal. That's old news. Who cares? Do you really think a DUI if you are rich and famous is a felony?"

Charles asked, *"Do you know what the Texas War of Independence was about?"*

207

"About slavery. So what? What are most wars about? The haves and the have nots. That's history, that's Texas, and I'm not ashamed. It happened."

When the conversation turned to religion, all three admitted to being atheists. They criticized my beliefs for which I did not apologize. I ended the evening, standing and saying, *"Charles, I find you offensive. Please excuse me. Good evening."*

Sleep was fitful. Never had I encountered three against one. Travels were usually with like-minded folks, and, if not, mutual respect averted rude exchanges such as the one I had experienced.

The days at sea brought more welcome rest, bridge and Trivial Pursuit. The ship crossed the International Date Line on Friday, June 13, and the next day it was again Friday, June 13. Just that weirdness gave the trip an extra star. Ever accommodating, the cruise line offered Jewish services both Fridays. The ship's newsletter posted the days as May 13 A and May 13 B, never mentioning the dreaded Friday the 13th.

Ever the smart ass, I questioned my bridge, trivia, and dinner acquaintances, *"Do you know why Friday the 13th is deemed unlucky?"*

Not one person knew the answer, not even the smart Brits or the Aussies. *"That was the day the king of France ordered the arrest of the Knights Templar who were subsequently tortured and burned to death and their assets seized by the French crown."*

No need to go into the why and wherefore; the information is easily found on the Internet if you are interested. For an extra dose of smart ass, I added, *"But some of them escaped to America with much of the treasures, and Nicholas Cage discovered the enormous stash in caverns under Washington D.C."*

Very few of them caught the humor or had seen the movie. I had a lot of explaining, but at least it added some fun and conversation to pass the time during six days at sea.

Jet lag normally has no affect on me, but this trip consisted of eight days of setting the clock forward one hour. Coupled with the time difference landing in Japan and then progressing across the northern Pacific, gaining the time back with no interlude to adjust, my sleep patterns suffered. Even my Fitbit asked, *"What's up?"*

I awoke one morning to discover my bad eye was filled with blood — just a ruptured blood vessel, nothing serious but ugly to view and tedious to explain. One of the Brits on the Trivia team was a doctor and, of course, he noticed it immediately, reassuring me it was not serious. The team continued to hover in first or second place. Competition was fierce for the points that would entitle the team players to purchase key chains, fountain pens, coasters, or tee shirts with the ship's logo.

My bridge partner Ellen introduced me to an Irish Cream martini, following an extended dinner one evening. We didn't score so well the next day at bridge.

I played bridge one afternoon with a lovely lady from Argentina. I dined that evening with her and her husband, a French speaking Swiss who owned a ranch in Uruguay. They were traveling from Argentina to Alaska, then to Chicago and New York and on to Switzerland to their villa for three months, since winter was imminent in South America. He was quite charming and told me of his farm/ranch where he raised corn and grains. She spent weekdays at their home in Buenos Aires while he tended to the farm. They were just an example of the people encountered on strange journeys a bit off the beaten path.

One particularly boring day I wore a shirt of my mother's, a sparkly tuxedo shirt covered in cowboy boots lined in glitter. When packing I always chose some things of my mother's because her taste was exquisite, as well as Texas flashy and expensive. The shirt was at least 25-years-old. I received many compliments on the shirt and even an offer to buy the shirt. My Indian butler even commented, *"You are looking very nice, Mrs. Klein."*

Many blouses I wore sported glitter and when I wore a simple silk shirt, the cool British ladies on the Trivia team joked, *"Where is the glitter today?"*

As the ship sailed in moderate seas, I learned about the Aleutian Islands, about 2,500 of them stretching over 5,000 miles. The ship's course paralleled this island chain, part of Alaska and home to over 40 million seabirds. The scenery was fantastic, volcanic islands topped with snow, like an inverted ice cream cone. The Alaska Maritime National Wildlife Refuge was established by President Teddy Roosevelt.

After five days at sea, the ship was scheduled to dock in Dutch Harbor on the Aleutian island of Amaknak, which lies within the city limits of Unalaska and is connected to Unalaska by a bridge. Dutch Harbor is one of the largest fishing ports in the United States.

The Aleut or Unangan have lived on Unalaska Island for thousands of years. The Russian fur trade reached Unalaska in 1759. Dutch Harbor was so named by the Russians because they believed that a Dutch vessel was the first European ship to enter the harbor.

The seas calmed to the extent that the ship floated in an ocean of fog, and the ship was denied access to the harbor due to the danger of navigating through the fog. Disappointment ran rampant as the passengers missed out on touring the World War II Visitor Center, the Grand Aleutian Hotel, the Museum of the Aleutians, and the Holy Ascension Cathedral.

Instead, we were destined to spend another two days at sea. The blood in my eye dissolved, bridge occupied the afternoons, and Trivial Pursuit the early evenings.

An excellent lecture provided information on Kodiak Island, our next port of call. Kodiak Island is the second largest island of the United States, second to the largest island of Hawaii and similar in size to the state of Connecticut.

The island is known for the bear and salmon; commercial fishing is king. I learned that salmon on the west coast migrate, lay eggs, and die, but the salmon that migrate on the east coast do not die because the older rivers contain sufficient nutrients for the salmon to return to the ocean.

Despite its small population, about 13,500, Kodiak is among the busiest fishing ports in the United States. Kodiak harbor is an important supply point for small communities on the Aleutian Islands and the Alaskan Peninsula. Visitors to the island either fly out to a remote lodge for fishing, kayaking or bear viewing, or stay in town to access whatever pursuits they can reach with the limited road system.

Chief among the attractions is the 1.6 million acre Kodiak National Wildlife Refuge, lying partly on Kodiak Island and partly on Afognak Island to the north, where spotting the enormous Kodiak brown bears is the main goal of the trip.

The Russians' presence on the island dates from the late 1700's, and their culture is still evident. In 1912 a volcano on the mainland devastated the island, and in 1964 a severe earthquake and tsunami destroyed the town.

The largest coast guard station in the United States is in Kodiak, and even through the climate is harsh, visitors fly in to shop at the super Walmart. The Alaska ferry visits Kodiak, a 30-hour trip from Seward.

At last, those of us suffering from cabin fever were given the opportunity to leave the ship. I was met by a lady guide who drove and owned her own van and escorted a group of us through Kodiak. She was a substitute teacher who flies in to teach at five remote schools.

Our first stop was at a Russian Orthodox Seminary, one of three in the United States. The purpose of the seminary is to train native Americans as teachers to combat substance abuse in the native population. Unemployment in the villages is 90 percent. Subsistence living is hunting, fishing, and barter.

The church was founded in 1794, and St. Herman of Alaska converted the natives by example. His journey to the mission took years when he traveled from Finland to Kodiak. St. Herman died in 1838.

The local high school has 800 students, their mascot is the Kodiak bear, and one of their cheers is "Maul them and smile."

I was shocked to learn that only 1 percent of Alaska is privately owned. The ptarmigan is the state bird. Kodiak receives about 74 inches of rain per year, and the tides run nine feet.

From the seminary and chapel we visited the Northern Exposure Art Gallery and visited the Fisherman's Church where we were served Russian teacakes and borscht while being serenaded by a Balalaika band. A drive along the coast took us by the Coast Guard facility and to a equine center where we viewed an eagle nest, complete with mother and eaglets.

Late afternoon found the Trivia team in good spirits even though we had dropped to second place. I dined that evening with some of the team members on steak and lobster.

While most travelers rave about the gourmet food on cruise ships, I was finding that the food lacked flavor. Presentation surpassed tastiness. Perhaps that was because the meat and vegetables were frozen. They had to be since the ship was either at sea or docked at small inaccessible ports. Maybe it was lack of seasoning. I just know the food did nothing to stir my appetite. I guess I'm spoiled by my garden and ranch-roaming meat.

Early the following morning as I checked my itinerary I noticed that the return flight was on June 20, not May 20. Panic ensued. How could I have been so stupid, not to look at the second page of the itinerary or notice the wrong month. On top of that, the bad eye that had cleared up was once again filled with blood.

The girls at the desk dialed the airline and after holding for 30 minutes and then explaining my ordeal, I was rescheduled to leave at midnight five hours later than the original flight. With a sigh of relief, as well as some apprehension, I continued the day.

Homer, Alaska, the Halibut Fishing Capital of the World, greeted the ship. The scenic setting on Kachemak Bay surrounded by mountains, spruce forests and glaciers makes Homer unique. The city lies at the base of a four-mile long sand spit and was founded in the late 1800's as a gold-prospecting camp. A popular local bumper sticker characterizes the town as "Homer - A quaint little drinking village with a fishing problem."

Extreme tides ranging from 14 to 28 feet are not unusual. The town boasts a population of about 5,000 but services over 10,000 who fly in to enjoy McDonalds.

Five active volcanos are in the area; fortunately they were at rest while I visited the Pratt Museum, an art gallery and a cultural and natural history museum rolled into one. The museum has an exhibit on the 1989 Exxon Valdez oil spill, botanical gardens, nature trails, and native displays. I spied on wildlife through robotic video cameras set up on a seabird rookery at the McNeil River Bear Sanctuary. That was pretty neat.

I visited the Norman Lowell Gallery, viewing a collection of world class art depicting Alaskan landscapes and unique collectibles, and the Alaska Islands and Ocean Visitors Center before returning to the ship for the final day of Trivia.

Our team won and enjoyed a private cocktail party in a luxury suite before I returned to the lobby and redeemed my points for two tee shirts. I was ready to go home with a bloody eye, a sleepless night ahead of flying through three airports, and a flat tire waiting in the Texas heat.

When the ship docked the final day in Seward, the skies were overcast and the temperature in the 40's. I boarded the Grandview Cruise Train for a scenic four and a half hour ride along 126 miles of the Kenai Peninsula. The little town of Seward with fewer that 3,000 citizens was founded in 1903 when survey crews arrived and began planning a route to the interior. Coal is shipped from Seward to China and Japan.

The scenery was fantastic with lots of rushing streams, thick forests, patchy snow, lakes, beaver dams and the Chugatch Mountains. The guide in my train car was an interesting lady from Kentucky, retired military. She works six months of the year in Alaska and returns to her family in Kentucky for the winter.

I noticed that the plastic glass from which I drank water on the train read, "Made from corn, certified compostable."

The train made a quick stop in the town of Moose Pass, population 250, as we slowly moved toward Anchorage, enjoying the beautiful countryside.

From the train I boarded a small tour bus with another informative guide, also retired military.

Anchorage is the largest city in Alaska, founded in 1915, with a population of about 300,000. The tallest mountain in America is Mt. Denali, formerly known as Mt. McKinley, at 20,320 feet.

We visited Earthquake Park, the largest float plane base on Lake Hood and Lake Spenard. I learned that the floats for the small planes can cost up to $20,000. A problem with geese on an island in the lake interrupting the flights was solved by putting pigs on the island. The pigs ate the bird eggs, and the birds learned not to come back.

Alaska has more pilots and planes than any other state, the post office is open every day of the year, and Anchorage is the second busiest cargo airport in the United States, second only to Memphis.

The longest street in Anchorage is less than nine miles, and there are over 200 miles of bike trails with special underpasses for bikes. The city boasts over 300 parks. Diesel costs $2.29.

A common affliction of Alaskans is SAD, seasonal affective disorder, obviously an ailment due to the weather, one I am experiencing as I write. It is mid-July in Texas.

During the Anchorage Winter Festival, they play snowshoe baseball. Of the 740,000 people in Alaska, 40 percent live in Anchorage. Over 70 percent of the people living in Alaska are not born there. From Alaska you can fly anywhere in the northern hemisphere without refueling. The median age of 37 is the youngest in the United States. There are three seasons in Alaska - almost winter, winter, and still winter.

213

The average low temperature in the summer is 45 degrees, and the average high is 63 degrees. Alaska rates second per capita in Spam consumption next to Hawaii and first in duct tape use per capita.

So much for the fun trivial facts/entertainment from the guide, before stopping at the Anchorage Museum where we enjoyed a light lunch before exploring the museum. We then traveled to the outskirts of Anchorage to visit the Alaska Native Heritage Center to learn about the rich heritage of Alaska's 11 major cultural groups.

The tour bus left us at a local hotel's hospitality room with uncomfortable chairs and our luggage to await the appropriate shuttle to the airport. Mine was at 9 p.m., and the current time was 6. My flight was scheduled to depart about midnight.

I can't tell you what I did for three hours except I was miserable, made small talk with some of the other travelers, walked around, and finally went to the airport where I waited for more hours. The bustling airport somewhat revived me, but I couldn't drink coffee to stay alert since I would be changing planes in Portland and Salt Lake City before arriving in San Antonio early afternoon to deal with a flat tire and a three-hour drive home to the ranch. I wanted to sleep, but sleep eluded me, and anxiety reigned.

After a one-hour layover in Portland and a two-hour layover in Salt Lake City, I arrived in San Antonio, took the shuttle to the parking lot, and found the tire flat. The shuttle driver returned with a portable compressor and aired up the tire enough for instructions to drive to the big compressor where he filled the tire and said, *"There you go. Have a safe trip home."*

I stood in the Texas heat, exhausted from no sleep, eye filled with blood, and said, *"Would you let your wife or daughter drive three hours on deserted roads on this tire?"*

He looked me in the eye and said, *"Follow me. We'll figure out something."*

I drove to a shaded area under a pavilion and parked where he indicated. He drove away. I waited. Ten minutes later, he arrived, *"I found your Huckleberry."*

A heavy young man who worked for Security Parking was coming off shift and volunteered to change the tire. The owner's manual provided instructions and the whereabouts of the special tool to remove the spare tire. By the time the tire was changed there were two of them. I gave the shuttle driver $100; he handed it to the young man. It was 3 p.m.

San Antonio is not my favorite place; I wanted out of the city, thinking I could make it to Boerne and get a room. When I made it to Boerne, I figured I could make it to Kerrville and get a room. When I arrived in Kerrville, I knew I could drive to Garvin's Store and get a Diet Coke for a caffeine fix.

A mile past Garvin's Store, I pulled over and puked and puked. Those last miles were torture. When I opened the gate, I was too tired to kiss the dirt; instead I got out of the pickup, walked up the stairs, empty-handed to my bedroom, took off all my clothes, and crawled in bed. I was home.

72 Two Weeks

At last my daughter allowed me to have my six-year-old grandson for two weeks. I dangled the bait of taking him to swimming lessons. There is a special bond between us because he was born when his mother lived here at the ranch, and I was with him most every day for the first two years of his life.

At the age of 74, there isn't much left. I've had enough husbands, boyfriends, romance, and adventure. My life is full but often humdrum — keeping six houses, multiple vehicles, grounds, gardens, fences, animals. This bright young child kills the boredom and brings new life to me.

He calls me Grandma every morning with an intensity that makes me smile. *"Grandma, rise and shine."*

I teach him to measure ingredients and make pancakes. He's not very good yet at flipping them. I take him swimming here at the ranch below the dam in 18 inches of water. He wears a life preserver. I am in a lawn chair sitting in less then two feet of water. I indicate he should walk downstream. He stops, *"Grandma, don't you care about me?"*

We take potato chips to the creek. He offers me some. I tell him, *"I can't eat too many. Salt is not good when you are old. I might have a heart attack."*

"Okay, Grandma, you can't have any. I don't want you to die."

The time passed too quickly. Three times a week we drove to Uvalde for private swimming lessons. He had two 30-minute lessons each day. Between lessons we ate fast food — Wendy's, Taco Bell, McDonalds, Dairy Queen – and shopped at Walmart. I loved it because indulgence is alien to me. I'm German. With my grandson, anything was acceptable. Yes, I even ate Pop Tarts.

He was so serious. *"Grandma, am I going to grow taller than you?"*

"Yes, but I'll probably shrink before then."

"Why will you shrink?"

"When you grow old, you shrink, and then you die."

"I don't want you to die."

"I'll always be with you in spirit and in your memories."

The next day we are at Walmart. An elderly midget/dwarf walks by. My grandson does a double-take, looks at me, and asks, *"Are you going to shrink like her, Grandma?"*

"I hope I don't shrink that small."

The ranch cat met us at the back door one morning. Parlay had a mouse in his mouth. The head was hanging out. He ate the tail first, then the head. *"Look, Grandma, isn't that the neatest thing?"*

Why that child has to swing on my refrigerator door, I don't know, and why he has to sling in circles anything in his hand, I'll never understand, but when I threaten him with the fly swatter he pays attention, at least momentarily.

Every night he says his prayers, short and sweet. *"God bless Mommy and Daddy and my little brother and Grandma, and make the bad guys good. Amen."*

73 Santa Fe and the Opera

August is the best time to flee Texas. I decided it was also a good time to go to Fort Collins, Colorado, for a long overdue visit with my son Joe and his wife Carla. I booked a shuttle from the Denver airport, where I paid close attention to the surroundings, recalling rumors of weird murals, underground tunnels, and the horse sculpture/statue at the airport entrance. I felt no strange vibes and arrived at my son's home to enjoy the evening sunset and a tasty Mexican dinner at a local restaurant.

The next few days passed quickly with a pleasant visit, fun eating out, enjoying beer at the local brewery, and savoring the cooler weather. The San Antonio airport welcomed me from a nonstop flight with a blast of heat. San Antonio is one of the 10 largest cities in the United States, but the San Antonio International Airport has limited non-stop service to other major cities in the country and very few international nonstop flights that don't connect in Dallas or Houston.

Only three days were left before flying to Santa Fe to attend the opera and visit with my three brothers, and I wasn't expecting any problems. Two adult guests were booked at the lodge below my home on the hill. The property was clean, the doors unlocked, and a copy of the rules lay on the kitchen island.

As I drove down the hill to retrieve four days of mail, I observed four vehicles parked at the lodge and at least four or more adults and more children milling around. The time was 9 a.m. I stopped, left the pickup engine running, and walked to the gate where I was met by a young woman. When I asked, *"Who are you?"* she replied with a name that wasn't on the booking reservation. A little confused, I suggested she might be at the wrong property. That's when the conversation turned to shit. She insisted she had a right to be there and gave the name of the ranch, Ambush Hill.

I retrieved my mail, returned to my computer, and confirmed that the reservation was for two adults for two nights in the name of a man. She was waiting when I returned with the computer printout. I observed three men drinking beer and a toddler in diapers.

I asked them to leave; she asked for a cash refund. I refused, saying it was all paid through Homeaway, and refunds were handled in the same manner. She threatened to post a bad review. I drove back up the hill, called Homeaway, and was assured that I was right in asking them to leave. The terms of the property rental had been violated. The listing clearly says six adults maximum, not suitable for small children, obvious since there are only three beds, one king and two queens. I could only guess where all 14 of them had slept the night before. An hour and a half passed before I heard them leave.

The review she posted was angry and contained numerous misspelled words. Homeaway emailed that they were investigating and that if I didn't reply within a certain period of time, my property might be suspended. I replied, am currently in good standing, and in the process of having Homeaway either remove the review or attach my reply to the review.

And then the rain came. The drive to the San Antonio airport in the early morning hours was horrible for an old lady with one good eye. The center line of Interstate 10 faded in the thunderstorms, and had I not been in the left lane and unable to change lanes, I would have abandoned the trip.

The flight to Houston was delayed due to the same thunderstorms, and, yes, I had to fly to either Houston or Dallas to connect with a flight to Albuquerque, a choice of flying north or east to travel west. As a result the shuttle reserved for the ride to Santa Fe left two minutes before I arrived and I waited an additional hour before leaving the airport, thus allowing 10 minutes to check in the hotel, change clothes, and meet my brothers for the ride to the opera, no problem for a low maintenance, seasoned traveler.

Since my brother is a patron of the Santa Fe Opera, we enjoyed the privilege of drinks and spectacular scenery on an upper patio prior to the opera's opening. Only four other people were with us sharing the lovely evening air, and as I glanced their way, I noticed that one was a popular conservative pundit. I have a picture to prove it.

The opera, *"Don Giovanni,"* was wonderful but a bit long, and I confess I napped a short while before returning to the hotel shortly before midnight.

Morning found me in the private breakfast area, quite early because of the time difference, where I read the complimentary New York Times and drank coffee while waiting for friends and family. We chatted away most of the morning until we decided when and where to meet for lunch and take the free shuttle provided by the hotel, the neatest perk imaginable, to the restaurant on the square. The hotel in which we were all staying was a boutique wing of a larger hotel, a separate building that provided 24 hour butler service, free full breakfast in a private top story dining and patio area, free taxi service anywhere in town until late evening, and free happy hour with hot snacks, beer, and wine in the same area as breakfast. The difference in price was minimal if you put the pencil to it.

After a great New Mexico lunch of a huge shredded beef burrito that came with guacamole, beans, rice, and dessert, some of us walked and shopped, and others returned to the hotel. I shopped, not believing the outrageous prices, mentally calculating what my turquoise and coral jewelry was worth if the store prices were an honest indication.

Back at the hotel, I had a short time before meeting for our private happy hour and enjoying a light meal of chicken wings, cheese, crackers, fruit, and liver sausage before the opera.

Again, we had access to the private patio, illuminated by the spectacular sunset and caressed by a cool breeze, which remained so until an entourage of 11 security men escorted a Supreme Court justice to our space. We kept our distance.

The opera, Romeo and Juliet, was magnificent, set during the Civil War, and sung in French. Each cushioned seat is equipped with a small screen on the back. By pushing a button, the opera is translated into your preferred language.

I can only wonder how someone came up with the idea to set this classic opera in America in the 1860's, but the music and plot are universal and timeless. Brother John told us that one year Carmen was set on the Texas border, and that he did not enjoy that opera; however, at the end of Romeo and Juliet, he cried and said, *"That was one of the two best I've ever seen, the other being Salome."* Again I confess to taking a short nap during the second half.

The following day I spent the early morning with the newspaper and coffee, lunched with some of the group, and shopped the afternoon before meeting at happy hour and catching the shuttle to a reserved dinner at an exclusive high-priced restaurant for which Santa Fe is famous. The waiter remembered my brother from past years, and the elegance of the meal was only surpassed by the flavor of the food and the choice of wines, making it definitely an evening to remember.

A phone call summoned the hotel's shuttle bus, returning eight of us safely to the hotel. My night was restless, knowing I was to leave Santa Fe the next morning by reserved transportation to the Albuquerque airport. My plane left late, suffering delays due to the thunderstorms still lingering over Texas, allowing me to barely make the connection in Houston, finally arriving home in the shadows between dusk and dark, musing over a fantastic trip and even better, time spent with my brothers.

Strangely, as we grow older, we are finding more occasions to be together. My youngest brother David reminds us always of a picture of our father and his brothers and sisters taken at some family event that precluded the death of one of them the next week.

Every time he insists we take a picture together, whether at John's Christmas party, Allan's 70th birthday party, or David's honorary speech at the Houston Literacy Foundation, we look at each other and wonder who of us will be the first to die. Fortunately, we smile, laugh, and do not dwell on the subject. My wish is that I go first so that I don't have to mourn the death of a brother.

74. **More**

Having read three books in the last two days leads toward reflection, not necessarily an uplifting exercise at 74. The purple Fitbit on my wrist probably thinks I'm dead, and my weekly steps taken average will be extremely low and the number of sleep hours unusually high. So what? Being a prisoner on the ranch is due to having paying guests in two of the homes listed on Homeaway/Vacation Rentals By Owners. Labor Day allows an extra day for short vacation excursions.

One of my favorite authors, Arturo Perez-Reverte, released a new book in June. I missed it but was thrilled to find and download *"What We Become: A Novel."* What a treat to spend the day reading and eating, a repeat of the day before.

The book focused on a man from the slums of South America who became a person of manners, style, and mystique in the world of the wealthy. The dance became his entrée.

He met a wealthy married woman, a passionate encounter ensued, his life continued as did hers. A decade later, their paths crossed, passion renewed, and their lives again diverged.

Three decades later a chance encounter engages them once again, this time with intrigue and lies, but the truth of their characters remained the same.

As the journey through the book transpired, the similarities to my longest relationship surfaced, unsettling what I planned to be a tranquil day.

She was a woman of substance and strength, and he was a man of ambition and opportunity without greed or jealousy. He knew where he had been, worked hard, and established a persona, not to be taken lightly, to be defended at all costs.

Raleigh, my second husband, was of Spanish descent, a product of the streets, who used his looks and skills to recruit girls he pimped to politicians and influential men. Raleigh was an extraordinary student of people. He perfected manners, his dress, the art of entering a room, lighting a cigarette, ordering a meal so that he charmed men and women alike, but beneath that veneer was the determination to succeed, whatever the cost.

If he discovered through gambling, drugs, or women that a married man who owned a car dealership preferred men, he used that knowledge to walk in the dealership and drive away in a new Lincoln without signing a paper.

A tailor from Thailand visited twice a year and designed his three piece suits. His shoes were polished, his nails groomed, his teeth white. He knew everyone, and everyone wanted to know him. When I was with him, I was Queen of the South, dressed in designer clothing, wearing nice jewelry. He carried a gold Dupont lighter, drank Dom Perignon, and spoke softly.

Arturo Perez-Reverte gave Raleigh back to me, and it was scary. I succumbed to his charms as did the woman in the book, and even though separated by death, he still haunts me most every day. The attraction was never physical though he was a handsome man; the magnet was his strength of purpose, the character he created and never abandoned. He was amoral and clinical in his treatment of men and women. Honor and respect, as well as brutality and violence, played a large part in his dealings. And in the end he remained true to himself. He knew more of loyalty than love, but, then, is there any difference between the two. Perhaps they are the same. One thing for certain, when I was with him, I felt safe.

Although the 15 years I was married to Raleigh, in truth, is only a small percentage of my 74 years, I must admit they were the years when I came alive, years when I learned and experienced the most and became alert, not enough to avoid further mistakes, but stimulated to live with courage and passion and without fear.

The years of traveling gave me an education in world history and culture, plus experiences dealing with all sorts of people, but the years with Raleigh taught me about observing people. After all, life is about people. For that matter, so is death.

I think the failure of the other marriages/relationships was not due to some flaw in my character, but rather because I was looking for a man with the strength of my father. Though he was small and insignificant physically, he was a man of substance. When Daddy entered a room, the world stopped and paid heed, and when he spoke we listened. I'll never forget a conversation with a Justice of the Peace in Polk County in the late 1970's, several years after my father died.

The person told me this story in not these exact words: "I never knew your father, but I'll never forget seeing him with the county judge. They were walking down the hall in the county courthouse.

Your father walked fast. The county judge was young and tall. Your father must have been in his 70's. He was wearing a Stetson hat, suit and tie, and talking with his hands. He told the judge, 'I told you I want that road closer to the lake, and you are not taking 120 acres of my land for a park. I'll donate 40 acres and give you the land for the road.' The judge said, 'Yes sir.'

I had never heard anyone talk to the county judge like that and asked someone, 'Who is that man?' She answered, 'That's Alvin Klein.'"

Most of my life I have been a scared little girl, waiting and hoping for a man with the strength of my father. But it's when I wasn't scared that I was most alive and had the most fun.

Medical Untruths

About nine years ago, I found the vision in one eye becoming blurred. At night sparklers distorted the vision in that same eye.

During a visit to my mother's after admitting the eye problem, she scheduled an appointment for me with her eye doctor, extolling his expertise in cataract surgery on both her eyes. Cataract surgery was scheduled with my selection of a lens that cost $800 and performed early one morning. The surgery took an hour extra, and as I awoke and felt the pain and heard the doctor asking for another lens, I knew something was wrong. They put me back to sleep, finished the procedure, and sent me back to my mother's where I stayed until the bandage was removed and I could see perfectly.

The doctor only told me that the $800 lens didn't work so he inserted a regular one. It only took a year for me to receive the refund from the hospital for the lens that was not implanted. Dumb me didn't question anything, and six months later while tilling my garden, the retina detached.

The vision in the eye was gone. When I realized the problem was not a broken blood vessel, I called an eye doctor in Uvalde, told the nurse it was an emergency, and I was coming in. They sent me to a retina specialist in San Antonio that same afternoon, and I was scheduled for surgery the following morning, time being of essence to save the vision in that eye.

A silicon band was placed in the eye to hold the retina together, and a gas bubble was inserted to push the retina against the back of the eye so that it would re-attach. As a result I was instructed to lie flat on my face 22 hours a day for two weeks. I can't describe that experience because I was most likely insane the entire time. I did succeed in saving some of the vision, although it was quite blurred.

At no time was I told that the cataract doctor placed the lens in front of the cornea instead of the back, that the cornea had been damaged during surgery. And again, dumb me never contacted the cataract doctor to discover exactly what happened. My main objective was to see and survive.

That first year after the detached retina, I spent hours driving to San Antonio every six weeks to have the eye checked, photographed, and renew a prescription for Prednisolone eyedrops, a corticosteriod said to be habit forming. When I asked the retina specialist about the addiction to the eye drops, he said it was no problem.

When I asked if I needed to take them forever, he said yes, that the drops reduced the chronic inflammation in the eye since the blood vessels to the eye were constricted from surgery.

And then a film grew over the damaged eye. According to the doctor this was common in about 40 percent of the cases. Surgery was scheduled to remove the film. The blurred vision was a bit better and I continued with the visits, reducing the frequency by choice, until I walked into the sliding glass doors in the guest lodge. The bad eye filled with blood as I made an emergency trip to San Antonio for a shot in the eye that hurt as much as you can imagine.

Again the eye stabilized as the specialist answered my questions as to the future of the eye. He assured me that as long as I took the drops, had the eye checked regularly, I would probably keep it, but if not and the pressure dropped too low, the eye would atrophy, and they would have to cut it out and insert a glass eye.

In the meantime my health was good; I went every year for the female test and complete blood work, comparing the written reports, until one year my Vitamin D was so low it was off the chart and I was advised to take a supplement. Dumb me should have asked for another blood test. I took 3000 units of Vitamin D each day until the bad eye was so full of grit I could not stand the pain. For that my retina specialist sent me to a cornea specialist where he sanded the grit off the bad eye, another horrible procedure. It was during this period that one of the doctors told me that the lens was implanted in front. Doctors don't talk bad about other doctors, in case you don't know that.

The cornea specialist recommended leaving the eye alone, my sentiments exactly. When I made an appointment with my retina specialist after the procedure, I waited an hour and a half before walking out and never returning. Instead, I made an appointment with another retina specialist who came one day a week to Kerrville, a shorter trip than to San Antonio. This specialist issued a prescription for a stronger eye drop that cost, even with my drug plan, $180. Without the drug plan the drops would be over $300.

And then I started seeing the sparklers in my good eye. Panic ensued. Blindness occupied my thoughts as I returned to my cornea specialist. He assured me there would be no problem. The cataract surgery went well. I see perfectly with my good eye, but I do not till my garden.

When I asked the doctor about the new drops for the bad eye, he told me they were too strong and not to take them. I canceled the next appointment with that retina specialist, relying on my cornea specialist whose offices now included a retina specialist with whom I spoke candidly.

He did an ultra sound on the bad eye, something no one had ever done. He said the eye looked good, the retina was attached and the pressure was low, but not bad low and said I might be a candidate for a cornea transplant. Not so dumb anymore, I made the appointment to talk to my cornea specialist about that possibility, but in the meantime did some research, and made the decision not to suffer a transplant as long as I could see perfectly out of one eye. The cornea doctor agreed.

And then I went on my Alaskan off-the-beaten-path adventure. When the blood vessels in the bad eye ruptured twice on the trip I surmised that the Prednisolone drops over the years had weakened the eye. Then I remembered the doctor who said there was not enough blood going to the eye to sustain a healthy pressure. There was certainly a lot of blood in the eye that I could see. I quit the drops and became sick with flu-like symptoms, the flu never erupting full blown. I figured it was caused by withdrawal from all the years of Prednisolone. Three weeks later, the vision in the bad eye gradually improved. On a visit to the cornea doctor for a wellness check on the good eye, I told him about the improved vision and the withdrawal. He did not disagree, and when he tested the pressure of the bad eye, it was normal, something that had not occurred in five years.

I'm still blind in the bad eye, but there is more light, the pressure is normal, and the good eye is perfect. What can I say? All the money and stupid pictures taken of the eye, the expensive eye drops, the miles and time to visit the doctor were a scam perpetrated by the medical profession that cost us taxpayers zillions of dollars. While I am not a doctor, this experience has framed my perception.

My advice is to ask questions, research, request duplicate tests, look at the pictures and results, and don't believe half of what you hear. Get second and third opinions, and take charge of your health. Remember the doctor works for you. Think of him as a mechanic working on your engine.

My mother inherited some land from her parents. They were poor, and this land meant a lot to her. A county authority planned a drainage ditch through the middle of her land. She went to an attorney and instructed him to legally force the authority to move the ditch to the edge of her property. When he replied that he would try to have it done, my mother told him. "I don't want to hear you will try. I want to hear that you will do it. If you can't assure me that you can, I will find someone else." Though those may not have been her exact words, they taught me a lesson I will never forget. When you hire someone to do a job, you're the one in charge. Remember it's your body, your health, your choice, and your money.

76 **Foodie**

During a recent conversation with my daughter-in-law, she commented, *"I'm reading a recipe book that goes into detail about the ritual of sharing food, quite interesting."*

I agree. It's not what you eat but who you eat it with. I really enjoy watching Anthony Bourdain, the traveler who eats all over the world. That's one of the interesting things I enjoy about traveling, eating the food. In fact, eating is one of my favorite things to do, next to cooking. Eating with Mother and her sisters was always such fun because while we were enjoying the meal, the subject of the next meal was always part of the conversation.

"Where was the best food in your travels?"

"There's always good food, but the best food I have ever eaten was in Vietnam and Cambodia because of the delicate flavors and the freshness. Ah, but I do remember a meal outdoors at a sheep station in New Zealand. It was a lamb stew with sweet potatoes, a dish I have duplicated with success, but one that hasn't quite caught on with my friends and family. I love sweet potatoes, probably because my grandmother raised them on the farm and my mother loved them."

One of my favorite dinner topics comes from asking what are the two foods on which you can survive indefinitely, each one having the necessary ingredients to sustain life. The answer is not bananas.

No one has ever answered correctly. The two foods are sweet potatoes and dates, another of my mother's favorites.

"Isn't the food good on cruise ships?"

"For me, not really. While the display is lovely, the flavor is usually quite bland and if you really think about it, the food has to be frozen prior to preparation."

When I leave the ranch, the first thing that comes to mind is where and what can I eat. I don't enjoy eating alone, which is quite limiting; and, unfortunately, my last two boyfriends were not foodies. In fact they are horrible eaters. I don't even cook for them anymore since vegetables are not to their liking, and they don't care for lamb.

Several times a week, I go to the freezer and retrieve wild pork, deer, or lamb and concoct a dish with the ranch meat and vegetables from the garden. Yesterday I thawed out a package of ground lamb and combined it with onions, garlic, carrots, green beans, okra, hot peppers, and lima beans, slowly smothering the combination in a black cast iron skillet. The dry spices I add may vary – cumin, turmeric, chili powder, epazote - as well as the fresh herbs from the garden – basil, dill, parsley, rosemary, thyme, mint. My boyfriend calls this dish veggie mush. It's not.

For this particular dish I only added a bit of chili powder, epazote, and cumin. Hot peppers from the garden are a staple in any dish I prepare. I grow poblano, serrano, jalapeño, tabasco, bell, cayenne, and chili pequins. I have to be careful when cooking for guests because I often add too many hot peppers. The alternative is to chop fresh peppers and serve them on the side.

Before the first freeze of the year I harvest the peppers, dehydrate them in the oven, and grind them into sprinkles. I also grow fresh hot peppers through the winter in the greenhouse.

I don't prepare sweets and desserts as I believe sugar is not healthy. Sugar makes me hyper. Usually I serve fresh fruit to be dipped in yogurt and brown sugar or buy some decadent pastry from the bakery at the local grocery store.

I believe that the body is an engine and should be given the best fuel. Food is the fuel and the medicine for the motor that keeps my body running smoothly.

My theory concerning dementia in older people centers around bone marrow. I believe animal fat is necessary for brain connections, perhaps a simplistic thought. The current trend is boneless meat, thus depriving the body of animal fat. I insist meat from the ranch is "bone in," and that fat is included in the ground meat. I enjoy bone marrow and fat trimmings. At 74 I can still add and subtract. At least, I think so.

One More Time

The time of day for an afternoon call to a friend arrived, an almost daily occurrence. We spoke of the presidential campaigns, the state of the world, the economy, the weather, our families, the local community, and, finally, ourselves, the day we were having – lonely, busy, lethargic, maniacal, or energetic – easy, over the privacy of a phone.

He asked, *"Are you going nuts, having not seen anyone in over a week?"*

"Not really, but I do miss someone to care for or share experiences. What about you?"

"Nope, I could never do it again."

Without thinking too deeply I offered, *"Oh I suppose if someone came along that would take me dancing, buy me dinner, cut up onions, and drink some wine with me while I cooked, and liked my food, I'd probably go for it."*

He was aghast. *"I can't believe you. After your experiences you would be a sucker for the same thing again? Would you let him move in?"*

"Definitely not in my house or any of the others on the ranch, though I might let him spend a night or two with me."

"Okay, I feel a little better, but I'd like to think you've learned by now not to be swayed by someone who pretended to like your veggie mush."

"Well, he'd have to be a pretty good dancer and know how to waltz, too."

231

78 **At Last**

At last, I come to the end of this book. The journey has been difficult, aging more so. I realize with time an eighth sense develops, the sense of forgiveness.

And as I've grown older, looking back and seeing the strangers within, observing the pictures of who I was, not believing but accepting who I now am, I accept those strangers were really me, and question if I was always the same. Was perception all there ever was, and is reality just a dream or imagination?

Seeing the strangers I have been, not recognizing myself, trying to stay blank, and accept that those other women were like grains of sand or ephemeral clouds, I overflow with forgiveness.

I believe the spirit lives beyond the senses, that the dead are among us, encouraging and commiserating.

Not a day goes by that I don't think of my mother, my father, aunts, uncles, cousins, friends, lovers, husbands, all gone and more on the way of leaving this reality, including myself.

I don't know where the years have gone or where I was when they passed. They've moved too swiftly, and there is no hope of slowing them down.

Rather than despairing, resorting to chemical dependency, and doing nothing, I intend to continue until my last breath, living rather than waiting for the inevitable.

I want to live long enough to screw up my grandchildren, making sure they have a fiery grandmother to remember. Every time I see my grandson, aged 6, I repeat with conviction, "Yes, your famous beautiful grandmother is here."

So far it has worked. He is a believer. His brother, at 24 months, has yet to be indoctrinated. I am depending on his older brother to continue the tradition in case I drop dead, which is a distinct possibility, but I don't plan to go down easy, which is the name of the most wonderful dog I ever knew. I hope he is waiting on the other side.

Most of all I thank the God who plays the music of nature and gifts me with the scenery I enjoy every fantastic morning of my blessed life.

Ambushed by America

Order Form

Sonja's books are available both in print and as ebooks online or directly from Ambush Publishing.

Fax Orders: Send this completed form to 1-830-234-3155

Telephone Orders: Call 1-830-234-3156

Email Orders: Visit sonja@ambushhillranch.com

Postal Orders: Send this completed form to:
Ambush Publishing PO Box 192, Barksdale, Texas 78828

Name: _____

Address: _____

_____

City:_____ State: _____ Zip:_____

Phone: _____ Email: _____

AMBUSHED BY AMERICA
Number of Copies _____   @$15.00/book Subtotal: $ _____

ROUNDTRIP FROM TEXAS
Number of Copies _____   @$15.95/book Subtotal $_____

HONK IF YOU MARRIED SONJA
Number of Copies _____   @ $15.00/book Subtotal $_____

Add $5.60 for priority shipping in United States
        Shipping: $ _____   Total: $_____

Make check or money order payable to Ambush Publishing.
If you wish to pay by credit card, go to www.sonjaroseklein.com

www.ingramcontent.com/pod-product-compliance
Lightning Source LLC
Chambersburg PA
CBHW022008100426
42736CB00041B/1037